TANDEM

Waterways In Europe

Roger Pilkington's handbook, guide and introduction
to the navigable rivers and canals of Europe takes
readers of Tandem's two previous books on the delights
of inland waterways, SLOW BOAT THROUGH
ENGLAND and SLOW BOAT THROUGH
PENNINE WATERS by Frederic Doerflinger, a step
further in their venturing. Like the earlier books, it
combines detailed instruction for the first-timer with
suggested itineraries based on the author's own
voyages, and has been brought right up to date by the
author for this edition.

The interesting viewpoint, the occasional warning to
the unwary stranger, the fascinating local anecdote or
legend, places to eat and convenient moorings which
the newcomer would never otherwise discover – these
are the sort of practical tips which neither the official
guide nor the rambling travel book provide.
Roger Pilkington has the know-how, gained during
more than twenty years of criss-crossing Europe in his
boat, *Thames Commodore*, and in WATERWAYS IN
EUROPE he makes it available to the increasing
number of holiday-makers who are turning to the
waterways for adventure and relaxation.

Waterways In Europe

Roger Pilkington

TANDEM
14 Gloucester Road, London SW7

First published in Great Britain by
John Murray (Publishers) Ltd, 1972

Revised and brought up to date by the author, and
published by Universal-Tandem Publishing Co. Ltd, 1974

Made and printed in Great Britain by
Hunt Barnard Printing Ltd., Aylesbury, Bucks.

CONTENTS

ILLUSTRATIONS

Waterways In Europe

FOREWORD

This book begins at the edge of the continental mainland of Europe. It does not deal with how to cross the English Channel or the North Sea, nor does it treat of navigation at sea or along the coasts. Its object is to be a guide to inland navigation on the continent, and I have written it for the yachtsman, inland cruiser, holiday boatman, and even for those who just like strolling along the towpath or spending a pleasant day on one of the many steamers and trip vessels which ply on the waterways of Europe.

Not every canal in Europe is described. Eastern Europe is omitted altogether, because however intriguing some of the waterways may be I doubt if any boating man wishes to spend his holidays trying to peer round the solid rump of a boorish guard who has been stationed by his hatchway to see that he does not land, take photographs, or even smile to the inhabitants. The Italian waterways are left out because they can only be entered from the Adriatic, and the Danube is passed over for the simple reason that it is still inaccessible without a passage of the Dardanelles. Some of the more colliery waterways of northern France are omitted because there are coal-heaps enough in Britain, and the Brittany canals are not included for the reason that those delightful waterways form a network unconnected with any other, and I have not yet navigated them myself. The key-note is that the canals and rivers here described are all ones which I know from my own voyages through more than twenty years of continental cruising. A guide must surely be authoritative, and it can only be so if the attractions of a particular waterway are dealt with from personal experience, and the ease or difficulty of any particular passage correctly given because the author has actually been that way himself.

I have also left out Holland, except where part of a main route such as the Rhine or Meuse may pass through Dutch territory. This is because almost every town or village in Holland is served by a canal, and there is no end to the catalogue of Dutch waterways. There are few locks, even the smallest place is usually equipped with a good quayside and a harbour-master, and facilities in general are so good and navigation so simple that the country is one for easy voyaging. For beginners it is ideal. Yet scenically the Dutch landscape is really very dull indeed. There are cows and windmills, and perhaps brilliant splashes of colour where the rows of tightly packed tulips glint in the spring sunlight, but the delight of Holland is in the towns and villages, which invariable seem to turn their best face toward the water. No city in the world can be so attractive to the boatman as Amsterdam, with the opportunity of endless voyages of exploration by dinghy among its spider's web structure of canals. Few little harbours can be more appealing than those around the Ijsselmeer, where engineers may have shut out the salt water but otherwise little seems to have changed since their peak of prosperity three centuries ago.

Besides, Holland is well served with waterways maps and guides, and is the only country to have a special office to deal with all matters concerning inland boating. The address is : Het Bureau voor Watertoerisme, Museumplein 5, Amsterdam-Z. The office publishes an annual *Almanak voor Watertoerisme,* containing details (in Dutch) of every creek and hamlet, and several dozens of useful diagrams of town harbours. There is no need to be a linguist to find this book invaluable.

On the other hand, I have included Sweden, because most of its canals are not well known and yet are accessible to any boatman who can reach the Baltic by inland waterways and cares to run up through the Danish isles and make a short coastal trip, and also to trailer-craft owners who take the North Sea ferry routes. Outside Canada there is nothing quite like the Swedish canals, and if remoteness is wanted then waterways such as the Kinda and Dalslands routes are ones without equal.

Denmark is left out for a good reason – it has no inland waterways other than harbour channels.

Norway has two canals, but the Tiste Navigation is not accessible from the sea – nor any longer by dry inclined plane as it was before 1960. However, it is available to trailer craft. The remarkable Telemark Canal, on which a steamer also runs, can be reached by a sea voyage to Skien, but my own two attempts to reach it have both been frustrated by storms. This canal runs through some remote country and in general is similar to the Swedish waterways.

The difficulties of a continental cruise are really very few. Given a boat either owned or hired, and a reasonable amount of sense, all the equipment is already to hand to make such a voyage possible. Yet there are certain things I have gradually come to learn over the years which make the success of such an enterprise more certain, and help to ensure that handling a small boat in heavily used commercial waterways is a delight rather than a road to neurosis, so I have included a number of quite practical tips for those who are new to such adventure.

Whereas the condition of most waterways in Britain is static or even deteriorating, other European countries pour money into canal engineering. It is unlikely that anyone will find a canal described in this book to have been subsequently closed; more likely it will have been enlarged, modernised, provided with new locks or an inclined plane to by-pass a former flight, and generally improved in the interests of traffic. This is not done for the convenience of yachts, but just because water transport is the cheapest and most efficient form of carrying heavy goods.

In Britain, the traditional narrow-boat with its ridiculous lading of 20 to 30 tons, and its living quarters which would be condemned by any responsible Medical Officer of Health, is now almost extinct. Its continental equivalent as a barge which can penetrate anywhere is ten times the size, the 350-ton standard barge of France and Belgium known as a *péniche* or *spits*. Thousands of these craft ply on the European network, carrying grain, bricks, flour, coal, wine, cement, timber or whatever needs to be transported in bulk from one place to another. Even these are too small for some purposes, and for real bulk handling and container-carrying the ship of the future is the 'Europaship' of 1,350 tons. Most through routes on the continent are already of 1,350-tonner or 'R.H.K.' dimensions, or are being enlarged to that standard. (The term R.H.K. stands for Rhein–Herne Kanal, the waterway which first set the dimensions for larger inland shipping.)

Compared with waterways in Britain even the smaller 'Class I' or 350-ton routes are of such dimensions that only exceptionally large yachts would be unable to pass through them, and for this reason I have not cluttered the text with precise dimensions of the works, unless they are less than Class I, which can accommodate craft 38·5 m. in length, 5·2 m. in breadth, with a height of 3·7 m. above the water and 1·8 m. below – which corresponds to a depth of water of 2·0 m. although in fact most French canals have already been increased to 2·2 m.

Not so long ago the continental waterways were almost unknown as a cruising ground. British yachts penetrated to Holland or sailed up the Seine to Paris, but they were few in number and usually of some size. In the 1950's one could voyage for a month without meeting another cruiser, and until the opening of the Moselle such German yachts as one might meet were speeding through the waterways on their way to the Mediterranean rather than enjoying the canalised rivers for their own sake. Nowadays the story is different. Boating enthusiasts reared on the shallow and weeded canals of England are beginning to realise that just across the English Channel there exists a network of waterways stretching from the Baltic to the Mediterranean, channels which pass through ancient cities or by vineyard slopes, through forests and over mountains, across the wild and sparsely populated areas of Sweden and the sun-baked salt flats of Provence. These are the canals and rivers which I here describe in detail, and I have tried to arrange them in an order which is convenient rather than rigidly formal. Marshalling by alphabet would be absurd, and to group the waterways by countries would be little better, particularly when some of them lead through several lands in succession. So I have adopted a fish-skeleton system of my own, taking a main waterway as the backbone and then describing one after the other the various ribs which are attached to it. Nor have I invariably started at the top of a river and worked down; always the keynote is the direction in which it is most likely to be navigated by a boatman coming from Britain or the North Sea.

There is a lure about water travel that to many people is irresistible. Perhaps the tempo and stress of modern life have something to do with it, for a person who spends much of his life in traffic jams on the way to work is not so inclined to pass his holidays in the same fashion. But there is more to it than that. Certainly the relative density of traffic is extremely small – a canal passing eighty boats a day is a busy one, whereas a motorway may register three thousand vehicles in an hour – and there are no yellow lines or parking meters or indeed any of the badgering about to which one is increasingly subjected on land, but instead there is a freedom in water travel which is more like that known to the mountaineer.

So, on board, off with the lines, and away.

ROGER PILKINGTON

St Aubin, Jersey

BASIC BOATING ABROAD

1. THE BOAT

Any boat up to 38 m. × 5 m. will be able to navigate most European waterways, provided it has not a fixed mast or a draught exceeding 1·80 m. (Where waterways have smaller dimensions they are stated under the appropriate section.) It is important that the craft should be sound, because outside Holland it is unlikely that you will be within 200 kms. of a yard of any description capable of doing structural or mechanical repairs. In particular, wooden craft are not easily repaired abroad; yards just do not like them. Most yards are in any case only accustomed to working on péniches or Europaships.

Trailer-boats are ideal for exploring Europe. It greatly increases the range if a boat can be towed overland to a launching site, but one should not assume that overnight accommodation on land will always be easy to find or even exist.

Hiring: Hire facilities in Holland are excellent, and boats are available all over the country. Details can best be obtained from the Bureau voor Watertoerisme (see p. 2). In Belgium hire craft are not available, and in Germany generally forbidden, maybe wisely when one considers the size of the commercial craft among which they would have to ply. Two good hire fleets offer craft in France. In the north, Saint Line Cruisers have bases on the Marne and the Canal du Nivernais. Address : Saint Line, La Collancelle, 58-Corbigny. In the south, Blue Line have a good fleet on the Canal du Midi and its connections. Address : Blue Line Cruisers (France) Ltd., Le Grand Bassin, 11-Castelnaudary.

In Sweden hire-cruisers and sailboats can be had at the various bases of Holiday Charter-Boats AB, Box 194, S-68101 Kristinehamn.

Charter: A few private boats take small parties, and their standard varies enormously. Names and addresses can be had from the offices of the various National Tourist Offices. Details of craft are not given here, because many of them do not stay in business long enough to make such a list reliable. However, for a larger party the *Palinurus* can be chartered on French waterways, and the same boat – which is a converted canal barge – can be joined on its scheduled runs, mostly in Burgundy. For details, write to S.G.T.R., 19 rue d'Athénes, Paris 19.

Trip-boats and steamers ply for short, or in some cases one- or two-week, voyages on many waterways. Several are mentioned under the appropriate sections, but details of cruises on European rivers, including the Danube, can be found in the *ABC Shipping-Guide*.

2. FORMALITIES

Papers: Most countries of Western Europe have minimal requirements in the way of papers and certificates for a yacht entering from abroad, and even those countries which insist on driving tests and a certificate of competence for their own nationals sensibly take the view that if a yacht succeeds in reaching them from elsewhere the skipper must know what he is about, so no master's ticket of any kind is required. All that is necessary for a powered boat is in general that the steersman should not be under sixteen – a provision none can quarrel with.

For the craft itself, Belgium and the Scandinavian countries do not demand any papers at all. The Hollanders only ask to see a current membership card of a boat club or similar society. Even a local waterways restoration society card will do. The only country which has specific demands which *must* be met is France. To navigate on French waterways, except the Seine below Rouen, and other tidal areas which count as sea, two papers are essential. Without them, no amount of cajolery, cigarettes, tears or fist-shaking will get you admitted. The documents are : a *Carnet de Passage en Douane*, obtainable at a small price from a motoring organisation or a sufficiently grand yachting association. This is a sort of guarantee that you will re-export the craft within a year, and the carnet will be stamped upon entry and exit by the customs. It is most important to see that this formality is carried out, or you will have trouble getting out of the country again. The stamping is easily overlooked at such places as Bordeaux, where one can steam up the river past the customs office without giving the matter a thought.

The *Permis de Circulation* is an authorisation, issued free, to make one return journey on a stated route. It is obtainable (allow six weeks) on a form to be had from the French National Tourist Office, 178 Piccadilly, London, W1V 0AL; or an area permit can be obtained over the counter from any office of the *Ponts et Chaussées, Service de la Navigation* – which includes the lock into the Bassin Carnot at Calais. The permit will be stamped at the various locks on the route that are designated as *Bureaux de Contrôle*. Trailer-craft also need this permit, and in some countries may only be admitted on a customs carnet. If in doubt, consult your motoring organisation when arranging for the shipment of the car and trailer.

Insurance: Most insurance policies specify cruising limits which will exclude the continent. Remember that it is vital to have the cover extended in advance. There may be no extra charge, but unless the policy has been endorsed you will be left high and dry if you try to make a claim for an accident outside the bounds. It is worthwhile specifying fairly wide geographical limits, ample to cover any side-trips you might decide to make on the spur of the moment. Always keep the policy aboard. You may be asked to produce it.

Canal dues: In HOLLAND these are non-existent on most waterways, but where a charge is made it will either be levied at a lock or at a swing-bridge, where a clog will be swung out on a fishing line to receive some small sum.

BELGIUM. For craft over 5 tons a charge is made to cover the voyage from the point of entry to the furthest destination in Belgium. It will be unlikely to exceed 5 or 10 pence, all locks and bridges included.

FRANCE. There are no charges, except for a few curious payments which have to be made for *not* using towage facilities in certain tunnels, etc. The only ones known to me are in the Pouilly-en-Auxios and Mont de Billy tunnels, and at the Loire crossing at Decize. A small charge may be made at sea-locks such as the Ecluse Carnot in Calais, these facilities belonging to the ports and not to the canal authority.

GERMANY. As one might expect, the arrangements differ and are complicated. The Moselle charge is about £1·25 per lock, but only if no barge or steamer is present, in which case the big ship pays and you go free. The same applies if the lock needs to be filled or emptied to prepare it for commercial craft coming the other way. On the Lahn, a card for a number of locks can be bought at a reduced price. The Dortmund–Ems, Wesel–Datteln, Rhine–Herne and similar canals are free, but not the Kiel Canal. The Neckar has varying rates, the Weser is gratis, the Ilmenau makes a modest charge.

LUXEMBOURG has only the Moselle and follows the German arrangement.

SWEDEN charges for the use of its canals. Usually the fee will be just a few pounds for the return trip, but it may cost you as much as £40, according to size, to go through the Göta route. Never mind; the experience is well worth the money.

3.   HOW FAR, HOW LONG

How far one can travel depends less upon the actual speed of the craft than upon the habits of yourself and your crew, for rapid progress will in any event be impossible because of locks, and speed limits – which should be observed. An early morning start, when the countryside is often at its best in the soft light and the glistening dew, makes all the difference. If under way by half past six one may reach the destination for the day before lunch and have plenty of time to explore the neighbourhood. Under an unhurried system of this kind I find that on waterways like the Meuse where locks are usually a few kilometres apart one can reckon on 40 to 50 kms. per day. On more heavily locked canals such as the Canal de Bourgogne it is easier to think in terms of 5 or 6 locks per hour, with a daily quota of 30 to 40 as enough to satisfy the most energetic members on board.

If in a hurry, which usually means having much less enjoyment of the voyage, one can cross France from the English Channel to the Mediterranean in 20 days, or reach Sweden in 12, probably exhausted.

Craft starting in Britain may easily lose valuable holiday time stormbound. If the holiday period is limited it is often a good idea to make the crossing during an earlier week-end of good weather and leave the craft ready in a port the other side. On the way home the boat can also be dumped at the coast to await a good opportunity.

Navigation times: These really depend upon the hours at which the locks and swing-bridges are worked. In HOLLAND, the times at which there are manned is variable. Some are open round the clock, especially on main commercial routes. Others are closed for all or part of the day on Sundays (and in that case also on Ascension Day and Whit Monday), but this varies from one province to another. It is always advisable when doing a long run to make sure that on Saturday evening you are not shut in between two bridges which will not open until Monday. Generally speaking, locks and bridges are likely to be available from 06.00 to 19.00, though in towns there are often periods of an hour or more during rush-hours when bridges remain closed to speed the road traffic.

BELGIUM has regular hours right across the country, and

these are, in summer : 06.00–19.30, and on Sundays 09.00–13.00. Later hours may operate on the Albert Canal if traffic is heavy.

FRANCE also has a nation-wide timetable, which in summer is 06.30 to 19.30 but draws in its horns gradually by an hour or two in mid-winter. Boatmen should remember that July 14th is the anniversary of the storming of the Bastille, and lock-keepers as well as others have a holiday, and sit in the market-place looking dejected. Easter Sunday is also a no-navigation day, and so are May 1st and November 11th.

In recent years the French government has thought that just occasionally a lock-keeper might like to eat at some point between 06.30 and 19.30. The system varies, but the commonest one is a complete standstill on the locks between 12.00 and 12.30.

GERMANY. Arrangements differ from one waterway to another. The Moselle locks are open all round the clock without interruption, whereas some canals do not open until 08.00.

SWEDEN has long hours of navigation, which vary somewhat from one waterway to another. The locks are open on Sundays.

Stoppages: There comes a time in the life of every canal when lock-gates need renewal, or some major repair has to be carried out which makes it necessary to drain a length and close it to navigation. These periods are usually planned well in advance, and the French publish an annual calendar of closures (*Liste des Chômages*) which will be sent to you on request when you apply for the *Permis de Circulation*. It can also be seen at any local office of the Ponts et Chaussées, Service de la Navigation. It is so designed that when one route is under repair an alternative is usually left open, but as the stoppages take place in the summer and may last up to six weeks it is important to discover in advance whether some vital link in your proposed route is not to be available. After a closure has finished, it is wise to allow three clear days for the assembled barges to move ahead and disperse.

In Germany and Belgium stoppages also occur, but less often, and usually there is an alternative lock or a way round. It is generally safe enough to enquire at the first lock or toll office on arrival in the country, but you can also ask the National Tourist Offices to discover for you in advance whether any stoppage is in the wind. In Sweden, repairs are carried out during the long winter closure.

Drought: Long dry spells can run down summit reservoirs so that a canal may be closed through several weeks for lack of water for locking. Obviously this can only apply to watershed canals, and therefore to France. Such stoppages cannot be foreseen for more than a week or two, but enough notice is always given to permit craft on the move to get clear. However, if you leave a boat in the stretch concerned, it may be imprisoned for weeks because the bed is dry and will remain so until after the next heavy rains. At certain locks there is a notice-board where all such impending items are announced. If you see a paper headed *Avis à la Batellerie* (Notice to Inland Shipping) then read it.

4. EQUIPMENT

Inland waterway cruising on the continent involves a certain amount of equipment, the chief item on the list being common sense on the part of the skipper. Other useful items are :

Boathook: As long as can be carried without causing an obstruction to trip over. Its use is mainly to push the stern out from the bank when leaving a mooring in a muddy or weedy position where the filter will become blocked if the engine is started, or the propeller will chew up gravel and boulders. It is also useful for a variety of jobs, such as retrieving ladies' handbags from locks. Occasionally it is invaluable for putting a crew member ashore, if he pole-vaults with it over the marshy edge or beds of reeds or nettles; the best one I ever had for this purpose was a Cambridge punt pole with a hook set on the end.

Whatever yachtsmen may say, a boathook should *not* be used when entering a lock, as sooner or later one of the boat windows will be smashed with it. Besides it implies incompetence. It also strikes terror into the hearts of bystanders and bargemasters if one enters a pen with the crew armed to the teeth as though about to attack.

It is useful to paint a ring round the role at the maximum draught of the boat, and one or two more rings at distances or 25 cms. or so above. A marked boathook is invaluable for sounding the approach to an unknown bank if the water is murky.

Bank anchors: At least three should be taken, and a really heavy hammer (3 or 4 kilos) to drive them into the ground. It is a good idea to be moderately certain there is no cable or pipe close under the surface before driving metal spikes into the ground, or your popularity locally will suffer a marked decline. The best type of bank anchor for holding and also for getting out of the ground again is a single-

fluked one ending in a ring. The fluke can occasionally be run up sharp on a grindstone at a smithy or a waterways maintenance yard.

The ring ensures that a noosed rope can be attached swiftly without tying a knot of any kind.

Anchor: An anchor will probably be useful to hold the boat out from a rocky shore in a river with some current, and it will serve to haul the boat out before proceeding. It is also an essential safety device when cruising on rivers such as the Rhine or Rhone. A heavy, stockless anchor is probably the best. The plough-share anchors favoured by yachtsmen for sand or mud will be quite useless on river beds of shingle or rock.

Quick release is essential. The anchor should not be lashed, nor stowed at the bottom of a locker, but ready for immediate dropping. The inboard end of the line or chain should be permanently secured to a ringbolt in the hull.

Mooring lines: Apart from a good supply of auxiliary lines, three mooring warps suitable also for lock-work should be carried. They will need to be not less than 30 m. in length, and with a noose at least 1 m. long to cope with large stone bollards.

Ladder hook: On a short line (about 2 or 3 m.). See p. 49.

Fenders: Locks more than anything else raise the question of fenders, which must be thick and resilient enough to act as a real cushion if the boat weaves or is pressed hard against the lock wall. The side of the pen is sure to be dirty and slimy, and however smart those expensive white sausages may look when you leave home, they will not do so for long. In a lock they will pick up all the dirt, and as the boat moves they will act like ink-rollers to transfer all the filth to the hull. Besides, you are certain to lose them, caught in ladder recesses or mixed up with the gate girders. Much better is to have a fender which will not revolve, and will either not be lost at all or is so cheap that to lose it is no tragedy.

For fairly small craft which only present up to 3 m. of

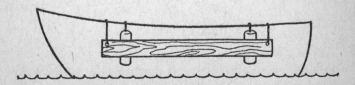

vitally fenderable length amidships, there is no doubt at all
that the best fender is merely a board placed lengthwise and
held clear of the side by a suitably thick white sausage or
similar pad at either end. Otherwise there is everything to
be said for old tyres, except that unless small they are not
very pleasing to the eye, and they have a tendency to make
black marks on the boat. These difficulties can, however, be
got over.

Small tough tyres are not easily acquired. The wear and
tear on the wheels of milk-carts is insufficient to keep up a
good supply. But a small and even tougher tyre can easily
be made by taking an ordinary motor tyre – picked up free
and with showered blessings on your head at any garage
near the canal – and cutting it across. A hacksaw will be
needed, because of the wire in the rims, and as there may be
metal strands in the worn tread it is a good idea to wear
gloves for the operation. A tyre can easily be slit by a sharp
blow on the butt of a ship's knife, and the next job is to make
four holes by cutting out small triangles of three slits each,
as shown in the diagram. The tyre can then be rolled up on

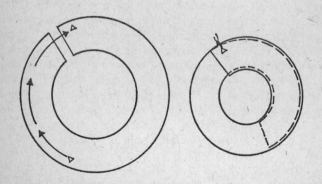

itself and secured by passing a piece of line through the two
pairs of holes when they are superimposed, and tying it
above them.

Two more holes are cut about 20 cms. apart in one side, and a piece of strong plastic line passed through and finished

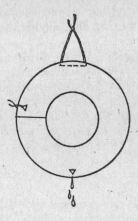

off with a knot, locked by melting. A final hole at the bottom of the opposite side will help drainage.

One now has a very stout fender with a hanging loop, which will of course have been made just right for hanging on your bitts. To prevent blackening of the hull it can be hung against a shield of rubber carpet underlay, or the same material can be cut in the round and stuck to the tyre with a rubber adhesive. The great thing is to have proper suspen-

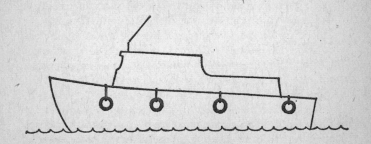

sion points for fenders at the positions where they are needed
– a matter usually quite overlooked by boat builders. The
fenders can then quickly be slipped on when required. On
my own boat I carry four such fenders on each side, which
is enough to hold her out all along her length and give good
resilience.

Gloves: Lock winding can be hard on the hands. Many
bargemen use gloves with stout studded leather palms. These
are easily obtained at chandleries, and are usually stocked
by fuelling barges.

Hosepipe and tap fittings: The hose will need to be a
sound one, at least 30 m. in length. (See p. 58.)

5. UNDER WAY

On the water you can go where you wish, stop where you
want to, and within reasonable limits live the day in your
own way without being hemmed in by the timetable of
others. You can choose your own view for the evening halt,
and just because most of the waterways have been the route
of communication for hundreds of years the cities and towns
along them will turn their best and mellowed face toward
the boatman, while sending the motorist round a diversion
that leads between the gasworks and the slaughterhouse.
From the water the world is yours, and you share it with
others who, even though their living may depend upon their
voyaging, enjoy it as much as yourself and can usually be
relied upon to be courteous, considerate and friendly.

In return for the good-natured interest shown by the men
who work the boats of Europe one should always bear in
mind that they are not on holiday. They may enjoy cruising
through France or Germany in the long summer days, or
pulling in for the night near a favourite village inn, but
boating is their livelihood. As a French bargeman once put
it, *'Nous, nous travaillons, mais vous – vous vous promenez!'*
This being so, and bearing in mind that the numbers of
cruisers is always increasing, a holiday boatman should

always try not to hold up commercial craft. A laden barge plodding ahead of you from one canal pound to the next may be a slight irritation, but when at last there is a chance of overtaking you should exercise a certain amount of judgment. It is almost indecent to squeeze past when the next lock is only a minute or two ahead, and although it is impossible to formulate an exact rule I myself reckon that one should only overtake a barge if by so doing one is not going to hold it up for more than a minute or two. This is another way of saying that after overtaking your job is to get into the next lock as quickly as possible, work it energetically, and speed the emptying or filling for the following barge in every possible way – for example, by dropping the paddles on the gates before leaving.

Really it is only a matter of consideration and understanding and trying to put yourself in the other man's position. For instance, nothing is likely to cause more ill-feeling than to pass a lumbering slow-boat, delay it, and then promptly stop in the next reach for a bathe, or to buy the *vin ordinaire,* or merely to have lunch on deck while admiring the view. On the whole, bargemen are extremely courteous and will ease off and beckon you past if there is no lock within the next few minutes ahead, and similar behaviour from 'promenaders' is always appreciated.

Barge etiquette: In large locks and at busy quaysides you will be in the company of barges. It is often necessary to lie against them, but you should remember that the barge is not just a transport vehicle. It is the family home. You should not make fast without first asking permission – which will be readily granted. Barges tend to lie against each other in such a way that they do not look straight into the accommodation of the neighbour, and it is only polite to follow suit and make fast well ahead of the wheelhouse and cabin.

Before going ashore, enquire whether the ship is leaving within the next few hours. Often a barge may be on call at short notice for lading, so the skipper will tell you he intends to leave; yet when you return he is still there. This is not an indication that he was being unfriendly, but merely that his

3

number has not come up at the regional lading bureau as soon as expected.

If all is well, go ashore across the boat, but invariably round the bow end. It is considered bad manners to cross in front of the wheelhouse or round the stern. If you should enter the wheelhouse to speak to the skipper, take off your shoes; this is a ritual which keeps the boat clean inside, and you will notice that many bargemen are continually changing their shoes. If you return aboard with dusty or muddy shoes, take them off before walking round outside the hold.

Barge families have many friends, but have no idea when they will meet them again. If you are following a barge you may notice some excitement when a particular craft is sighted coming the other way. As soon as both families realise that they are meeting friends they may not have seen for a year or more the women run up to the bow, and as the two ships slowly pass they will walk backwards the whole length of the vessels, talking. In this brief half minute all the news and greetings since the previous encounter have to be exchanged, and as the sterns pass each other the skippers usually step out for a sentence or two such as 'Have you seen Georges?' or 'Maybe find you at Conflans over Christmas.' These brief meetings are almost the only social life a boat family may have, and they will not want to have them interrupted by some impatient yachtsman blowing on his hooter because he wants to pass.

Rule of the road: Always keep to the right. The only exceptions are when blue flagging on open rivers, or meeting bank-hauled craft on canals. These cases are dealt with separately (pp. 36 and 40).

Speed limits are variable, and are generally about 5 km./hr., although larger waterways such as the Rhine have none and the general rule is devil-take-the-hindmost. Where special limits apply they are clearly given on a signboard. The limits are imposed to prevent damage to the banks by the wash set up by a passing barge, and it is the wash which matters. If your craft makes no wash (probably a hydrodynamic impossibility) no one is likely to object if you go somewhat faster than the general limit; but special local limits may be enforced by clocking, whether you make any wash or no. If on the other hand your craft makes an unusually heavy wash, you should be content to travel below the general speed limit.

Sound signals: In general it is enough to signal . for 'going right', . . for 'going left', and . . . for 'engines are going astern'. However, several others are also customary :

– – – 'I wish to pass the lock, or swing-bridge'.

. 'I understand' (in reply to instructions shouted by a loudspeaker in some strange tongue).

. . . . 'I can't manoeuvre'.

. . . . . 'You must not overtake me'.

– 'Look out', or 'take that confounded fishing punt out of my course'.

Flags: A yacht should fly its national ensign *and no other* at the stern. It is proper and polite to show the courtesy flag of the country in which you find yourself, flying it from the starboard halyard of the mast. It is also good manners to make sure that this ensign is the right way up, and that somebody is detailed to change it when you cross national boundaries – a thing easily forgotten. Where the frontier runs down a river (Rhine, Moselle, Lys, etc.) it is legitimate to fly two courtesy flags, each one on the corresponding side of the boat.

In BELGIUM it is customary to fly on a short staff at the bow a red flag with a white square. This means you are a boat in commission. The signal is not so stupid as it sounds, for it enables a skipper to see that where a dozen barges are moored outside a lock only the one or two showing this flag are waiting to enter. In HOLLAND the same flag is used by towing and towed craft to show they are part of an assemblage. Before cutting across between barges it is well to make sure that no such flag is being shown – which would indicate the existence of towage hawsers, possibly just submerged. In GERMANY the towage signals are much clearer; the tug hoists a yellow barrel with black and white rings at either end, whilst the last and *only* the last towed vessel in the line shows a yellow ball.

A red flag on a staff projecting from the side of a stationary vessel means that passing craft should slow and reduce their wash. A black pennant with a silver cross or a design of oak leaves in place of the ensign means that somebody has died aboard the boat – a not uncommon event when families have no other home. It should be treated with sensible respect, and one should never try to make fast alongside.

The one really important flag signal is the blue meeting flag. It is used only on rivers, and is run out on a staff on the starboard side, opposite the steering position – which is where you should also display it. Some of the larger vessels replace the flag by a blue roller blind in the same position, and this is much easier to see than a flag edgeways on. The signal means that the approaching vessel is going to meet you starboard to starboard instead of port to port, and its chief use is by craft moving upstream and taking advantage of the current shadow of the next shoal ahead. It is sensible except in a very small boat to answer flagging by flagging, to show you know what is happening. On the Rhine, about half the vessels you meet will be flagging you, so it is wise to have one member of the crew detailed to watch approaching craft through the binoculars and report all blue flags and blinds, and to haul your own answering signal in or out according to the steersman's orders.

At night the blue flag is replaced by a white flashing light in the same position, and it can be answered by winking a flashlamp. On the Rhone it is fashionable for the larger vessels to blink a green light on the starboard side, even by day, to indicate that they are going to do a starboard meet.

On busy open waterways such as the Rhine, a barge may mount an identical blue flag (but not a roller blind) at the yard-arm of the mast near the bow. This flag is hauled up by a long line from the wheelhouse, and lowered again by a weight. It means 'I am engaged in overtaking', and though this fact might seem obvious, it is not necessarily clear who is overtaking whom when four or five ships and tow-trains are abreast. There is no need for a yacht to fly this signal.

Lock signals: On electric locks or swing-bridges, one (or two) red lights obviously means 'no entry'. One (or two) green lights means 'proceed'. One red and one green means that the lock is being prepared for you. On some Dutch locks a sort of parrot cage is hauled up a mast instead. Up means stop, down means enter.

Some Dutch locks occasionally display a large blue pennant bearing the mysterious word *Spuien.* This means that the lock is being used as a sluice, to let surplus water or more probably a lot of floating filth out of the upper reach. The lock will probably be open at both ends, and have a current of a few knots running through it. Bring up well before the pen, and ask the keeper if you may run through. If he allows you to do so, use great care and run straight down the centre line without hesitating.

Tunnels: These are characteristic of French canals, especially where they cross a watershed. Some are several kilometres long. Even if able to see the other end you should not run in without permission from the *gardien,* who may be the keeper of the previous lock, because the tunnel may be followed by a narrow section in which a boat is already approaching. Obviously certain very short tunnels such as Malpas on the Canal du Midi can be entered when the view is clear.

For tunnel-running there are only two essentials. First, decline firmly to make the passage behind the special towing tug, where there is one. It is impossible to steer most yachts when towed at snail's pace. Second, a good searchlight is very necessary. A kilometre or two inside the hill it can be very dark, even if the tunnel is theoretically lit, which few are. To steer straight needs enormous concentration. I find it helpful if the searchlight is held to pick out the bow, and beyond it the waterline in the tunnel some 30 m. ahead on one side. Accommodation lights turned on inside the boat can help to light the walls abeam, provided none of them can dazzle the steersman.

Bridges: Where a bridge has a number of arches, they will be marked as follows :

White disc:	Arch is navigable
Green disc:	Arch is navigable
Red disc:	Arch is not navigable
Red-white-red striped board:	No entry from that direction
One yellow diamond:	You may use this arch
Two yellow diamonds:	You *must* use this arch

Navigable arches may also have near either side a red and white diamond bisected vertically. The navigable passage is between the two white halves only.

Ferries are common on many rivers, and also on some large canals (Kiel, Amsterdam–Rhine, etc.). It is always advisable to give a short blast when perhaps one minute distant, and take careful note of how the ferry operates. Some are held by a pulley on an overhead cable and present no problem, but the *gierpont* type found in some Dutch rivers needs care, because it is held by a long cable anchored several hundred metres upstream and suspended from a row

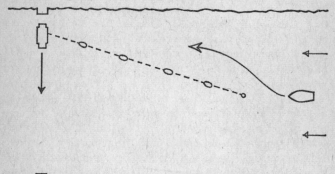

of little boats or floats. If the ferry is moving, keep to the half of the river from which it has started and pass behind it. Otherwise you can find yourself in a wedge-shaped trap.

Dredgers are abundant, especially on rivers. Some are improving the channels, others are merely taking the gravel. There will be cables to anchors and also to one bank (sometimes to both). It is safe to pass only on the side of the dredger which displays either a white disc or a board divided horizontally into red and white halves. A rusty white disc and a faded red one can be almost indistinguishable, so be sure you have the message correctly.

Meeting and overtaking: To meet an oncoming barge in a canal involves a certain technique. If the barge is unladen there should be no difficulty except that in a high wind from the side the barge may be obliged to occupy more of the waterway than otherwise, and you need merely keep going without much slackening of speed, keeping as far to your own (right) side of the waterways as prudence will allow. But the effect of a fully laden barge is very different, for it is not gliding over the water, nor cleaving it, but rather more pushing it out of the way while it passes.

If, as is usual on French canals, the ship is laden to within a few inches of the bottom of the waterway, its skipper will not be able to run close to the side when meeting you, though he will at least move over in due time toward his own side of the actual channel. As he approaches, the bluff bow will shove the water ahead, piling it up by perhaps as much as a foot. At the same time the propeller is driving the water back from the stern, and the result is that the water from the hump at the bow streams very swiftly round the sides to fill up the cavity. The water from your half of the canal will do very much the same. The effect is to force your boat somewhat toward the bank, and then as soon as the roll of bow-wave has passed you to sweep you onward but also somewhat toward the stern of the barge.

Most barges will ease off, which makes things much easier, but in any event the technique for easy meeting is to keep just to the right of the centre and aim straight down the waterway, even if this brings the barge itself squarely into your sights. The wheel should be handled by somebody capable of steering straight without weaving; from the barge skipper's point of view there is nothing so maddening as an oncoming yacht which turns its bow first one way, then the other, as though the steersman is undecided, incompetent, inebriate, or all three.

Keep ploughing ahead, but at a reduced speed, until the barge is no more than ten seconds away, and then incline your bow definitely toward your side of the waterway. He will do the same, and if his stern comes over alarmingly in your direction have no fears. It will soon move the other way.

Your engine should be running at dead slow until his wheelhouse is passing you, when you should accelerate a little to shoot clear and into his wake. When meeting, you should never put the propeller out of gear, as you will be much more manoeuvrable if you keep steerage way on your boat.

The only exception to meeting port to port in a canal is if the oncoming craft is being towed from the bank by a tractor or horses. Though increasingly rare, bank-hauling still exists in central France, and a hauled barge is of course easier to meet in that it has no motor causing a strong-draw-back of the water. On the other hand, it should be obvious that the craft must be passed on the side away from the tow-path and towline.

Overtaking involves a different technique, and can be quite difficult. It is forbidden where the appropriate sign is shown, a white rectangle edged with red, on which are two parallel arrows crossed by a diagonal red line. It is also not allowed within a short distance of a lock, the actual 'proper' distance being a matter more of manners than of rules. In France the winning post is often set on the bank; bearing the words *Limite de trématage* (or sometimes *trémattage*) it marks the point beyond which one may not overtake (*trémater,* or *dépasser*). As a practical rule you may assume that if following one lock behind a laden barge you will need a pound of at least 1½ kms. to catch it and overtake. My own practice is to wait until such a pound is coming, then help the bargeman wind the lock-gear and say I would like to pass him in the next pound (French, *bief*; in German, *Haltung*). Such a request is appreciated and never refused. What bargemasters do not like is a continual harrying from the rear.

In a waterway of limited breadth and depth, two boats proceeding in the same direction, and abreast, can easily drive all the water back so that they both hit the bottom or are thrown together. It is really essential that the barge should ease off somewhat and move over before you pass, and if treated with courtesy the skipper will oblige. As soon as you see the churning behind his screw slacken off, run up towards his port quarter and wait to be beckoned on. Keep as far from the barge as you can (which may be no more than one metre) and make up past it, remembering that there will be a definite drag toward it. All will probably go excellently until you are nearly up to his bow, when you are surprised to find that you are no longer overtaking your neighbour.

The reason is simple. Barges are somewhat blunt at the bow, and instead of cleaving the water they push it up as a mound in front. This heap of water continually streams away to rush past the bow on either side. It may easily be flowing at 2 knots, and that is why you appear to be stuck. At this point, but not before, you should accelerate and climb over the wave, cutting in ahead of the bow of the barge as soon as you have 2 or 3 metres of clear water between you. Your boat will then be on the water the barge is pushing forward, and you will benefit immediately from the shove. It is then safe to turn round and wave your thanks for the skipper's courtesy in letting you by.

On a canal your own boat is not very likely to be overtaken, but on rivers such as the Rhine you may find ships of 2,000 tons coming past at considerable speed. Always keep a sharp eye astern, and when a big fellow starts forging past you, steer deliberately away from him. The suction can be enough to draw a light boat right into the stern of the large one. In my old *Commodore,* which had a weight of only about 7 tons, I was twice struck by overtaking vessels, the skippers of which were quite as surprised as I was.

Washerwomen: Apart from barges and cruisers, other classes of customers use the waterways. In France, the national shortage of rural plumbing is such that even in the second half of the 20th century the canal authority provides washing bays where women take their linen to launder it in the not necessarily very clean water of the canal. The washing bay is usually a sort of concrete pit in which the woman kneels or stands to pound and scrub the clothes on a sill which is an inch or two above the canal level. It is necessary to ease right off when approaching such a laundry, for even a very small wave will either sweep the clothing into the canal, or run over the sill and fill the pit in which the *laveuse* is kneeling.

Fishermen: The other and commoner user is the angler. Whereas professional fishermen who cast nets in even such unlikely places as the Kiel Canal have enough sense not to obstruct the shipping, there is no escaping the fact that a small percentage of holiday and week-end anglers are either exceedingly stupid, or neurotic, or both. I have had anglers cast their lines straight across the bow of my craft all the way from Flushing to Port St Louis du Rhône. Anglers of this kind appear to think that the canal was placed there by providence and the water engineers entirely for their amusement. I have even known an angler fish from the lock-gates and become hysterical when the keeper pressed the button to open them to let out the shipping.

In a fast-flowing river such as the Rhone it may be impossible for any ship, large or small, to make progress upstream unless making at least 8 knots – and setting up a considerable wash. Yet an angler will stand on a low stone at the water's edge with his canvas chair, chest of drawers, lunch, bottle of wine, spare clothing and boxes of bait all spread about within inches of the water, and start to yell and gesticulate at the approaching waves, or shout to the boatman to go to the other side of the river and not disturb his float. Others will sit on a quay wall and be indignant that a boat should draw in toward it at all.

Though the majority of fishermen are pleasant, good-humoured men who appreciate the fact that you slow down so as not to send the wash over their tethered punt, one should always regard an angler as at least a potential lunatic. Probably the best way to deal with fishermen is to reduce wash to reasonable proportions, wave and look encouraging, but absolutely refuse to take their suggestions about how you should navigate – or what you should do with yourself. If they insist on casting across the channel, give one long blast and proceed on your way undaunted. If they monopolise the quayside, give one long blast and draw in against them, regardless. Voluble expressions of angler's neurasthenia are best countered by smiling pretence that the man is talking about the weather being so good, or so bad, as the case may be. The point is to realise that anglers may have a fishing licence, but absolutely no authority to obstruct navigation.

Man overboard: It depends where it happens. In a warm canal in midsummer it can be pleasant to have an unexpected swim, but in a river in mid-winter it can be dangerous. Apart from elementary action such as throwing a lifebuoy near but not at the person if the circumstances demand it, the most important thing is to avoid hitting them with the screw. Any person allowed to steer your boat should understand very clearly that if somebody falls off the boat under way the wheel should immediately be turned *toward* him. This will swing the stern well clear of the point where he will surface.

It is not always easy to climb back aboard a boat. While a ladder is being lowered, or a string of nooses made in a rope, let the person hold a short line hung over the side, but be sure that the motor is in neutral. If it is necessary to manoeuvre out of the path of oncoming traffic, do so at very slow speed and not until the person in the water is securely held twice his own length ahead of the propeller.

6. LOCKMANSHIP

Although on the major waterways electrically operated locks of large dimensions are the rule, small, one-boat, hand-operated locks are characteristic of almost all French waterways as well as Swedish canals and some of the smallest German navigations. Though there should be a lock-keeper in attendance it is still your job to work half the paddles and gates once your boat is inside. If the lock has to be got ready, this is customarily done by the keeper alone, but much time can be saved by having a crew member leap ashore and get to work shutting gates, and closing or opening paddles. Naturally he should first look down the canal beyond the lock and be sure there is not a boat approaching from the opposite direction and within about eight minutes' range – this being the time needed to fill, enter, empty, and leave the lock.

While the shore-man is getting busy, you can lie off and wait, remembering that preparing the lock will cause a considerable flow in the canal. It is unwise to be less than 50 metres from the gates, because at a lesser distance the draw-off above a lock can be quite strong, or the swirl below the lock difficult to cope with. One can hold the boat on the engine, but it is more satisfactory (particularly if you are awaiting a craft from the other direction) to have a means of mooring which will hold the boat in such a way that the screw and cooling intake is kept clear of the stones, mud and other debris along the shore, and the engine can be turned off. After twenty years of French canals I am convinced that for simplicity nothing can compare with a grapple. This is a sort of three- or four-pronged hook heavy enough to throw and attached to about 20 m. or more of light line. It can easily be heaved over the bank and into a bush, or very often the mere rough ground will provide enough grip for it to bite.

When waiting above a lock, the current will be from behind. Run the bow firmly into the edge of the low bank and fling the grapple ashore level with the stern. Make sure it is holding, and then make fast aft, leaving the stern far enough out to give an angle of about 30° with the bank. The flow will hold your boat in that position.

If waiting below a lock, the flow will be from ahead. Again, run the bow firmly into the bank and then fling the

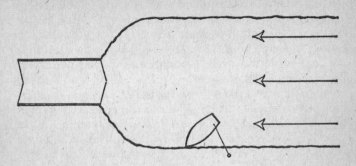

grapple ashore a boat's length upstream. Make fast amidships on the outer side of the boat, or at the stern if enough line is available, so that the boat projects at about 70° from the bank.

When ready to leave, the grapple will probably come free if given a sudden jerk on the line. If not, it will certainly drag out when you go astern to line up for the lock. If by any chance it has lodged round a tree or over a riparian chicken-run just fling the line ashore and let the shore-man go back and extract it while the pen is filling or emptying.

The procedure for going *up* a lock is easy. The moment the gates begin to open and you are sure there is no barge coming out, make for the opening at enough speed to avoid being swung by the slowly eddying water below the gates.

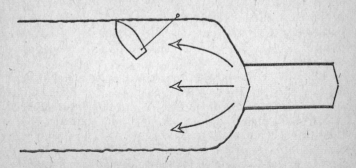

Or, if you prefer, wait until you can see that the eddy has stopped. Run in confidently and bring up close inside the bottom gates, but with direct access to a ladder, which is usually a short way inside on one side of the lock but near the far end on the other. Certain canals have ladders only on the actual gates; if so, run close enough (and slowly enough) for one of the party to step off neatly on to the gate-ladder, or the stone platform just at the entrance. It is important that somebody is put ashore as you enter, to place your lines and shut the gate on that side – unless of course you have already dumped somebody to prepare the lock.

The lines should have large nooses, which can easily be dropped or thrown over bollards, and they should be hauled in tight and made fast *at once,* because the top gates are often leaking or the keeper may have the habit of leaving half a paddle up to cause a flow which will help to shut the lower gates. How you moor will depend partly on where the bollards are, and they are not likely to have been installed with yachts in mind.

When a lock fills, the water surges in at the bottom of the upper gates. You will soon discover that this produces a violent flow *down*stream at the upper end, and a strong if less turbulent flow *up*stream above the bottom gates. About one third of the way up the lock from the bottom gates is an area where the net motion is neither fore nor aft but a calm vertical rise. This is the patch of water your boat should be sitting on.

It is not a good idea to have the stern line attached to a bollard by the lower gates and the bow line near the upper gates. The boat will start weaving to and fro across the lock and you may be powerless to stop it charging the opposite wall. Given a bollard aft of the middle of the lock, an excellent system is to place both lines on the same pin. This also has the advantage that your ladder man may be able to carry both nooses up over his shoulder – in which case, make sure there is slack enough for him not to be dragged off his ladder. Lines should be continually drawn in *and made fast,* not held in the hand, as the boat rises. You may also find it a help to leave the screw running slowly, to help keep the bow line under tension and give some rigidity to your position, at least during the first and most violent minute or two of filling.

Meanwhile, your man ashore should be busy. (It may be the steersman himself. My wife and I have never had any difficulty in running through hundreds of locks without others to help. It is all a matter of proper allocation of jobs.) It is no use putting somebody ashore who has not strength enough to be useful, for his first job is to shut the gate behind you on his side, and then see that the paddles are dropped, not with a bang but winding them down quickly. When winding either up or down he should keep his eye on the ratchet pawl, and if it slips, and the handle starts whizzing round, he should on no account try to stop it with his hand – or any other part of his anatomy .He will only get a broken wrist, or arm. He should make himself scarce as quickly as possible before the handle flies off the spindle and hits him on the head.

He next walks up the lock to the top gates, takes up the handle hanging on them, and starts to wind the paddles up. In France the lock paddles nearly always have a high- and a low-geared spindle. The high gear is good hard work but it is much quicker. Besides, even the most decrepit of lady lock-keepers disdains the low gear as sissy.

There are three important points to watch. First, in the belief that aged machinery benefits from vigorous greasing, many keepers have so ladled thick grease over the rack and pinion that it lies in black heaps on the staging. The captain will appreciate it if this mess is not trodden in and brought back to the deck. Secondly, if the handle is correctly held, you will not get your arms greased either, or bang your elbow on the rack. You should stand to wind the handle up-and-over *away* from you, but the important point is to have the hand nearest the mechanism palm upwards, and the outer hand palm downwards. Though at first this may seem strange, the upturn of your inner hand automatically draws your elbow clear of the works.

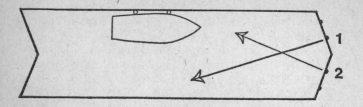

Lastly, the correct paddle should be raised first. This is the one nearest the mitre of the gates and on the same side of the lock as your boat.

The water will shoot right clear of the craft and not rush between it and the wall – with alarming consequences for anyone trying to hold the boat steady. The paddle adjacent to it on the other gate should next be raised, and while this is being done you can tackle either of the others.

With all paddles open you have about two minutes in which to lean against the rail and make lock conversation about the weather, whether there are any craft not far behind you, the problem of the year's vintage, the delights of the countryside, and any other topics which come to mind. The top gates will then be ready to open, and the first heave on the handle is best given just as one of the slight forward surges easily seen on the water is pushing in the same direction as yourself.

As the water rises in the lock, whoever is aboard has the job of tightening up the lines. When the boat reaches lockside level he will find it easiest to leave the stern line secure but jump ashore holding the loose end of the bow line which has been passed round the bow bitts. He can then control the whole movement admirably, and as the line will now have to be let *out* a little, there will be no risk of jamming on an ever-tightening knot. The moment the gates begin to open he can throw both lines back on board and hold the boat in position with his hands ready to push it out when everyone else is aboard.

Locking down involves the same paddle work, though it

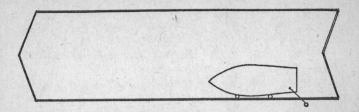

is immaterial which paddle is opened first. However, making fast is much simpler, because the motion of the water is merely to drop evenly all over the lock. Fore and aft mooring is quite unnecessary. A single light line is enough, which can be put over a bollard astern of the boat, led round bitts preferably on the quarter, and easily held in the hand.

If the noose is large enough, the line can be flicked off when you have reached the bottom of the lock, and hauled aboard.

Another excellent system is to have a hook on a line only 2 m. long. The hook can be dropped over a ladder rung and the other end of the line hand-held or made fast loosely opposite the ladder. As the water drops, the hook has merely to be moved down, two or three rungs at a time.

When ready to leave, you will of course still have somebody ashore, who has been opening one of the lower gates. Unless he is as gentle a jumper as a cat the boat will not be improved by his leaping off the lock-side to land with a thud on the deck far below. In many locks he can easily come down the ladder, but in some cases it will be necessary to pick him up on the stone platform at the foot of the steps below the bullnose of the lower gates. When pausing to collect him, remember that emptying the lock is likely to have caused a swirl below it.

The next class of lock is the French one of usual Class I dimensions (38.5 m. × 5.25 m.), but mechanised in that electric or hydraulic power has been added to work the existing machinery. These locks operate quickly and efficiently, and the flow of water is usually more even. There is no need to leave the boat or jump ashore, though it may be useful for someone quickly to run up a ladder with the lines while the gates are shutting. These locks have no signals; when the gates are open, you go in.

In large electric locks (Rhone, Moselle, G.C.A., Dortmund–Ems, etc.) it is usual to make a yacht come in last and to fill up a small hole at the rear of the sardine mass of shipping, even if it arrived there ahead of the rest. Listen carefully for shouted instructions trickling from the bankside loudspeakers : *'Das Sportboot bleibt zurück, und fährt erst nach dem Motorschiff in die Schleuse'*, or some such order. One toot on your hooter means you have got the message. If you look puzzled, the captain of a nearby barge will indicate by signs what is expected of you. On some canals (e.g. the Albert and the Maas–Waal canals) a long instruction is shouted, telling all the boats by name how they are to pack themselves in. Your name for the occasion is likely to be *Vedette, Sportboot* or *Jacht.*

Really it is much better to be at the front, because the water comes in down the centre line without any turbulence, and at the front one avoids the difficulty of trying to pull in within a metre or so of a big ship which has left its screw turning and the rudder hard over to keep close to the wall with minimum effort. If requested, bargemasters will usually turn off the engine, but some seem quite unable to grasp that you will be driven about like a cork in a whirlpool if their jet stream is directed at you. Again, when the time comes to leave the lock, the ships will give a puff and a chuff and pull back the throttle. At this moment you must be held extremely fast, and securely too. Do not attempt to let go until the last ship is at least 50 m. ahead of you, and preferably just reaching the gates. All this trouble may be avoided by a swift dash up to the lockhouse and a well-tuned request to be allowed up front – though some lock-keepers may not grant your request, explaining that if the holding hawser of a 2,000-tonner breaks as it approaches your transom you might wish you had stayed at the rear after all.

Many of the largest modern locks have rising bollards

which float on tanks in recesses in the wall, and so rise or fall with the water. These make locking very simple, as there is no need to let the lines in or out. Others (e.g. the International Moselle) have small recessed bollards every 2 metres of the ascent, but they are so placed that one cannot have access to two rows of them if aboard any craft smaller than a French standard barge. It is not such a good idea when rising to have both nooses on one bollard, as you can easily drift out while trying to get them both on the next one. 'Topping and tailing' is probably better, but involves continually driving forward to move the bow line up, then back to do the same with the stern line.

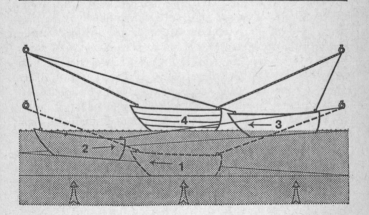

Easiest, if space permits, is to ask if you may lie alongside a big ship and use him as a rising bollard – not forgetting that you will need to detach yourself, push over, and make fast to the wall before he turns on the power to leave.

If alone in a large modern lock, do not move out of the pen until the exit light goes green, even if the gates are already open. There may be underwater devices (sinking gates, etc.) which need to be fully retracted before a boat can safely leave. In very deep locks it is often the practice to blow a siren or hooter when the raising or lowering is about to begin. If by chance you should not be ready, because your craft is not attached or a line is jammed, give one *long* blast on your hooter to warn the lock-keeper to hold his hand.

Tipping: At some large locks a small tip is customary. When showing the papers see how much the barge captains put down on the table, and do likewise. Tipping is not usual at small French locks – and even at only fr. 0.50 would work out very expensive on, for instance, the Canal de Bourgogne. But there is sometimes a case for it, particularly when some old dear has slaved away in pouring rain to open an almost derelict pair of gates.

Perhaps it is good that the days are gone when money could buy everything. No copper handshake will nowadays induce a lock-keeper to stay on duty so that you can pass through his lock a few minutes after hours, and risk getting the sack for doing so. This is not to say that he may never do so, but just that he will do it out of kindness at his own suggestion, and not for shekels of yours. It is not just the fact that on some waterways acceptance of a tip brings instant dismissal, but that the social order has changed.

On the other hand it is natural to want to thank in some way an individual who has gone to particular trouble to help you, and the question is – how. To this there is no answer that will hold good under all circumstances. Probably the best way is to assess the conditions and act accordingly. If the lock-keeper is an old and crippled pensioner, perhaps a widow scraping a living on some unfrequented waterway such as the Montauban arm or the River Seille, then it seems reasonable to give a franc or more for the mere passage through. But at smarter, more prosperous locks this will not do. One could hardly expect the white-coated white-collar men of the International Moselle to be overjoyed at the sight of a few pence. Like most, what they really appreciate is the personal contact, a few minutes' chat over a cigarette while the lock is filling, some remarks about their garden or their lush pot-plants in the electrically heated cabin, the prospects for their youngsters. Yet sometimes one wants to do rather more.

Some years ago I hit upon a solution which has since proved very satisfactory. There cannot be a lock-keeper anywhere in the world who is not either a stamp collector himself, or has not a son, niece, godchild or some other acquaintance who is an amateur philatelist. I keep on board a box of used stamps saved from the mail at home throughout the year, and bring it out when occasion demands so that the keeper or his son, niece, godchild or whoever it may be can rootle in it and help themselves. This is extremely popular; it shows a certain amount of personal interest and avoids all the embarrassments connected with passing a franc, or mark or guilder. I am not suggesting that everyone boating on the continent should do the same, but just that on the waterways we all nowadays live and move and have our being in a society where social differences are entirely lacking and the tipper–tippee relationship no longer exists.

7. MOORING

Stopping in a waterway is not quite as simple as making fast in a harbour. Other craft passing may make a wash which bumps your boat against stones or tree roots, and laden barges in modest canals will cause a draw-off which will put great strain on your lines and their attachments. In rivers there is also the matter of the current and how to use it.

Mooring alongside a wall or wharf with plenty of water

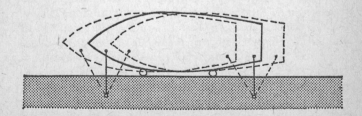

is the easiest situation. There are probably rings and bollards, and little is necessary but to make fast fore and aft with fenders over the side. However, passing barges will tend to drive the boat to and fro, which may be annoying.

It is much better to have *both* ends of your craft held from *both* directions.

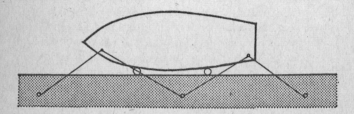

Some canals have not a single quay or pontoon in a hundred kilometres. You have no option but to moor against the bank, where there is likely to be little water and plenty of stones or other debris, or at least some good juicy mud to block the cooling system. It is a good idea to select a suitable spot and come in at an angle of about 45°, the engine being turned off just before you run on the mud or into the reeds.

Good stout trees may be available for mooring, but you will not be popular if you have lines tight across the towpath and forcibly dismount cyclists coming by in the dark. Lock-keepers and others often use cars and motor-cycles on the towpath, and for this reason lines across it are in fact forbidden, unless they are either flat on the ground or some three metres above it – neither of which is likely to be feasible. Small bushes and saplings are tempting, but if you use them as bollards you may find that the draw-off of an approaching barge will tear them out of the ground and swing you across the path of a vessel which cannot immediately stop and may embed its 350 tons of mass in the side of your boat. Better is to use bank anchors (see p. 28) capable of exerting a really firm hold, and to steady your mooring by the cross method.

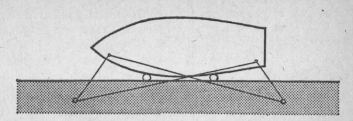

This will prevent you sawing along the bank, and the bow or stern being pulled out into the channel.

Where the bank is rough or rocky, you will want to keep the stern out. This is most easily done with a gang-plank which has a small loop of rope, or possibly a hole, at the inshore end.

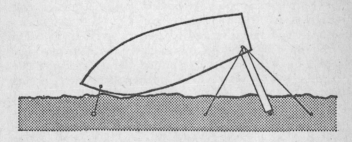

The three-point hold given to the boatward end of the plank makes for great security.

The gang-plank can also be used to keep the stern out from a high wall edged by stones or accumulated rubbish.

In rivers where heavy traffic causes a ceaseless and violent wash, it is nothing short of dangerous to moor to any structure at all, even to an anchored barge. Your lines may be snapped or the bitts pulled out of the deck; and even if the actual mooring survives you will receive a most unpleasant buffeting. On the Rhine, for example, any berthing along the river itself is unwise. A backwater or harbour should always be your goal for stopping.

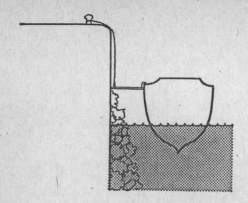

Rivers with even a modest flow demand mooring with the bow upstream. The anchor can be used to hold you out from the bank, the gang-plank to prevent you being too far out, and to help with getting ashore.

River pontoons are tricky, because if they tip on the wash of big ships they will do so at a different speed from your boat. The result is a banging and clattering, and probably a scoring of the paintwork. It is preferable to have the lines

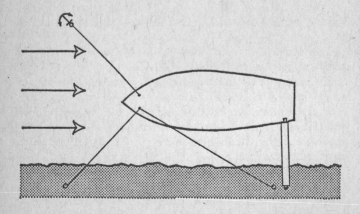

made fast above and below the pontoon gangway, and to come alongside only after dropping the anchor out in the stream. When the chain is tightened, your boat will be held close to the pontoon but not against it, so the lying will be much better.

8. SUPPLIES

Fuel: Diesel, petrol and two-stroke mixture are easily obtainable in the Low Countries. In the Swedish canals you may risk running out of fuel unless you top up at each of the infrequent fuelling points, and in France it is essential to keep an eye on the gauge as pumps are quite rare. In France, ships use domestic heating oil or *Gaz Oil* (pronounced Guzzwull), which is really diesel oil but without so high a duty.

In Germany, fuel can be had duty-free provided you ask the customs post at the entry point for a *Betriebsbuch* in which you enter daily the hours of running the motors, and an *Empfangsbescheinigungsheftchen,* which is merely a little booklet of fuelling receipts, one of which will be made out by each fuel-barge or depot which supplies you. This provides an enormous saving in cost. Major German rivers are copiously provided with vast and efficient fuelling boats and floating chandleries. The Lahn and the Left-handed Canals are probably the only waterways where fuel is not abundant.

Drinking water: Available also at Yacht Clubs and in many commercial ports, water is usually to be had at certain locks on any canal or river navigation. The hose may be ready and waiting on the lock-side, in which case you should have the stopper out so that the pipe can be put in the moment you enter. If any traffic is coming the other way you will have to stop watering and leave the lock as soon as the gates are open.

In France, water is hard to find. The barge people tend to drink wine or mineral water, and wash with a bucket. It is vital to have adequate tankage, and to impress on any friends not used to boats that they must not run water to

waste. There may not be another tap for 200 kms. With
France in mind, my *Thames Commodore* was fitted with
tanks to take 1,200 litres, and has never run dry. This may
seem a large amount, but with cooking and washing one
can well allow 20 litres per day per person.

Some locks have a tap but no hose, so you should always
have one ready. The hose carried aboard should not be less
than 30 m. in length, and a plastic one which kinks or sags
together when stowed in hot weather is quite useless. A
sensible, stout, rubber-and-canvas hose is a good investment.
French, and in fact all continental tap fittings, are likely to
be different to your own, and the correct species should be
bought at the first possible ironmongers in the country concerned, and securely fixed to your hose.

Water tanks are best installed in two sections, which can
be used independently. Then at least you know when you
are half way through your stock and need to start looking
carefully for taps. Much water can also be saved if washing-
up and rinsing is done with already hot river water cun-
ningly diverted from the cooling exit pipe to the sink by a
two-way tap.

Gas: If your own boat has a gas installation for cooking
or heating, it is well to realise (which some boat-builders do
not) that the brand of cylinder you use may not be available
abroad, and that the fittings of other brands will not connect
with your pipes. If in doubt ask the makers, and not the
local store which happens to supply you. Even if assured
that your customary brand can be obtained in the country
you are visiting, you still need to consider that it may be a
rarity. As you will not wish to walk 50 kms. for a fresh
cylinder of British type, you may find it much simpler to
have your pipe fitting changed in advance to take the
cylinders of *Camping Gaz International,* which can be
found in even the smallest towns across the whole continent,
are stocked by floating ship-shops, and are freely inter-
changeable from one country to another.

Mail: Some people seem to think that the world will stop
turning if they cannot have their mail forwarded to them.

If you are going to have letters sent on, the natural thing to do is to give a Poste Restante (Postlagernd, General Delivery) address at a series of towns through which you are going to pass. This is not such a good idea as it seems, and it can result in such inconvenience that I personally refuse to take friends who leave Poste Restante addresses.

The reason is simple : to extract mail from a post office you obviously have to be there when it is open. Post office hours are often peculiar. Many do not open until nine in the morning, and shut from twelve to three. All will be closed on Sunday, and probably most of Saturday. There is also a good chance that you will arrive on the patronal festival of a local saint and find the place closed. So you may have to hang about for a day or more, merely to discover that nobody has even sent you a postcard.

The solution is equally simple. You need only adopt the mail system of the barges, and have the mail addressed to a lock. Obviously the lock must be open if you can go through. The locks at any small town, or at a waterways junction, or at the entrance to a canal or, in fact, almost anywhere will have a mail board, on which your letters will be displayed. If you do not know in advance where the locks are you can discover them from canal maps, or from the details of the waterways given in this book.

Mail should be addressed to you personally, but your name should be followed by the name of the boat (*bateau, Schiff, båt, jacht*) in capital letters, as this is the identifying name that the keeper will see when you come sailing in. A simple mail address might run like this :

> Mr J. Reader,
> Bateau 'TIGER LILY'
> Écluse de Gray,
> GRAY (Haute Saône).

The corresponding term for lock would be in German *Schleuse,* in Dutch and in Flemish *Sluis,* in Swedish *Sluss.*

Telegrams: You need have no worries that you cannot be found in case of emergency. The continental waterways mostly have their own private telephone systems, and where they do not you can safely rely upon the ingenuity of the post office. After all, there are many thousands of barges scattered over the countryside, and the authorities are very used to finding them swiftly. A telegram addressed to you with only such a vague address as Bateau TIGER LILY, Canal du Rhône au Rhin, France, will reach you swiftly, for although the canal may be more than 200 kms. long the telephone system will quickly locate you and see that you are stopped at the next lock. Once again, the vital name is that of the boat, not yourself.

Currency: Continental banks have quite as strange hours as British ones, but they vary. Some German banks open at seven in the morning, and French ones frequently take a three-hour siesta at midday. You will not be able to change money on Saturday or Sunday unless you are close to a frontier-post used by road traffic – as at Remich on the Moselle – although in real emergency a hotel may oblige by changing a modest amount.

THE WATERWAYS

The canals and rivers described in this section are grouped as far as possible in areas. *Starboard* means on the right in the direction in which the waterway is being described. *Port* similarly means on the left. The initial R in the description of a river course means on the right bank when facing downstream – which will be on your left when going upstream. Similarly L means on the left bank, which is on the right when going upstream. In the navigation notes, $\frac{1}{3}$L means one third of the way across the river from the left bank (facing downstream), and $\frac{1}{3}$R means one third of the way across from the right bank. This terminology is standard in continental navigation manuals.

Certain rivers are described as being navigable according to the 'Thirds Rule'. This merely means that on comparatively straight stretches one stays in the centre, but that on bends the channel will be found nearer the outside of the curve and one should steer a course roughly one third of the way across the stream from the outside of the bend. Travelling down stream this would be $\frac{1}{3}$R on a curve to the left (port), $\frac{1}{3}$L on a bend to the right (starboard).

INTRA-COASTAL WATERWAY,
FRANCE–BELGIUM–HOLLAND

All the ports from Calais northward to Zeeland (except Blankenberghe) are connected by canals which run a short distance behind the coast and provide small craft with a sheltered passage in any weather. Dimensions are standard French, or larger. Starting from Calais the route is as follows :

Port of Calais. The ship-lock into the Bassin Carnot beyond the car ferry terminal opens for some time either side of high water (Dover + 0.17). Report to the lock office beforehand, and also to the customs office on the quay across the basin from the packet boats, making sure that the *Carnet de Passage* is duly stamped there, and the *Volet d'Entrée* removed.

The lock-keeper will want to see the *Permis de Circulation;* but in the case of a craft taking this route on the spur of the moment he will issue a pass as far as the Belgian frontier, free of charge. At the further end of the basin a barge-lock leads into the Canal de Calais, which turns sharp left under a bridge. There are good moorings against the quay straight ahead, instead of turning left, and this is the most convenient point from which to visit the city.

CALAIS was taken by King Edward III in 1347. At the end of a fearful siege the monarch demanded unconditional surrender, intending to execute the entire garrison, but was persuaded to settle for six chief citizens, barefoot and with ropes round their necks. The successful intervention of

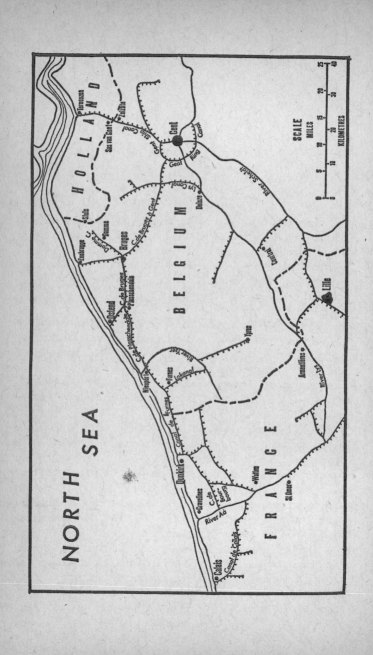

Queen Philippa saved their lives and she restored the men to their families. Rodin's famous bronze of Eustache St Pierre and his five companions stands outside the 19th-century gothic city hall, and another copy beside the House of Lords in London. Calais was re-peopled with English families and remained an English borough with two Members of Parliament until 1558, when it was recaptured by the Duke of Guise. No traces of the English occupation remain.

In the rebuilt market square of the new town a burned-out tower with its bells fallen and fused with the heat has been left as an eloquent memorial to the city's destruction in the Second World War.

Canal de Calais. 29·5 kms. long, this is a fenland waterway crossing a landscape of wide fields of black earth furrowed by rootling pigs. One lock, at Henuin, beyond which the canal meanders a little before reaching the R. Aa. Turn left or right. Both routes lead to Dunkirk.

River Aa. Turning left, the stately Aa leads as a tree-lined avenue down to Gravelines (13 kms.) with another outlet to the sea at high water (Dover + 0.36), but after only 7·5 kms. the Canal de Bourbourg leads off to the right (see below).

Turning right instead of left at the end of the Canal de Calais, after only 4·5 kms. the main route from Dunkirk to Paris is reached at Watten. Turn left at this junction into the widened Canal de la Haute Colme, which rejoins the Canal de Bourbourg after 8 kms. This second route is quicker, because there are no locks, but it is less picturesque.

Canal de Bourbourg. Length 21 kms. Locks 2, at the junction with the R. Aa (up) and in Bourbourg (down).

The passage across the meadows and through Bourbourg itself is winding and rural, faded farm hamlets lying pale and lonely under the wide fenland sky. Traffic is negligible.

After the junction with the Canal de la Haute Colme the

waterway becomes broad and wide, having been enlarged
to Europaship standards, and 11·5 uneventful kilometres
lead to the Lock of Jeu de Mail in Dunkirk.

The outlet to the sea is through the docks, via the short
link immediately opposite the end of the Canal de Bourbourg. To reach Belgium, turn right from the Canal de
Bourbourg into the Canal de Jonction. Beyond the barges
there is good alongside mooring on the port hand, for shopping. A short way ahead is the Ecluse de Furnes leading into
the Canal de Furnes.

DUNKIRK was also English, but only for three years (1659–
62), and its chief fame in the 17th century was as a base for
corsairs (pirates). It was almost entirely destroyed in 1940
during the evacuation of more than one third of a million
British and allied soldiers, many of whom were picked up
by yachts.

Canal de Furnes. Length 25 kms. Locks 1, at Furnes.

This almost straight and uneventful waterway cuts across
the flat land behind the dunes. There is little traffic. Just
beyond the bridge at Ghyvelde (10·5 kms.) there is a French
customs jetty on the right, where the *Carnet* must be
presented and the *Volet de Sortie* stamped and removed.
After another 2·5 kms. the canal has unobtrusively slipped
into Belgium, the Belgian customs post being on the right
just short of the town of Furnes. Formalities are minimal.
At the lockhouse in Furnes a permit to the furthest destination in Belgium must be obtained for a few pence.

It was on the Belgian section short of Furnes that in 1876
Commander W. J. C. Moens in the steam-yacht *Ytene*
joined forces with a French barge to pull down a bridge
when the keeper tried to extort money. Though commend-
able, such behaviour is nowadays inadvisable, as no gun-
boats can get up the canal to shoot a way out.

FURNES (VEURNE) is a quiet Flemish town with an excellent and modern commercial harbour basin offering good
mooring. The central square is surrounded by little step-
gabled houses of brick, some with magnificently ornamented

eaves, others with ironwork dating from the Spanish occupation in the 16th century. Dominated by the great churches of St Walburga (c. 1600) and St Nicholas (13th to 15th centuries), Furnes has a sombre air which is reflected in the annual procession of black-hooded penitents bearing crosses on the last Sunday in July, and the procession of the Cross on the Sunday before 3rd May.

At the lock another waterway, the Lokanal, leads off to the right in the direction of the Yser and the canal to YPRES (IEPER), where little of the medieval town survived the furious battle for the Ypres Salient in the First World War. Ahead, the Canal de Furnes runs almost straight to NIEUPORT (NIEUWPOORT), at the mouth of the Yser, and ends at a large round tidal pond into which open the locks of the Canal de Furnes, the River Yser (leading to Ypres, but not a through route beyond) and the Canal de Plasschendale. Before high water (Dover + 0.57) all the locks are opened and craft pass across the basin. If undecided whether to continue by canal there is time enough to lock out, run down the tideway to inspect the state of the sea outside, and return if necessary to lock in to another waterway. Nieuport is primarily a fishing port with drifters lying along the quay, but the yacht harbour further down the outlet to the sea offers hospitable moorings. The town is also renowned for its eels cooked in many different ways, and as the end of the Western Front in 1914–18. The statue of King Albert on his horse stands in a large circular memorial by the locks, and nearby is the bust of the lock-keeper Geeraert who held back the Germans by using the paddles to flood the land. On the last Sunday of June the sea is solemnly blessed – as it has been since 1486.

Canal de Plasschendale. Length 22 kms. No locks. An uneventful waterway which runs from Nieuport to its junction with the Canal de Bruges at Plasschendale lock (usually open right through). Just short of the junction it is crossed by a railway swing-bridge on the busy Ostend–Brussels line. Trains are so frequent, especially at commuter time, and the bridge operation so cumbrous, that the span can only be swung at specified times and for a very few minutes. Waiting barges do not always get through at the first attempt. It is important to establish and maintain your place in the queue – but on no account to jump it, because the bridge is round a corner and oncoming craft are not easily seen.

From Plasschendale onwards the waterways can be used by barges of 600 tons, and will eventually take 2,000-ton craft.

Canal de Bruges. From the top of Ostend docks (outlet to the sea, two locks) this canal runs to the junction with the Canal de Plasschendale and thence to Bruges. Length 21 kms. No locks. At the toll-house beside the swing-bridge at the junction a pass must be obtained for a boat coming from Ostend.

The canal is not straight, but winds a little between its tall lines of poplars, and is as though out of a Flemish painting. The water is peaty and black with a somewhat acrid smell, but there are much worse aromas ahead. Within an hour the incomparable tower of Bruges belfry can be seen across the fields.

At the entrance to Bruges there are several swing-bridges which open in concert subject to the exigencies of rush-hour road traffic, shunting goods wagons across the canal, and the bridge-keeper being involved in an argument with a cyclist. *Caution:* If a whole covey of barges is coming down from Bruges round lock, do not attempt to force a passage between one and the next but wait for the signal.

OSTEND besides being a ferry port and a base for fishing boats, is the chief resort of the Belgian coast, with casino and restaurants and the bow of *H.M.S. Vindictive* from the Zeebrugge raid of the First World War. The sea is blessed on the first Sunday in July. Fair mooring at the North Sea Yacht Club in the tidal harbour, but better in the basin.

BRUGES. At the entrance to the town a lock on the port hand leads into the Canal to Zeebrugge (i.e. Sea-Bruges), a vast waterway and another outlet to the sea. Next, to starboard and beyond the distillery, is a smaller lock leading into the Coupure, the original canal through the city. The Coupure provides a good mooring when staying in the city, though it is closed at the weekend. It is well polluted with sewage, and lines dropped in the water should only be handled with gloves. On account of the smell, leave the lavatory pumped dry.

Caution: Bites from Coupure-living mosquitos should be treated with antiseptic and if anyone falls in they should be taken to hospital at once for a thorough cleaning inside and out. In spite of these menaces the mooring is one of the most beautiful imaginable, the sound of bells tinkling down through the branches of the trees on the medieval quays. An alternative mooring is beyond the round lock, in the second entrance to the Coupure.

An unusual experience is to get a dinghy into the Coupure, hauling it over the road if necessary, and then to row at night through the many little medieval canals which wind about the city as far as the willow-fringed Lake of Love (Minnewater) with its swans, a basin which at the height of the city's prosperity in the 13th century saw the arrival of as many as 150 ships or lighters in one day. In the Grand Place the incomparable belfry of the 12th century contains the fine carillon on which the municipal carilloneur gives concerts several mornings a week in the summer – though the 49 bells are hard to hear above the traffic and one can best listen from the canals or from the town ramparts along the ring canal. The 'Pageant of the Holy Blood' takes place every five years, in years ending with 2 or 7, and nothing could better evoke the splendour of medieval Flemish life in a city which is still unbelievably age-old and was once fabulously wealthy. But even without these additions a walk along the cobbled quays where the gabled houses are mirrored in the black water is an experience never forgotten.

Immediately beyond the first Coupure entrance is the Bruges round lock or Dammepoortsluis, a stone basin with three gates instead of two. The one ahead is the route to Gent, but in the side a smaller entrance leads into the Damme canal and thence to Sluis. If going to DAMME

(5 kms.) tell the lock-keeper so that the water level can be held while you make your exit. This almost deserted little town on the canal which centuries ago was the main trade artery of Bruges, was formerly a seaport. A small trip-boat runs from the Dammepoortsluis, or one can lock down and go in one's own boat. Allegedly Damme was the residence of the medieval joker Till Eulenspiegel (see also *Elbe–Trave Canal*).

Canal de Bruges à Gent. From the Dammepoortsluis to the Gent Ring canal. Length 40 kms. No locks. Not scenically notable, this waterway smells unpleasantly of flax-retting effluent which comes in via the Lys Canal, which crosses it about 10 kms. short of Gent (Ghent, Gand). Half a day can be spent in an unusual side-trip by turning right into the Lys Canal to Deinze (one lock) then left to the Lock of Astene on the River Lys (q.v.; to the right the Lys provides an adequate but not very beautiful route via Courtrai and Armentières to St Omer and the Canal de Calais.) Astene Lock is normally closed, and in fact is so rarely opened that great strength may be required to creak the paddles open, but the installation is manned and the keeper can be per- suaded to telephone for permission for a boat to pass. The prohibition is to prevent the terrible effluvia of the Upper Lys from entering the long meanders of the elegant river down to Gent, a stretch lined with manors, riverside inns, and hamlets reminiscent of the Upper Thames. A cruise down this winding section of the Lys is sheer delight, for even if the water is rather black the begonias in the water- side flower-beds of stately homes slash the sombre river with the brilliance of their reflections.

Gent Ring Canal. One lock. The former route through Gent being closed, craft reaching the city from the west can only take this modern by-pass which curves round to join the Gent Ship Canal near the docks. At the far end turn left for Holland and the Scheldt estuary; or right for Gent city centre, the Upper Scheldt to Antwerp and Brussels, or the Lys to Astene lock (see above).

By far the best berth in GENT is at the quay in the dead end opposite the side of the Palais de Justice. From the Ring Canal turn right, bear left beyond the railway bridge and follow through the barge docks until a right angle bend to the right leads into the Kastelsluis lock. Beyond this, follow the pleasant town canal until it opens out into another waterway which in fact is the Upper Scheldt. Turn right. Beyond the Brusselsepoortsluis lock, double back sharp right into the Lys, which soon curves hard left to a narrows (the Ketelvaart) between the back of the Palais de Justice and some old houses much battered by the impact of barges. At the end of this cut turn right into the dead end and moor beneath the trees.

For a brief run-down on the history of the city, Gent has a miniature Son-et-Lumière model in the Belfry with a commentary available in English, and one can see that not much has changed in the last few hundred years. Some of the canal warehouses on the Graslei (Quai. aux Herbes) date back to the 13th century. *Caution:* Though extremely romantic, the old canals of Gent are probably more polluted than any others in Europe and seethe with bubbling corruption. Do not attempt to wash or rinse any utensils over the side, and leave the deck scrubbing till later. As at Bruges, try to avoid flushing the lavatory.

Gent Ship Canal. Length 35 kms. One lock, normally open right through. This canal reaches the Scheldt estuary at Terneuzen in the Dutch province of Zeeuwsch Vlaanderen, and is a vast waterway for ocean-goers. The Belgian customs jetty is at Sas van Gent, a short way beyond Zelzate on the starboard side heading north. Stop for clearance (minimal delay). Next to the customs house is the Belgian navigation office, where incoming craft should acquire a permit. The Dutch customs are 1 km. further down on the opposite (port) side. Clearance is immediate and no waterways permit is needed.

TERNEUZEN is a pleasant and typical canal-end town with no other *raison d'être,* and was the home of the *Flying*

Dutchman. On reaching the outskirts take the first cut on the starboard side, to the barge lock. Yachts may not use the big-ship locks. Locking out is around high water (Dover + 2.37), before which the dozens of waiting barges spring into life and fight for the gap in the lifting bridge, in the town centre. This is an easy place to be crushed. It is wisest to lay off and fill the last small space at the back of a lock which will resemble a much-magnified tin of sardines containing thirty or more barges of every size. While waiting one can climb the water tower and see what the Scheldt and the Zeeland islands are like. To the right the river leads up to Hansweerd and the South Beveland Canal; to the left it runs down to Flushing and the Walcheren Canal. Either of these routes will lead through the islands toward Rotterdam, the Rhine, Friesland, the Kiel Canal and Scandinavia.

Caution: The exit into the Scheldt should be taken fast, but also with care. There is a bad swirl at some states of tide, the current setting on to the rocky mole. If your boat should be wrecked it will not be the first British yacht to come to grief at this spot. If unfamiliar with such exits, carefully watch the barge ahead and follow his track. Keep a sharp look-out for incoming craft, and for ocean-goers clipping close past the dyke outside.

RIVER RHINE AND CONNECTIONS

River Rhine. Navigable from Rheinfelden bridge to the sea. Length 882 kms. to Hoek van Holland. Locks 2 Swiss, 8 French.

Navigation: On the Rhine more than anywhere else it is essential to know exactly what you are doing, and to have a boat that can be relied upon to do it. The current is swift (6 knots is not at all unusual in the Bingen defile, and 5 all the way from Lauterbourg to Strasbourg), and most of the ships are so large they might not even feel a slight thump if they ran you down, whilst some are cocked so high at the bow when unladen that the water within 200 m. ahead is invisible to the steersman. The traffic behaves according to very definite sailing directions, and though some yachtsmen have adopted the principle of merely dodging out of the way it is much more restful, and more reassuring to other traffic and your own next of kin, if you behave according to the rules. Certainly between Koblenz and Strasbourg it would be foolish to run the Rhine without following the course as set out (in French, German and Dutch) with excellent clarity in the 101-sheet volume of charts entitled *Le Rhin. Guide pour la Navigation,* published by the French School of Pilotage of the Rhine and available from Editions de la Navigation du Rhin, 3 Route du Rhin, Strasbourg-Neudorf; or from Schiffahrtsverlag Rheinschiffahrt, Haus Oberrhein, Rheinvorland, Mannheim, and stocked by many chandlers.

That guide sets out the directions so clearly that no details of the course need here be given. But the principle is simple. To prevent erosion and assist scouring, the Dutch

reaches with relatively little fall are groyned all the way from Sliedrecht up. These groynes are high, broad, and usually several feet above the water. Close to their ends the current is greatly reduced, or even reversed, and groyne-crawling will take even a really slow boat up the river. The groynes continue (though less visible) to beyond Cologne, and they are usually joined by a gravel shoal, the outer edge of which is likely to be buoyed. Throughout this lower half of the river ships tend to keep to the right on the straights but not necessarily on the bends. It is important to note that the principle of up-going craft taking the inside of the bend does not necessarily apply. The up-going ships are always where the current is slackest and that will be in the current shadow of the next shoal ahead.

In the gorge the directions should be followed with great care, because the river bed contains rocks outside the navigation channel. It is sensible here to have an anchor ready for a quick drop in emergency. Half the accidents on the whole river occur in the Bingen defile, and however competent you may be you can still feel surprised when the tow-cable parts on a 2,000-ton motorless lighter which then swings sideways and starts careering broadside down the river toward you.

From Speyer upstream the river was much straightened out in the 19th century (81 kms. were chopped off its length between Strasbourg and Basle alone) and this made it flow so swiftly that it became altogether unnavigable until groynes were added in alternate sets to throw the water from side to side and take the exuberance out of it. This means that the channel (and current shadows) change sides about every $1\frac{1}{2}$ kms. and so should you.

Above Strasbourg there are no problems except that the free run through Basle is fast and constricted by the bridge piers. Watch for back-runs on to the buttresses – a useful practice at all Rhine bridges.

Pilotage: The only stretch on which pilotage is customary except for ships which continually ply on the Rhine is in the gorge above Koblenz. However, it is quite unnecessary for a yacht or cruiser. Provided you are familiar with fast rivers, understand the blue flag system and have a copy of the *Guide pour la Navigation,* you can perfectly well proceed on your own. If not, or if you have read too many exaggerated tales of the terrors of the Rhine, then pilots are available at Bad Salzig, at St Goar, and (for the return journey) at Bingen.

Lock dues: Below Switzerland navigation of the Rhine costs nothing, the G.C.A. locks being authorised and guaranteed toll-free by the Treaty of Versailles. A small charge is made for the Swiss locks at Birsfelden and Augst.

The Rhine, which flows through Switzerland, France, Germany and Holland, is one of the world's most famous rivers, and from Roman times onward it has been the scene of bloody battles as well as an artery of trade. The main transport route of the Common Market countries it is now the river with more traffic than any other, and some fifteen thousand barges – many of them the largest in Europe – run between Rhine ports or take the Rhine on the way to its navigable tributaries. Coasters regularly run up to Cologne, and occasionally even to the Swiss port of Basle. Huge passenger vessels ply in the summer months, the river is crossed by scores of ferries, and although cruisers are relatively uncommon one may meet everything from eights to eel-boats. The entire river is administered by the Central Commission for the Rhine, on which Britain (of all surprising countries) is represented.

Scenically the Rhine varies greatly. In the section above Basle the river sweeps fast and grey along the southern edge of the Black Forest. Below the city and all the way to Strasbourg it is diverted into the Grand Canal d'Alsace, an enormous and rather featureless waterway in French territory, built for hydro-electric purposes under authority of the Treaty of Versailles and only recently completed. To either side the land rises to a height of more than 1,000 m., but the plain is broad and both the Vosges and Black Forest hills are at a distance of several kilometres. Near Breisach a line of volcanic vineyard hills (the Kaiserstuhl) appears alongside the river, but thereafter the mountains again keep their distance all the way to Karlsruhe, where they peter out.

For the whole course from Basle to Worms the river itself is somewhat uninteresting, except for its traffic. The long and straight canal cuts of Alsace give way to seemingly endless copses of poplar, and swampy thickets. Not a single town or village dares to venture within range of what once was a broad and variable river bed, unless it has its feet planted firmly on a rise which will serve as a defence from the floods.

At Worms the vineyards appear again, alternating with patches of industry until below Mainz, where the Rhine flows broad and majestic past famous wine villages such as Ingelheim and Oestrich, Hattenheim and Geisenheim, to Rüdesheim where it pulls in its belt, puts on pace, and rushes through the defile of the Binger Loch into the 64 famous kilometres of the Rhine gorge with castle ruins perched on almost every crag of the brown and slaty rock, all the way to the confluence with the Moselle at Koblenz.

Once again industry alternates with the vintners until the last of the vines appear on the hillsides of the Siebengebirge, a group of volcanic hills opposite Bonn. From here to the Dutch frontier the natural scenery is flat and featureless and the glory of the Rhine lies in its noble cities such as Cologne, the fantastic turmoil and smoke of Duisburg and the Ruhr, and the ever-increasing surge of traffic. In Holland the river seems to lose its determination, some of it dividing off to the right and splitting again to form the R. Geldersche IJssel which empties into the IJsselmeer, and the R. Lek which flows through Arnhem and eventually rejoins the other route (the R. Waal) on the edge of Rotterdam. Although the Lek is a pleasant alternative route it can be shallow in dry weather, and three barrages with locks have recently been added to overcome this tendency – though when there is plenty of water the locks are by-passed.

Most traffic will of course use the Waal, which begins by deciding to wash the feet of Nijmegen's hill. From here onward small brickworks and shipyards are scattered along the banks at intervals between lush pastures cropped by cows and occasional faded little towns of mellow brick. Below Gorinchem the ship-building begins in earnest, and continues almost unbroken to the tug-chopped waters of Rotterdam, beyond which the Rhine (now confusingly called the Nieuwe Maas or New Meuse) passes Maassluis and reaches the Europort and the North Sea under the title of Nieuwe Waterweg.

The waterways leading off the Rhine are :

Oude Maas, L, to Voorne Canal and Hellevoetsluis
R. Schie, R, to Schiedam and Delft
Rhine–Schie Canal, R, to Delft
R. IJssel, R (see *Inland Route, Channel to the Baltic*)
R. Lek, R (alternative route)
Dordtsche Kil, L (see *Inland Route, Channel to the Baltic*)
Wantij, L, to the Nieuwe Merwede
Nieuwe Merwede, L, to the Hollands Diep
Steenenhoek Canal, R, to the Merwede Canal
Merwede Canal, R, to Utrecht
Afgedamde Maas, L, to the Bergsche Maas
St Andries Cut, L, junction with the Maas (Meuse)
Amsterdam–Rhine Canal, R, to Amsterdam
Maas–Waal Canal, L, to the Maas (Meuse)
Pannerden Canal, R (branch which becomes the R. Lek)
Spoy Canal, L (q.v.)
Wesel–Datteln Canal, R (q.v.)
R. Ruhr, R, and Duisburg basins (see also *Rhine–Herne Canal*)
R. Moselle, L (q.v.)
R. Lahn, R (q.v.)
R. Main, R (q.v.)
R. Neckar, R (q.v.)
Canal de la Marne au Rhin, L (q.v.)
Canal du Rhône au Rhin, L (q.v.), Rhinau branch
Canal du Rhône au Rhin, L (q.v.), Colmar branch
Canal du Rhône au Rhin, L (q.v.), main line.

Moorings: The course of the river will here be covered in an upward direction, this being the way in which most yachts from Britain will encounter it.

MAASSLUIS, the first tolerable mooring after entry at Hoek van Holland, may offer a corner near where the railway bridge crosses the harbour, but probably alongside tugs or working craft in a state of almost neurotic readiness to dash out.

ROTTERDAM. To escape the incessant wash and yet not be lost in some far-flung forgotten basin, either pass through the Parksluizen lock into the Rhine–Schie Canal if going that way; or continue upstream to the next opening, R, which is the *K.R. & Z.V. De Maas,* a most hospitable club which will not pester you but has its own excellent restaurant on a bullnose built out into the river. Nearby are the park with the Euromast for a fantastic view of ships on the move, the quay of the Spido trip-boats for visits to the docks and the Delta works, and a tram stop. Rotterdam is primarily a port but it is notable for one of the first attempts at a pedestrian precinct, the Lijnbaan area not far from the Central Station.

For DORDRECHT see *Inland Route, Channel to the Baltic.*

SLIEDRECHT has a harbour shut away behind an island, with easy lying alongside. GORINCHEM has awkward lying in the fore-harbour, but easy stopping in the town canal if heading for Utrecht. The best way of visiting Loevestein castle is by trip-boat from Gorinchem. The moated fortress is renowned for the escape of Hugo Grotius, the international lawyer. ZALTBOMMEL has possible mooring on the loading quay just inside the public harbour, which is the second entrance (the first being a shipyard basin). The most picturesque small town on the Dutch Rhine, it has a municipal weigh-house and many little gabled buildings of the 16th and 17th centuries as well as some wealthy burgher residences of the 18th. TIEL, just short of the entrance to the Amsterdam–Rhine Canal, has a loading quay at which barges often spend the night. The carillon is heard pleasantly over the roofs of this quiet little town of shippers.

At NIJMEGEN find a berth in the pleasant basin, the next opening (2 kms.) above the Maas–Waal Canal. *Caution:* The current flows fast past the entrance. Keep going, but blow off for the entry. Inside, there is usually little water close to the wall to port, or straight ahead, but more toward the further end of the basin. This is a convenient mooring from which to visit the town on its unexpected hill. Apart from its historic associations with the Peace of Nijmegen (1678) and the British defeat in 1944, Nijmegen's chief surviving attractions are the town hall and public weigh-house near the Groote Kerk church on the hilltop. Both are fine buildings of the 17th century, and the town hall is where the Peace was signed.

LOBITH. For customs clearance on *downstream* voyages only, enter cautiously the bay first on the right below the waterfront when travelling *downstream*, and aim straight for the slipway until abeam of the jetties of grocers and customs men. Then turn 90° and run straight in. Do not cut the corner. A joint customs office will be found at the far end of the short waterfront.

EMMERICH. For customs clearance in *upstream* direction only, a halt must be made here. Pass the waterfront with its prominent depth-gauge dial, and enter the first harbour, R. The customs jetty is inside on the left, and you will probably be allowed to lie there while shopping.

WESEL has a commercial harbour on the river bend, but much better lying is in the Wassersporthafen, an excellent municipal marina laid out in a large disused gravel pit, R, further downstream. Though outside the not very notable town, the harbour has its own simple restaurant on the inner flood bank. *Caution:* Do not have all your lines tied in inextricable knots by an army of exceedingly helpful but unknowledgeable week-end boatmen.

The harbours of WALSUM and HAMBORN are best left unvisited except by those wishing to turn their boats black. DUISBURG has two possibilities – apart from a further 30 kms. of 'quays' or coal-heaps. Both are entered right underneath the Rhine bridge. To starboard (L) is the quiet basin of HOMBERG; to port the opening of the RUHRORT tug harbour. It is easy to find a berth along one of the many tugs not currently working. Harbour trips are available but you can do your own thing and spend hours touring the dock basins.

At DÜSSELDORF there is a hospitable yacht harbour just downstream of the first (Theodor Heuss) bridge or one can moor up among the coasters in the port. Pass all three bridges and on the bend enter the port with its series of basins. Keep left and left again into the corner of the first basin. If asked why you are there, fail to comprehend. Düsseldorf's Königs-allee (the 'Kö') is reckoned to be the smartest street fashion-wise in Germany. It is bisected by an ornamental canal and flanked with cafés. The town has two rival skyscrapers (almost) and the Mannesmann one has a lift for a splendid view of the Rhine. The town makes a beer ('Alt') very like a good English bitter, and above the Theodor Heuss bridge there is a pleasant floating inn in a small disused harbour. Outside (14 kms., by bus) you can visit the residence of your own relations, Neanderthal man, at Neanderthal.

Many possible moorings along the lower German reaches are purely industrial and not to be recommended, but at HITDORF there is a yacht harbour, R, the last reasonable halt before COLOGNE, where one should pass through the three-arched Hohenzollern railway bridge near the cathedral, continue past the passenger jetties L and under the road bridge, then hug the bank L and pass under the span of a swing-bridge into the Rheinauhafen. The most convenient berth for the town centre and a reasonably quiet one, is in the corner by the steps to starboard immediately on entering.

Cologne's cathedral was six centuries in building, and is a shrine for the alleged relics of the Three Magi. Its twin spires are best seen from the river, upstream of the Rhein-auhafen. Beside it is the entrance to the Dionysius Mosaic which was discovered perfectly preserved when digging an air-raid shelter, and is second only to that at Nennig on the

Moselle (q.v.). Cologne is an ecclesiastical city but also an industrial one, and after half a day in the old town just behind the waterfront the boatman is likely to want to move on up river.

The next stopping point should of course be BONN, and it is almost incredible that the Bundesrepublik government should inhabit Beethoven's birth-town and yet not provide a facility of any kind for even a barge to draw in. So Bonn has to be left unvisited, unless one returns to it from the very next possible mooring, which is at HONNEF 13 kms. up-stream. Behind the island of the Grafenwerth R is a back-water, and a short way inside the entrance are the jetties and pontoons of a yacht club. *Caution:* Watch the depth at the entrance, downstream of the Grafenwerth spit.

Close beside the mooring is the terminus of the tram-railway to Königswinter and Bonn, and this provides an easy means of visiting them.

KONIGSWINTER is still a favourite resort, as it was in the Grand Tour days, with a promenade beside the river. A mountain railway ascends the Drachenfels (over 300 m.) behind the town, with a fine view across to the Eifel Hills, and in the foreground the Rolandsbogen arch, reconstituted relic of where Roland of the Chanson de Geste died after seeing his true love's funeral at the Nonnenwerth convent, on the island opposite Honnef. From this top the whole of the Siebengebirge range can be visited along tracks entirely free of motors. At Bonn one can leave the delegates and ambassadors to do their own things, and limit oneself to the Beethovenhaus, a pleasant little dwelling containing every-thing from original scores to genuine ear trumpets. One's admiration of the composer does not suffer from a visit to this house.

OBERWINTER harbour is just above the Nonnenwerth, L. It is lined with broken rock and only mooring on work boats is possible, or at the pontoons of the Bonn Yacht Club. Heavy traffic roars past all night on the road, and to reach the village street to shop is quite a dangerous sally. BROHL has a harbour of similar dimensions, but at the inner end to moor is not quite so difficult.

For KOBLENZ see under *River Moselle*. An alternative stopping place at anchor or perhaps on the grassy bank of the park, is in the Rheinlache, a backwater L about 1 km. upstream of the road bridge. For OBERLAHNSTEIN see *River Lahn*. There is a harbour of refuge opposite Wellmich, L, known as AM HUND, and 2 kms. further upstream another at ST GOAR, where one can probably make fast to some deserted craft. St Goar is a small and typical Rhine town of half-timbered and slate houses, named after the hermit said to have been the first Rhine pilot. It is overlooked by the vast ruins of Rheinfels castle, destroyed by the French in 1794 and now the venue for the festivities of the Hansa of St Goar, an old guild revived which has jollifications in August. From St Goar a ferry crosses to St Goarshausen with Castle Cat and Castle Mouse, from which the Rheinfels was at last successfully bombarded after six centuries of successful preying upon the shipping. From these castles a path leads 2 kms. to the LORELEI rock at the foot of which is the some-what inhospitable Lorelei harbour of refuge where one can overnight for want of anything better. *Caution:* Do not look at any beautiful maiden who may appear, combing her golden coiffure with a comb of gold.

OBERWESEL has the best harbour along all the Gebirg-strecke or gorge. Its entry is easy, about 1 km. L above the Seven Sisters reef. Being the last possible halt of any kind before the climb through the Bingen rapids it is a good place to pause, drawing in near the far end on a proper vertical quayside. The town still has eighteen watchtowers and bastions and is overlooked by the Schönburg. In Oberwesel some small but excellent wine-cellars are open to the public.

BINGEN has a harbour of refuge L, but it is not easy to moor in and is too far from the town. However, the town also has a river port with a great length of vertical quay-side, where there is hardly any wash because the ships are over on the other side. Bingen is a somewhat industrialised town at the confluence with the R. Nahe (not navigable but famous for its wines). A much more attractive berth is to be

had at RÜDESHEIM, in a quiet harbour tucked away in the
trees above the town R, the entrance being opposite the upstream end of the Rüdesheim ait.

Although Rüdesheim with its inns lining the Drosselgasse
probably has more tourists delivered to it in packages by
road, rail and ship than any other German village, it is not
so dreadful as one might suppose. A chair-lift carries you
over the vineyards to the Niederwald memorial (the 'Watch
on the Rhine') erected in 1871. The statue of Germania is
seven metres round the hips. Down in the town one may
visit wine-cellars and the Asbach brandy distillery, but if
one wants to know more about the wine-making process it
is better to enquire in a less-frequented village. However, the
museum in the Brömserburg has an excellent collection of
vintners' machinery, and implements and glass going back
to Roman times.

There are only two moorings available along the 25 kms.
of broad reach leading up to Mainz. At NIEDERWALLUF there
is an anchorage, R, with a yacht harbour behind the training dike. *Caution:* When the river is low do not enter unless
the radio indicates a rise approaching from upstream.
SCHIERSTEIN has a proper harbour containing yachts, barges
loading, and soldiery messing about in boats. The entrance
is under the elegant curve of the footbridge, R.

At MAINZ the massive waterfront is not suitable and is
lashed by waves, but $1\frac{1}{2}$ kms. downstream of the centre is a
large port basin, the Zollhafen. Turn left on entering and
moor near the end. You will not be too far from the city
centre. Once an electoral see of powerful and sometimes
rather military archbishops, Mainz is a pale shadow of what
once it was. The World Printing Museum (Liebfrauenplatz
5) has a fascinating collection of printing devices and manu-
scripts, and in the reconstruction of the workshop in which
Gutenberg printed the Bible (at Mainz, in 1455) typesetting
and printing as practised five centuries ago can actually be
watched. Near the opera, the *Haus des deutschen Weins* has
hundreds of wines available at the table.

A harbour is available at OPPENHEIM, L, primarily a wine

town, opposite the monument commemorating the landing of the LZ4, first 'successful" Zeppelin, on its flight from the Lake of Konstanz. (Success was limited, the next day the airship was burnt out near Stuttgart.)

The best landing at WORMS is in the Handelshafen, about 1 km. above the railway bridge L. Worms has an ancient Jewish cemetery (11th century onward) and is also the original home of Liebfraumilch – though the name now applies to mass factory blends – but its great claim to fame is for the Imperial Diet of 1521 before which Martin Luther had to appear. The Victorian gothic Luther memorial shows him with his fore-runners, including Wycliffe, and his staunch supporters the Landgraf of Hessen and the Elector of Saxony.

MANNHEIM has large docks and miles of quays, but the best mooring is out of the main stream, either in the Mühlauhafen, or in the Binnenhafen which is reached by turning into the R. Neckar and noting the opening to starboard, 1 km. up. Mannheim was the seat of the Elector Palatine after the sack of Heidelberg by the French (see *R. Neckar*) and so is relatively modern (1689). The town is geometrically laid out behind the electoral palace, the largest baroque residence in the country. SPEYER has a modern industrial harbour above the bridge, but more convenient mooring is in the smaller old harbour on the bend L, downstream of the bridge, with a good quay wall under the cranes. Though sacked by Louis XIV the great 11th-century cathedral has been rebuilt, and has a large basin outside the portal to serve as a sanctuary for criminals. There is an old quarter of one-time fishermen and shippers near the old harbour, and across the bridge is a museum which shows the history of wine-making through 2,000 years and has an ancient wine-tavern, reconstructed. Apart from an industrial harbour at GERMERSHEIM, and the entrance to an old arm of the river at SONDERNHEIM, both of which can be used if necessary, the next halt is at KARLSRUHE. Here there is a single port entrance leading to six basins. Bear to port on entering, then keep straight ahead all the way to the end, about 2 kms. Moor on the good quay just short of the left-hand corner. Although now an industrial town with a population of a quarter of a million, Karlsruhe was originally laid out fan-wise around the residence when the Margraf of Baden moved there in the early 18th century, as the result of a dream. He is buried in the curious pyramid in the market-place.

NEUBURGWEIER, 16 kms. upstream, is the German customs post and one must draw in, whether going up or down the river. Just above the barge-roads and signal station is a small creek R with jetties for the patrol launches, an easy mooring.

LAUTERBOURG has a large but bleak and messy harbour, not anywhere near the town; between there and Strasbourg (more than 50 kms.) there are gravel-pits and old short-circuited branches of the river which are very often badly silted, but one of these, the first opening R after the railway bridge 14 kms. above Lauterbourg, is the IFFEZHEIM creek, leading within a few hundred metres to the Baden-Baden yacht club, with good moorings and a clubhouse. The small harbour at GREFFERN is usable except when the river is low, but there can be bad drawing-off. KEHL has large and long basins R just above the mouth of the R. Kinzig (not navigable), but port and town alike are dismal and messy. It is only 2 kms. further to the north entrance of the Port of Strasbourg L.

STRASBOURG. The best mooring on all the Rhine is available in the city, and it only needs finding. After passing the signal station at the entrance, continue straight ahead for 300 m., then turn half right to the Écluse Nord. Through the lock, carry on into the Canal de la Marne au Rhin leaving the large Bassin des Remparts to port. About 100 m. up the canal there is a customs jetty on the right, where you must call and show the papers. Then follow the canal through two bridges to a large water cross-roads and turn left into the River Ill, following the bend round. Head upstream (there is plenty of water) until you pass the twin-spired St Paul's church on the starboard side. Two bridges further you come to a junction, with a large block of flats in the angle. Opposite the flats in the Canal des Faux Remparts is the side of a former lock, with a lawn and flower-beds. If drawing more than 0·80 m. this should be your mooring. However, the intrepidly adventurous can continue up the Ill for a further 1¼ kms. Continually the river becomes narrower and swifter, but after six bridges it begins to divide. The extreme right-hand branch leads to a lock immediately above which is the good quay of La Petite France, with the magnificent half-timbered Gerwerstub or Maison des Tanneurs just ahead of it. On leaving you can proceed ahead through the swing-bridge, pass another bridge, and tunnel under the fort to emerge into a broad river section. After one more bridge turn left and you are soon at the Écluse de l'Hôpital of the Canal du Rhône au Rhin, which leads back into the dock basins of the main port.

Strasbourg is the capital of Alsace, the fifth largest of all French ports, a centre of the Reformation, seat of the Council of Europe, a university city and one where buildings of great taste and beauty appear on every hand. The old city within its ring of waterways is dominated by the cathedral with its single spire off-centre. The façade was built by Maître Erwin in 1284. Inside the cathedral is the famous pillar of angels (13th century) and the astronomical clock (19th century) with its innumerable mechanical jacks, biblical and allegorical. Beside the Ill is the palace of the Cardinals Rohan, including the one who attempted to win the favour of Marie-Antoinette with a necklace acquired on the never-never, and further upstream stands the old customs house, now a restaurant. Most famous of the brick and timber houses with rows of the dormer windows so characteristic of Strasbourg is the Maison Kammerzell, but the Rue du Bain-aux-Plantes by the Petite France mooring has a very fine row of less pretentious ones, including the Lohkäs inn with its mechanical organ. Among Strasbourg specialities are onion tart and choucroute garni, with fine wines of Alsace.

Leaving Strasbourg by the southern lock one comes to

the Grand Canal d'Alsace, where stopping is of course
possible at the locks, which tend to be far from civilisation.
However, immediately past the Kaiserstuhl hills and at the
approach to Vogelgrün lock the old course of the Rhine
curves away to port. On the port hand BREISACH has a maintenance harbour with access for yachts and a little further
ahead a good jetty. Although the town is in Germany,
customs formalities are not involved. The town is partly
cramped on a rocky mound and is dominated by the 14th-
century cathedral on the summit. Inside is a painting by
Martin Schongauer (d. 1491) and the astonishing carved
altar-piece (1526) by the 'Meister H.L.' (Hans Liefrink?)
who is said to have created it to win the approval of his
beloved's father – in which he succeeded. Across the river
in France is the desolate disused fortress of Neuf Brisach
(17th century) inside which a town of sorts survives, somewhat forgotten.

Breisach is the point from which to visit the Kaiserstuhl
hills, renowned for the wines of Achkarren, Bickensohl,
Kiechlingsbergen and other villages – wines so good that
they are not wasted on export to Britain. At Breisach and
Ihringen one can visit vintners' establishments. An excursion
can also be made by bus or train to the university town of
Freiburg-im-Breisgau at the foot of the Black Forest (17
kms.)

After the last G.C.A. lock at Kembs the course rejoins the
river for the final 4 kms. to BASLE. Enter the Kleinhüningen
harbour, R, and moor immediately inside on your left.
Swiss customs are in the shed nearby. This harbour is Switzerland's main importing base and is packed with Rhine
barges. At the end of the basin is an extremely well-designed
museum of the history of Rhine shipping, and on the inner
side of the same basin a lift leads to a platform on the roof
of a tall warehouse, from which there is a fine view of the
port, the outer mole of which ends in a pylon which marks
the point (actually in the river nearby) where three countries meet. From near the museum a tram goes to the centre
of Basle, a city renowned for banking more than for beauty,

although the area around the cathedral is not without a certain degree of quiet charm.

Above the second and very ill-designed Swiss lock at Augst the small harbour L tends to be silted, but one can stop at the steamer stage a little further ahead, L, at KAISERAUGST. The name thinly disguises that of Caesar Augustus, and behind the village one quickly comes to the remains of the Roman town of Augusta Raurica (from 44 B.C.) with theatre and forum, and one Roman house reconstituted and furnished. *Caution:* If leaving your boat at the stage, check the steamer timetable first.

RHEINFELDEN has a loading port R for the German town, a very dull modern place compared with the old Swiss town across the river, where one may be able to draw in cautiously to the right of the island, or conceivably on it. Sounding is advisable if drawing in on the Swiss side, though there is good depth at the German staging. *Caution:* The current is strong. Make sure your lines are well secured, and put down the anchor as an extra precaution.

Spoy Canal or Cleves Waterway. From the R. Rhine at km. 864 to Kleve (Cleves). Length 10 kms. One lock at Brienen (closed on Sundays). Draught 2 m., headroom unlimited.

Navigation: No hazards, except that one pays to be locked through at Brienen. The waterway is used by 600-ton barges which should be met with extreme caution, especially in the long and narrow canal section above the lock. The keeper will always know if the route ahead is clear; if not, it is advisable to wait.

Most of the route is a backwater or disused arm of the Rhine. Even if one is not going to make the unusual side-trip from the Rhine to Kleve, the waterway itself provides a good place to spend the night out of the wash of shipping. The entrance is on the starboard hand, 1 km. below Lobith customs roads and just inside Holland. A short way up the course a jetty marks the frontier, and one should make fast and walk over the bank and across the field to the German customs shed, where the officer will be so surprised he may be unable to think of anything to say or do. Up to the lock, which is more than half-way to Kleve, the course is a dead river with cattle paddling at the edge and humans bathing. A fisherman may lay nets, but not across your bow. Then at Brienen the scene changes, and a narrow artificial cut leads in rather Dutch fashion directly to Kleve, where there is a surprisingly modern commercial port.

Moorings: Below BRIENEN LOCK there is a peaceful anchorage, or very small craft may use the pontoon of the Yacht Club. On the bank is a grove surrounding a poignant memorial to a teenager who in the 19th century was drowned when saving others in a Rhine flood. KLEVE provides good mooring alongside at the wharf, from which it may be necessary tactfully to dislodge fishermen. The town is new, but the castle of the Dukes of Cleves survives in splendour on the hilltop and its weather vane of a swan reminds one that the dead arm of the Rhine up which one has come is the waterway associated with the legend of Lohengrin and his sad return to the castle of the Holy Grail, after rescuing the daughter of the Duke. The same castle was later the home of the unfortunate Anne who was persuaded to become the fourth wife of King Henry VIII.

Wesel–Datteln Canal. From the R. Rhine at Wesel to the Dortmund–Ems Canal at Datteln. Length 60 kms. Locks 6.

This canal, which is really a lateral canal to the R. Lippe, parallels the Rhine–Herne Canal and is about 25 kms. further north. It is modern and efficient, and in contrast to its older brother it passes through undisturbed country which, if often hidden behind high banks, is at least not belching smoke. Apart from the not very large manufacturing town of Dorsten it passes through no industrial centres at all, and is much to be preferred by yachts making for the Mittelland Canal. The waterway is part of the main route for Eastern European ships carrying grain to Rotterdam and has very heavy traffic – so heavy that although the locks have been doubled one may have to wait awhile. However, craft coming up the Rhine from Holland will find it the quicker as well as the more pleasant of the two alternative routes.

Moorings: DORSTEN has an industrial harbour. Otherwise only above the locks – where it may be difficult to find a space.

Rhine–Herne Canal. From the R. Rhine at Ruhrort to the Dortmund–Ems Canal at Herne. Length 46 kms. Locks 7.

This canal, which is on the route to the Weser and Elbe for craft coming down the Rhine, is heavily used by coal-barges and ships carrying iron ore and scrap to the foundries along its course. It passes through one of the most heavily industrialised areas of the world, and although it can easily be run in half a day the boat will afterwards need a complete wash-down with detergent to remove the rain of coal dust and sticky tar which has dropped upon it from the Ruhr sky. The canal skirts such renowned places as Bottrop, Essen, Gelsenkirchen and Wanne-Eickel, passing through their industrial outskirts rather than the town centres. It is not necessary to describe these places further than to say that much of the prosperity of the Bundesrepublik depends upon their activity, and that one of the most prevalent diseases is known in Germany as Managerkrankheit.

Moorings: Certainly not.

River Moselle. Navigable from Frouard (near Nancy) to the R. Rhine at Koblenz. Length 317 kms. Locks French, 10 (or more, according to the progress of reconstruction above Metz); Luxembourgish, 2; German, 10. On the German section most of the ship-locks have small electric do-it-yourself pens alongside, for boats up to 3 m. beam. See note 1 on p. 283.

Navigation: As a modern locked waterway the Moselle presents no problems at all, but an excellent chart-book can be bought at the locks at either end of the International section (Königsmacker lock when proceeding downstream, Koblenz when coming up). In some places the groynes of the old river have not been removed, so it is very unwise to stray outside the buoyed channel in these areas. Where there are no buoys it can be assumed that the river is deep from shore to shore.

Lock dues are payable at the Luxembourgish and German locks only, and are not charged if you either use the do-it-yourself pen, or are in the company of a barge or passenger boat. The fee is more than £1 per lock but it can often be avoided by planning your departure from an overnight stop to coincide with the arrival at a lock of a passenger vessel going in the same direction. A useful tip is to help yourself to a timetable at one of the jetties; this will give exact times all the way down the river from Trier to Koblenz. Barges can also be used to pay your dues, but it should be remembered that there is usually a dead period in the docks at Thionville and Hagondange between Friday evening and Monday morning. This two-day gap in the shipping will spread down most of the river, becoming correspondingly later with increasing distance from Lorraine.

Passenger boats: Steamers of various lines ply between Koblenz and Trier, Trier and Remich and Sierck-les-Bains and Remich. There are river trips from Metz also, and individual trip-boats ply from other points, especially Trier, Bernkastel, Cochem and Koblenz.

Though used as a waterway by the Romans the Moselle only became fully navigable to the Rhine in 1964, since when enlargement and modernisation of the upper reaches has also been put in hand. This programme already provides navigation of Euroship dimensions right up to Frouard, where there is a modern port for Nancy. Above Toul the river is also navigable for some 20 kms. and that section is described briefly under the *Canal de l'Est, Branch Sud* (q.v.).

The Moselle is one of the most famous of European streams, the praises of its scenery having been sung first by Ausonius (d. 392) in his poem *Mosella,* whilst authors from Venantius Fortunatus (6th century) onward have described their happy, wine-washed journeys down the Moselle by boat. It is best navigated downstream, for in that direction the scenery becomes continually better, ending in the magnificent confluence with the Rhine. From Nancy to Metz the course is the revamped and improved 'Moselle Canalisée' made navigable by the French in the 1860's. This stretch of valley has patches of industry, particularly near Frouard and at Pont-à-Mousson, but to either side there are hills and occasionally the crumbled remains of ancient castles, whilst at Ars the river passes the arches of a massive Roman aqueduct which once spanned the valley.

From Metz to Thionville the course is mainly down a straight and relatively broad lateral canal, the 'Camifemo' cut in the 1930's to open up the industrial basin of Lorraine to barge traffic. Here the scene is one of foundries and coke-ovens and shining modern casting halls, but a mere 30 kms. down from Metz the lock at Thionville leads out into the International Moselle Waterway, opened in 1964 as a joint enterprise of France, Luxembourg and Germany and a fine example of how well a major engineering undertaking can be achieved without spoiling the landscape. On the contrary, the Moselle has probably never looked better.

The industry of Thionville is quickly left astern, and before the frontier is reached the first vineyards appear. At Apach lock the river leaves France and becomes German (Saarland) on the right bank, Luxembourgish on the left. French customs clearance is on the lock-side, German is under way without even slowing down, by fast customs cutter, Luxembourgish is at Schengen jetty below the lock, but only if you are going to stop there.

The villages on the Luxembourg bank are without exception hamlets of vintners. Built of mellow limestone and redolent of the scented smoke of vine-roots they are unsophisticated and unspoiled. The German shore is less interesting here, for the best vintages occur further down. At the confluence of the R. Sure, L (not navigable), the Moselle becomes entirely German. Luxembourg customs are cleared at the road post by the road bridge over the Sure, and the German on Wasserbillig quay.

Soon the river is joined by the water of the R. Saar, R navigable only for 2 or 3 kilometres, with caution. (It is the higher reaches which are used by barges, and they are approached from the summit pound of the *Canal de la Marne au Rhin*, q.v.). Past Trier the Moselle increases quickly in splendour to wind between forest hills and steep vineyard slopes which increase continually in height as one famous wine village after another drifts by – Piesport, Bernkastel, Traben and Trarbach, Reil, Zell, Cochem and Cond, Alken and Winningen. A softer, gentler gorge than that of the Rhine, the Moselle nevertheless has its castle ruins, many of which were once the fortresses of militant bishops, but vines are the predominant feature and it is on wine that the prosperity of the Moselle villages depends.

As a cruising ground the International Moselle is unsurpassed. It is safe, clean, and without any navigational problems. It is a river on which one could happily spend several weeks.

Moorings: PONT-A-MOUSSON. On the river wall just above the bridge L, or on the grassy bank of the meadow, R, opposite the bathing area at the entrance to the town. The former Jesuit university, founded 1572, with the octagon towers of St Martin's church (15th century) give the waterfront an unexpected elegance. In the Place Duroc the house of the Seven Deadly Sins demonstrates them in sculpture. A pleasant walk is to scramble up the hill, the Butte de Mousson, to the remnants of the vast feudal castle of the Dukes of Bar, with a superb view over the meandering river in its wide plain.

METZ has one of the pleasantest moorings upstream of Germany. At the approach to the town pass under a bridge and immediately cut away to starboard, leaving the navigation channel to port, and running 80 m. above the top of the weir. Follow this branch of the river past the bathing area and turn left at the next junction. Draw in immediately above the bridge, on the low wall topped by railings, having previously turned your boat to head upstream. If this berth should be occupied, take the same position below the bridge.

The city has many splendours, particularly St Étienne Cathedral with its 13th-century municipal belfry containing a bell which sounds at midday but otherwise is only used on special occasions, the 7th-century church of St Pierre aux Nonnains, the wide expanse of the Esplanade, and the arcaded Place St Louis, once a medieval market of money-changers. In summer the '*Fête de la Mirabelle*' (plum) is an occasion for a procession of floats and bands and a magnificent display of fireworks.

THIONVILLE is probably best passed by, but at SIERCK-LES-BAINS one can cautiously approach the retaining wall immediately opposite the railway signal and visit the remains of the medieval castle above the river.

REMICH has a fine quay for pleasure craft only, from which one can also visit the St Martin cellars of sparkling wine and the village of Schwedsbengen, where at the summer wine festival the village fountain actually runs with genuine wine, free to all. Across Remich bridge the Roman villa at Nennig is about twenty minutes on foot, with a fine mosaic of amphitheatre scenes, animals and musical instruments. Downstream, all moorings are on the Luxembourg side, there being a good quay at WORMELDANGE, mooring above the lock at GREVENMACHER, a river quay and a vast inland port at MERTERT and a pleasant long quay at the traditional bargemen's town of WASSERBILLIG. To see the Roman memorial column at IGEL one must anchor and row ashore.

All down the German river there are large landing-stages, but these belong to the K/D (Köln–Düsseldorfer) line of passenger ships and should on no account be used, as a steamer may turn up at any moment. There are other stages also which belong to trip-boats, and one should never moor at those either without specific permission from the skipper concerned – who may well be very willing to offer the facility outside his hours of running. '*Anlegen verboten*' should be taken seriously when seen painted on a jetty or pontoon.

For TRIER, the facilities are a disgrace. The only harbours are a small maintenance harbour above the lock, with a detour of several kilometres to reach the city, and the modern commercial port situated in a busless void half an hour's voyage downstream of the town bridges. However, it is possible with great care to pass both bridges, double back into the dead arm R. and anchor just short of the bridge and above the steamer jetties. The very small pontoon of the local club is much too subject to the wash of passing traffic and to drawing-off.

Trier was the capital of Roman Gaul, and is liberally sprinkled with remains – the Porta Nigra, two sets of baths, the amphitheatre, and mosaics and carvings in the museum. But Trier was also Electoral and Archiepiscopal and the great cathedral is from Roman times onward. The rococo St Paulinus' church by Balthasar Neumann commemorates the martyrs under Diocletian. The apostle Matthias is buried in the St Matthias church. Two medieval cranes survive on the river bank, and the upper of the two road bridges is built on Roman buttresses. The Zurlauben quarter behind the steamer jetties was formerly the abode of fishermen and shippers, as the motifs on the houses suggest.

SCHWEICH, a dull village away from the river, has a small port for pleasure craft L, just short of the ferry-house. TRITTENHEIM has a small pontoon, but very tight bracing is essential because of the wash on the bend from large ships. NEUMAGEN also has a jetty for public use. This is one of the most interesting halts, for here the Emperor Constantine had his summer palace and many notable carvings (now in the museum at Trier) have been dug up. A copy of the famous tombstone of a Roman entrepreneur, showing a 4th-century Moselle wine barge, is near the church, as is also a statue of Ausonius the poet, tutor to the Constantine boys. Constantine's cross seen in the sky is in the arms painted on the town hall, where is preserved a copy of the letter recalling that Neumagen wine broke the years of deadlock which preceded the Treaty of Münster (see *Dortmund–Ems Canal*).

The first really good mooring is at KUES, L, about 1 km. upstream of Bernkastel bridge. This is a large harbour with a good quay. Kues has the house of the theologian Cusanus (d. 1464) alongside the quay, and near the bridge the hospital he built, still in use. BERNKASTEL is a resort for package tours but the gaily painted half-timbered houses of its

market-place are delightful. The greatest wine festival in
Europe takes place in Bernkastel and Kues the first week-
end in September, with a whole street of stalls from vintner
villages along half of the German reaches. It starts on the
Friday night with a firework display over the river and the
burning of the castle associated with the famous 'Doktor'
wine.

At ZELL there is an excellent quay for visiting boats,
immediately below the footbridge. Zell is almost running
with wine, especially '*Schwarzer Katz*'. From Kaimt on the
further shore a track leads to the Marienburg, a former
convent with perhaps the most astonishing view to be had
along the valley, looking down upon Pünderich. A shorter
ascent is from ALF, where there is a small harbour on the
bend L. There is a bleak harbour of refuge at SENHEIM, but
at BEILSTEIN one should anchor close to the further shore L
and row over to see one of the tightest cramped Moselle
villages, dominated by Castle Metternich. For COCHEM, a
favourite resort at the foot of a towering floodlit castle
restored in the 19th century, moor at COND opposite, where
there is a proper yacht harbour, and take the ferry across.

In the backwater at TREIS, R, there is limited mooring at
a privately run marina. Treis is the best mooring for the
walk from Karden to Burg Eltz, an amazing medieval rock-
perched fortress complex, hidden in the depths of the forest
above the Elz trout river. BRODENBACH has a harbour R, but
care should be taken to give the point a wide berth when
entering. ALKEN has a public jetty and is overtowered by the
medieval Burg Thurandt, an Electoral castle which was the
scene of a famous siege in 1246, in the course of which one
of the defending knights escaped to summon help. For
several hours boulders bound in moss were rolled down
the hill from the castle until the besiegers became tired of
investigating the strange missiles. Eventually one of them
contained the knight, who lay still until dark and then
escaped from his mossy container. This event is commemora-
ted in the Moosmannsfest on the third Sunday of Lent,
when a boy is wrapped in moss and carried through the

town. Alken also has a gay wine festival in September.

At KOBLENZ the best mooring is below the lock and beyond the three bridges. Turn the long promontory of the lock cut and double back, bringing up about 50 m. short of the bridge, outside the former Electoral Palace (of the Trier arch-bishops). Deutsches Eck, the point of the confluence with the Rhine, is an impressive place and a good one from which to watch the dense Rhine traffic, even if the gigantic Kaiser Wilhelm I on horseback has vanished. Across the Rhine by ferry, a chair-lift takes you to Ehrenbreitstein, a massive fortress rebuilt in the 1820's and with a magnificent view over both rivers and the confluence. Other attractions at Koblenz include an opera, the habit of 'setting the Rhine on fire' by fireworks every summer, and the Weindorf, or Wine Village, immediately upstream of the road bridge (Pfaffendorferbrücke) over the Rhine. Here several typical inns from wine villages serve everything from sausage and sauerkraut up to a good meal, with a great choice of wines and in an atmosphere which is not too strikingly artificial, if rather designed for the packaged visitor.

River Lahn. Navigable from its confluence with the R. Rhine at Niederlahnstein to above Limburg. Length 67 kms. Locks 12. Smallest, 34 m. × 5·3 m. Draught permissible, 1·6 m. Small craft such as canoes may penetrate to Weilburg and the only German canal tunnel.

Navigation: The Lahn drains a considerable upland area and can rise after heavy rain to give a flood river which may in places (below Dausenau and Hollerich) run at 5 kms. in the hour, or more. But usually the current is slight and presents no problems. Several of the locks have power-stations nearby and the swift outfall from these can be tricky enough to make it inadvisable to meet an oncoming boat at those particular points. The one below Hollerich lock is badly placed on a sharp bend, and the very strong outfall below Scheidt lock is set right in the bend and causes a powerful current. *Caution:* It is the custom among Lahn barges to keep to the left at this point, and to be sure of avoiding a collision it is as well to ask at Kalkofen lock whether or not a boat is being locked down into that reach; and if so, to hang in the stream at least 200 m. below the power-station until it has passed.

The hydro-electric intake above Kalkofen lock is also able to exert a considerable pull. It is wisest to keep well back until the lock is ready, when descending.

Lahn locks have unusual signals in the form of discs which are turned edgewise and horizontal when the lock is not available for an approaching boat. *Lock dues* are modest. They can be paid at any lock, but a card to cover ten locks can be bought at a reduced price and shown for stamping at each lock until it is fully cancelled.

The Lahn is one of the easiest and most delightful cruising rivers in Western Europe. It carries little traffic, has efficient locks, and its steep wooded valley is at any time of year beautiful, unspoiled, and with plenty of interest. The villages abound with good inns, there are pleasant forest walks close at hand, and the water is clean for bathing.

Moorings: At OBERLAHNSTEIN in the harbour, first entry on the starboard hand above the Rhine confluence. The harbour is commercial and rather dirty but the mooring is convenient as a foot-tunnel leads under the railway to the shops. Above the town and reached by a steeply climbing track is the castle keep of Lahneck, floodlit in summer and with refreshments and sometimes open-air theatricals. On the NIEDERLAHNSTEIN side, pass through the lock and draw in at the bank immediately above it, R. Niederlahnstein was formerly an important town of shippers, and the customs house is now an inn with Goethe connections.

In BAD EMS a boat drawing more than 40 cms. will be unable to come alongside because of stones. Anchor in the right-hand half of the stream, below the first bridge and opposite the Kurhaus. This anchorage has the unusual attraction of free concerts by the Kurhaus orchestra. *Caution:* Do not be deceived by the inviting appearance of a handsome quay to starboard, there being no water there. The town has many memories of semi-alcoholic and fashionable royalty and aristocracy, and although now completely welfare-stated it has a genuine elegance. A geyser gushes hot and high close by the river and one can climb the hill of the Concordia Tower for one of the finest river views in Germany. A water-ballast gravity railway runs up the Malberg.

At DAUSENAU and OBERNHOF anchoring or mooring with springs to hold the ship several feet from the shore, are the only possibilities. Obernhof is a compact little village of half-timbered houses and is the only place on the Lahn with vine-yards. Arnstein monastery is a quarter hour's walk distant.

NASSAU has deep water along the bank, R, just above the suspension bridge. A path winds up the hill opposite and leads to the humble ruins of the ancestral home of Dutch and Luxembourg and even British royalty. In summer an orange flag is sometimes flown.

BALDUINSTEIN provides undisturbed mooring in a disused lock-cut, R. Double back and moor to the bank. From the village a path climbs to the vast and still inhabited castle-palace of the Waldecks, Castle Schaumburg, open to visitors and provided with a smart restaurant. This is probably the best excursion in all the valley.

DIEZ has a small water authority harbour between the second bridge and the lock, starboard side, where one can moor with permission of the superintendent. Failing this, draw in alongside above the weir, R. The castle of Diez is a medieval and rambling building cramped on a sturdy rock. Once a prison, it is now a hikers' hostel.

At LIMBURG there is good lying in the disused loading bay, immediately above the lock, with permission of the lock-keeper. Limburg is one of the most delightful cathedral towns in Germany. The Katzenturm bridge-gate, the mill-walk beside the river, the steep and narrow alleys of slate-hung houses, the archiepiscopal palace and cathedral tower-ing over the more common dwellings make an unforgettable impression. One can also run further up the river and anchor off DIETKIRCHEN to visit the astonishing cliff-top twin-towered church where St Lubentius is buried.

River Main. Navigable from its junction with the canal section of the Rhine–Main–Danube ship route at Bamberg to the R. Rhine at Mainz. Length 392 kms. Locks 37. The river is part of the whole R–M–D project which is scheduled for completion in 1981. At present navigation extends as far as Nuremberg, 57 kms. beyond Bamberg.

Lock fees are calculated on horse-power of the engines, but are not levied when a pleasure craft is in the company of barges.

Passenger boats: There are no regular services along all the Main. Steamers of the K/D Rhine Line run up as far as Frankfurt, and local runs – some of them lengthy – are made by trip-boats from Frankfurt, Miltenberg, Wertheim, Würzburg and Schweinfurt. On the Regnitz a trip-boat runs from Bamberg, near the town hall.

The Main is one of Germany's longest rivers, and drains the Schwäbische Alb and considerable areas of Bavaria. Two branches of the river unite near Bamberg (which itself is on the R. Regnitz, see below) and from the junction of these united streams with the R. Regnitz the Main is immediately navigable for Europaships, though only as the result of very large-scale works. The countryside down to Schweinfurt is not specially notable, but there is no industry – and indeed very little above Aschaffenburg, which still lies more than 300 kms. ahead. Below Schweinfurt the Main quickly becomes more monastic, winding between limestone hills often crowned with convents and pilgrimage churches rich in carvings. Soon the vineyards begin, and after Kitzingen the river flows past slopes of some of the most renowned German vintages of dry white wines such as are sold in 'bocksbeutel' flagons, culminating with the Stein and Marienburg slopes at Würzburg itself, an ecclesiastical city second only to Bamberg. Before Gemünden the open country has given way to forest, first the Rhön and then the splendid mixed woods of the Spessart on the right bank, later joined by the Odenwald on the left. The forests continue all the way to Miltenberg, where the trees begin to draw back and leave the river to flow steadily toward Aschaffenburg. Then by way of Hanau the Main approaches the industrial spread of Frankfurt and Höchst, finally flowing through another patch of vineyards at Hochheim (called 'Hockem' by the English in the 17th century, whence the term Hock) and running to its end at Kostheim opposite the city of Mainz.

A river of age-old villages and market towns, the Main nevertheless carries considerable traffic all the way, though particularly in its lower reaches. The 300-metre rafts which once were a somewhat alarming constituent of the traffic have gone, and so have the chain-ships and their chain, which was laid in the river bed all the way from the Rhine to Bamberg. The Main is an easy cruising river, edged by an inexhaustible supply of wine, half-timbered Franconian houses of great beauty, cathedrals and churches, and its hinterland is rich in Bavarian baroque, much of it very well known. It is a peaceful river with abundant opportunity for side-trips into some of Bavaria's most attractive country.

As the river is still only accessible from its confluence with the Rhine, it will be dealt with here in an upstream direction.

Moorings: FRANKFURT-AM-MAIN. Beyond the Autobahn bridge pass under two rail and two road bridges, then draw in anywhere on the long quay R by the trees and before reaching the landing stages of the K/D steamers. Little of the older part of the town survived 1945, but what there is will be found very close to the mooring, clustered round the Römer, a reconstructed enclave of 15th-century houses. The city has a modern opera house – one of the finest in Germany, and with German champagne in the intervals – and a notable zoo. OFFENBACH is a sprawling suburb town, where one can moor to the wall above the lock rather than in the dirty water of the harbour basin. There is an intriguing museum of leather working, with 2,700 pairs of shoes, one of them 6,000 years old, and the historical section on the evolution of the female handbag should enthrall lady members of your crew.

SELIGENSTADT has difficult mooring on the wall close to the castle – difficult because of the wash from traffic shoot-

ing the bend below Grosswelzheim lock. It is a small market
town, said to owe its name (Blessed Town) to Charlemagne's
dictum that blessed should that place be where he might
find his daughter, who had eloped with his secretary Egin-
hard. Emma is said to have been so strong a girl that she
carried her lover on her back to avoid detection from two
sets of foot-prints in the snow. The couple were first imprisoned at Dausenau on the Lahn, but may later have
escaped.

ASCHAFFENBURG has an old harbour, with the remains of
a chain-ship at the foot of the castle, but the whole basin
almost empties with the drawing-off of passing barges. It is
better to take the left fork just beyond the town bridge, into
the dead arm of the Main. There is an excellent quay wall
to port, safe from draw-off. On leaving, turn back and
double the point. Ahead the arm becomes a dead end.

The great features of Aschaffenburg are the vast Renaissance palace of the Electors of Mainz, now restored, and the
Stiftskirche church, both in red sandstone. The church has
paintings by Matthias Grünewald (d. 1528) and Lucas
Cranach (d. 1553), as well as an elegant external staircase
added during Renaissance times. Excellent fish from the
Main can be had at the *'Grüner Mann'* inn, by the bridge.

At WÖRTH, draw in on the short piece of wall immediately
above the ferry berth. Inside the slate-hung little town hall
is a panelled council-chamber with the insignia of the boatmen's guild and a detailed model of a chain-ship. For
KLINGENBERG, pass through Trennfurt lock and cross above
the weir (with suitable caution) to the sloping bank opposite
R. It is possible to moor to the trees away from the wash, to
sample the red wine of the vineyards behind the town. At
MILTENBERG all the jetties are private and in use, but at the
further end of the town there is a small loading bay, L, with
a good quay, and water alongside it. Miltenberg's market-
place is one of the most photographed in Germany. There
is a forlorn and forgotten Jewish Cemetery at the back of
the town. Note also the floodmarks on many of the houses.
A walk of three hours over the hills, or a short train ride

(8 kms.) up the Mudbach valley leads to Amorbach in the Odenwald, where concerts of baroque music are given on the rococo organ (1782) with a very piping tone. Amorbach has indirect associations with Queen Victoria, being the residence of the Leiningen family.

WERTHEIM is at the confluence with the R. Tauber, navigable for about 200 m. only. Turn to starboard into this river and moor at the old railway quay on your right, just short of the bridge. *Caution:* Examine the wall for projecting pieces of iron etc.

Wertheim is an excellent halt. The town has many fine half-timbered houses from the 16th and 17th centuries, and a range of fishermen's houses is opposite your mooring. The whole place is dominated by the remains of a red sandstone castle, the rings set in the wall alleged to be put there in defiance – 'If you can't break in, why not pull me home with you?' There are good excursions up the Tauber valley also, to Bad Mergentheim with its fine 16th-century castle of the Order of Teutonic Knights, where concerts and a music festival are held in the summer; Weikersheim with a castle of similar date belonging to the Hohenlohe family; and particularly Creglingen church with the Marienaltar, the most famous of all the works by the woodcarver Tilman Riemenschneider (d. 1531), two more altar-pieces by whom can be found further up the valley at Detwang and in the superb walled city of Rothenburg, standing complete and fortified on a spur above the Tauber.

MARKTHEIDENFELD has possible mooring on a somewhat sloping wall along the ornamental waterfront gardens, close to the anchors. Only 2 kms. upstream it is just possible to lie on the jetty in a few yards of creek R, at HAFENLOHR, a village which contains two one-man potteries, the owner working a small holding, digging the clay, making his articles and firing once in every few months. At LOHR there is a good quay for loading barges with timber, immediately beyond the bridge, R.

GEMÜNDEN is the confluence with the R. Fränkische Saale (not navigable), and although it is possible to penetrate as far as the row of fishermen's cottages the drawing-off by ships passing in the main river will ground you. Better is to stop in the large harbour of refuge below the town R, usually almost deserted. The further end is only a short walk from the Saale bridge in the town. From the market-place of Gemünden a path winds up the hillside to a ruined keep, from the top of which there is an alluring view over the Main valley. Excursions into the Rhön are easy, by bus or train, and from the town itself forest paths lead over hills up to 500 m. in height.

KARLSTADT has difficult mooring on the sloping wall R, exactly opposite the town watergate, but this situation at a long and almost deserted quay at the foot of high grey walls with hardly an aperture in them is like mooring in a picture from the middle ages. A climb to the ruined Karlsburg across the river gives an excellent view of the town, completely walled and with only one entrance in each side. Karlstadt has a good Riemenschneider in the church, a town hall clock-jack in the form of an amorous Swedish drummer conned by his Karlstadt love into beating the retreat and clearing the town of Gustavus Adolphus' soldiery, and a modern fountain commemorating the local celebrity Johannes Glauber (d. 1668) of Glauber's salt (or sodium sulphate).

VEITSHÖCHHEIM has passenger jetties, but these are in constant use. Anchor, or conceivably moor on the sloping wall R, in the shelter of the projecting groyne immediately ahead of them. This will give you the opportunity to consider whether you would have liked to be an 18th-century Prince-Bishop of Würzburg and own a second palace just for parties, with rococo gardens full of comic statuary (the dancing putti are famous), lakes, and suitably screened arbors for amorous intrigues.

For WÜRZBURG do not be tempted by the modern port. Pass the town lock, double back round the promontory, and choose a place on the long quayside R above the old bridge (15th century) with its twelve statues which between them give much of the history of the city. Würzburg is a place of great ecclesiastical glory. It has an old cathedral, and just to make sure a 'new' 18th-century one adjacent, the crypt of which contains the tomb of the Irish Saint Kilian (d. 689) who evangelised Franconia. His skull, in the 'old' cathedral, is brought out annually for a pilgrimage and jollification. The residence of the Prince-Bishops of the wealthy Schön-born family is a masterpiece of baroque, built by Balthasar Neumann (d. 1753), with a famous ceiling by Tiepolo and another by Zick. Baroque concerts are given in the hall. The hospice (Juliusspittal) founded by one of the Prince-Bishops is now the modern hospital but still retains its hostelry side and serves its own excellent wines in an inn on the hospital premises.

Crossing the bridge with its double row of heroes and saints you can follow a path (or take the bus) to the hilltop from which the great Marienburg fortress from the 12th century looks down upon your mooring. It contains the Mainfränkisches Museum with Riemenschneiders and many other Franconian masterpieces. Further upstream, by the next bridge, Neumann's Käppele chapel, a rococo fantasy, is reached by a double ornamental staircase which extends up the entire hillside past Stations of the Cross.

OCHSENFURT has a loading quay L below the bridge, but a more attractive berth is at the excellent landing in the gardens immediately through the bridge. Much of the town walls remain, and the town hall has an elaborate clock with clock-jacks of the mayor and councillors and a beautiful girl. At the hour, two oxen collide head-on, a reminder that Ochsenfurt means Oxford. This mooring is also the one from which to visit the vineyard village of Frickenhausen upstream.

MARKTBREIT has a quay beside the renaissance tower-crane and at KITZINGEN there is a long quay R above the bridge, whilst at VOLKACH a loading quay L by the bridge gives a chance to visit the church for yet more Riemenschneider carving, which was the subject of a theft in recent years and subsequent dramatic ransom by a German newspaper. For SCHWEINFURT pass the lock and turn the long spit to draw in at a quay with lawns and gardens and a footpath tunnel under the railway. Schweinfurt (Pigford) is renowned for ball-bearings, but one should not be discouraged. Its park-like mooring, where a piece of the first drum weir has been elevated into a monument, is a particularly peaceful one, and the rebuilt town has a colourful market. The next possible stop is at HASSFURT, which has an unfrequented commercial harbour just upstream of the town, R.

After 392 kms. the navigation of the Main as such ceases, and the channel becomes that of the R. Regnitz.

River Regnitz. Navigable for 3 kms. Locks 2. This is the first portion of the route of the former Ludwig's Canal opened in 1845 and officially closed in 1950, although in fact it had been virtually impassable for many years (see Negley Farson's *Sailing Across Europe,* 1926; Donald Maxwell's *A Cruise Across Europe,* 1906; and for an account when navigation was good R. B. Mansfield's *The Water Lily on the Danube,* 1853).

Soon after the R. Main leads away northward, the Regnitz forks. The left-hand branch becomes the modern R–M–D canal, at present featureless but open to the towns of Forch-heim, Erlangen (with a monument on the summit level of the Ludwig's Canal), Fürth, and Nuremberg, and not dealt with in this book because only this portion of the route is available and the descent to the Danube remains to be completed. This could be in 1981, but the opening date has already been pushed ahead by twelve years.

The right-hand and smaller branch is the one which leads into the heart of Bamberg, and though not a through route it provides some adventure and the chance to lie at what must be as picturesque a mooring as any in Europe.

Navigation: Take the starboard channel at the junction and keep within a few yards of the bank R until you reach a small but modern electric lock. Apply at the neighbour-ing power station for the keeper. *Caution:* Beware the out-flow from the turbines, which is beside the bottom approach.

At the next bridge a view opens up which is probably unparalleled on any navigation in Europe, the 300 m. row of compact and jumbled little fishermen's houses known as Kleinvenedig (Little Venice), the buildings bright in paint of every hue and gay with tiny gardens, window-boxes and pots of flowers. Many have their own small landing-stages, and the scene extends along the whole of the right bank of the Regnitz as far as an old crane from the horse-haulage days. From the upper end of the row of houses the river begins to shoal somewhat, and with a draught of 1 m. or over it would be difficult to pass the fleet passage by the town hall into the Nonnengraben. I have, however, done this easily by dinghy, and measured the depth. Whether by cruiser or dinghy, keep to the port channel. After two bridges in quick succession you will be in the deeper, relatively still water of the Nonnengraben which curves round beneath some tall half-timbered houses and past a pair of Ludwig's Canal cranes until after 400 m. it comes to a lock (No. 2 of the old canal) which is in service and with a keeper on duty – though it may be a long time since he saw a boat. Beyond the lock and swing-bridge the main course of the Regnitz opens out wide and wooded, with a bathing beach and restaurant amenity, and navigation possible for perhaps another 1 km. or more, beyond which the former navigation is derelict. *Caution:* If rowing beware of the current in the weir stream above the short lock-cut.

Mooring: BAMBERG. Immediately upstream of the first bridge after the electric lock it is possible to moor against the bank L, a spring being used to hold the boat out in the current, which can be stiff. Bamberg is, so to speak, Germany's Canterbury, and its grandeur is astonishing. Developed under the Emperor Heinrich II (d. 1024), it is an archiepiscopal see. The city underwent great enrichment during the baroque period. The Gothic cathedral contains the famous 'Bamberger Reiter' equestrian statue, and the tomb of Heinrich II and the Empress Kunigunde, by Reimenschneider. Of medical interest is the scene showing St Benedict operating on the Emperor for cholecystitis.

The town hall is equally well known, standing alone in

the torrent of the weir stream like a man-of-war and reached by two bridges on either side. On the Untere Brücke, the more downstream pair, is a slot-machine to turn on the floodlighting of Kleinvenedig, and a similar device is on the bridge by the mooring. If spending the night in Bamberg, you will find the lights going on several times hourly until long after midnight.

Outside the town a walk of 3 km. over the fields leads to Altenburg castle. A fine view of the city can be had from the top of the keep. Altenburg also has a bear-pit, complete with bear. The rococo pilgrimage church of Vierzehnheiligen is near Lichtenfels, 25 kms. north of Bamberg. It represents the ultimate in baroque, and was designed by Balthasar Neumann.

River Neckar. Navigable from Plochingen to the Rhine at Mannheim. Length 202 kms. Locks 27.

Navigation: Being a popular stream for canoeists, many of the locks have push-trolleys on inclined planes to carry very small boats over the step.

Lock dues are reduced or not levied if your craft is accompanied by commercial shipping. On the Neckar you will be an *Alleinschleuser* (solo locker), a *Mitschleuser* (locking with others) or possibly on Sunday afternoons a *Spätschleuser* (late locker) — each of which categories has a different rate.

Passenger boats: There are no through services up the Neckar, but river trips of varying length are available from Heidelberg, Neckarsteinach, Heilbronn and Stuttgart.

The Neckar becomes navigable only in the outer industrial suburbs of Stuttgart, where there are considerable docks from which Europaships carry finished motor vehicles (Mercedes) down to the Rhine and Rotterdam for export. Soon, however, it begins to meander through limestone slopes thick with vines which produce little-known and rather dry wines before, once again, flowing past motor factories at Neckarsulm (N.S.U.). Then the scenery changes, the castle crags approach the river, and the valley narrows until the Neckar is winding between the dense forests of the Odenwald and the Little Odenwald, the latter being really a northward continuation of the Black Forest. From Bad Wimpfen down to Heidelberg the river must rank as one of the most splendid in Europe, and although traffic is at times heavy the Neckar is nevertheless an excellent cruising ground with unspoiled villages strung along the greater part of its course. It is important not to be put off by the first few dull and canalised kilometres up from Mannheim. Quite shortly the river will prove its beauty.

Moorings: Because the river is not a through route it can only be entered at the confluence with the Rhine, and so its facilities will here be dealt with from Mannheim upstream.

MANNHEIM provides mooring facilities in the dock basins. For details see *River Rhine*.

At NECKARSHAUSEN it is possible to stop upstream of the railway bridge and nose carefully between the reed-beds to the river bank, L, with an abandoned quay. Walking over the railway-bridge footpath it is only a short distance into Ladenburg opposite. In the museum are relics from the Roman town, and the boatman will notice a piece of the haulage chain formerly laid along the river bed for the chain-ships. Motor enthusiasts can make a pilgrimage to the neo-gothic garage of Carl Benz (d. 1929).

HEIDELBERG has good facilities along the quay wall, L, below the old bridge with a turreted gateway close to the town centre. Inevitably the town has suffered from becoming a United States military base, but nothing can destroy the prospect of the red sandstone castle seen in the rosy evening light from the Philosophenweg across the river – a walk where boatmen as well as philosophers may still ruminate.

The castle belonged to the Electors Palatine and was sacked by Louis XIV. It is famous for its large wine cask (nearly fifty thousand gallons) in the cellar, but the castle buildings and the formal garden in front of the Friedrichsbau are perhaps more attractive. The Otto-Heinrichbau houses one of the best pharmaceutical museums in the world, and there is a complete rococo dispensary with all its apparatus and materials. Heidelberg's University, though modern by

Oxbridge standards, is nevertheless the oldest in Germany (14th century), and has produced many great men. A statue of Professor Bunsen with his burner is to be seen in the town. The gaol for ill-behaved students can also be seen, but its use was regrettably ended in 1914.

From near the market a cable railway climbs to the Königstuhl, 568 m., which of course has now to support an unsightly television mast. A walk down to the town gives attractive views over the Neckar valley, and is a pleasant way of gaining an impression of typical German forest hill country.

Heidelberg is also the most convenient place from which to visit Schwetzingen, accessible by tram and famous for asparagus and the whims of the Electors Palatine, for whom it was a summer residence. The vast gardens (in the French sense), laid out in the 18th century, contains lakes, walks, a temple or two, a mosque, and everything that baroque could think up. Particularly intriguing is the bath, filled by artificial birds perched in the shrubbery to dart water from their bills. The court theatre has an ingenious sloping stage with a false perspective carried on by the natural scenery when the doors at the rear are opened. Plays and sometimes chamber concerts are performed each summer in the Schwetzingen Festival.

NECKARGEMÜND has a proper quay, L, and at NECKAR-STEINACH there is mooring against a limited wall. The town has four separate castles, and another is across the river in Dilsberg. HIRSCHHORN has no quay, but the little town with houses perched on the walls and dominated by a castle stronghold is one of the most romantic sights on the river. EBERBACH with its annual cuckoo fair has the only respectable quay for many kilometres. ZWINGENBERG (moor against the old ferry ramp) is dominated by the great bulk of the castle which commands the passage up the Neckar. Residence in the summer of the Margraf of Baden, whose wife is sister of Prince Philip, Duke of Edinburgh, the castle is to a limited extent open to the public. By now the boatman will have discovered that mooring facilities along most of the river are not good and one must either stop round the back of lock approaches, or hang the stern well out to avoid bumps from the wash of heavy vessels. Very often the safest course is to anchor just offshore and use the dinghy as an attached ferry; in this way one can stop at NECKARZIMMERN and visit Hornberg castle, in which lived Götz von Berlich-ingen (d. 1562), Goethe hero and tough leader of many causes including the Peasants' Revolt, who was renowned for the iron fist fitted to replace a hand lost in the siege of Landshut.

At GUNDELSHEIM, as elsewhere, one can moor with per-mission on the back of the lower approach mole of the lock, but it is wise to sound the approach. Gundelsheim has a fine castle of the Order of Teutonic Knights, whilst at nearby Guttenberg the castle library contains nearly 100 wooden boxes carved to resemble books, each of a different wood and containing within it the scales, seeds, bark, etc. of that species.

BAD WIMPFEN is not an easy mooring, but there is a pon-toon below the bridge or one can anchor near the further shore. Once the fortress home of the Hohenstaufen Em-perors, the upper town is extremely picturesque and the castle with its imposing watchtower can be visited, even if the emperors are gone. At NECKARSULM there is a side channel, R, where mooring close in to the town centre is convenient for visiting the Zweirad (Two Wheeler) museum, housed in the castle of the Order of Teutonic Knights. Exhibits range from the Drais two-wheeler of 1817 to Daimler's motor-cycle of 1894, and there are early works by Alfred Krupp and Adam Opel. In HEILBRONN, the town of Kleist's heroine Kätchen, there is a mooring at the town quay. MARBACH has a jetty, and one may reach the village to see Schiller's birthplace and also the Schiller Museum, an excellent example of how disembowelled and enervated a writer becomes when museumised with portraits galore, translations into every pronounceable language, first edi-tions, and indeed everything but the essence of his work.

STUTTGART. Except for the docks, which are not convenient for the city, the best mooring is close below the lock at BAD CANSTATT, a spa suburb now overgrown by its larger neighbour, but still providing mineral waters. Motor enthusiasts will want to visit the Daimler-Benz museum at the Untertürkheim Mercedes works. Gottlieb Daimler (d. 1900) was himself a native of Canstatt, and the exhibits include his first motor-cycle, and also that of Carl Benz. The vehicles shown cover the whole era from 1883 up to the most modern cars, and nearly all the famous Mercedes racing cars are on show, including that of Juan Fangio. With luck, there is a chance of a ride in a vintage model.

Outside Stuttgart a television tower on a thin stalk tops a forested hill, and gives fine views over Swabia, but most of the town is a reconstruction of no great beauty. Near the river, 13 kms. downstream, but best reached by bus from Stuttgart, is Ludwigsburg with its vast baroque palace of the Dukes of Württemberg. The gardens and the deer park are pleasant places for a lazy afternoon.

Caution: Do not take a tour of the palace. There are 75 rooms, about 74 too many, and escape from the guide half-way through the round is impossible.

DORTMUND–EMS CANAL AND CONNECTIONS

Dortmund–Ems Canal. From Dortmund to the R. Ems at Emden docks. Length 267 kms. Locks 18 and one vertical lift.

Navigation: The canal is very heavily used, and is unusual in having an upper and a lower speed limit. No craft may travel at less than 6 km./hr.; nor, if laden, at more than 7. This more or less rules out the possibility of laden barges passing each other, but empty ships and yachts may travel at 9 and overtake. Water police patrol the canal (with no speed limit).

The waterways connecting with the Dortmund–Ems Canal are, from south to north :

Rhine–Herne Canal L (q.v.)
Datteln–Hamm Canal R (see below)
Wesel–Datteln Canal L (q.v.)
Mittelland Canal R (see below)
Ems–Vechte Canal L (see *Left-Handed Canals*).
Haren–Rütenbrock Canal L (see *Left-Handed Canals*)
Küsten Canal R (see *Inland Route, Channel–Baltic*)
R. Leda R (see *Inland Route, Channel–Baltic*)
Ems–Jade Canal R (see *Inland Route, Channel–Baltic*)

The Dortmund–Ems Canal, on which the prosperity of Emden rests, connects the whole of the Ruhr area with the north sea port, but it is also in its middle section the route by which traffic from all over Western Germany and from Rotterdam reaches the Mittelland Canal and thence Bremen

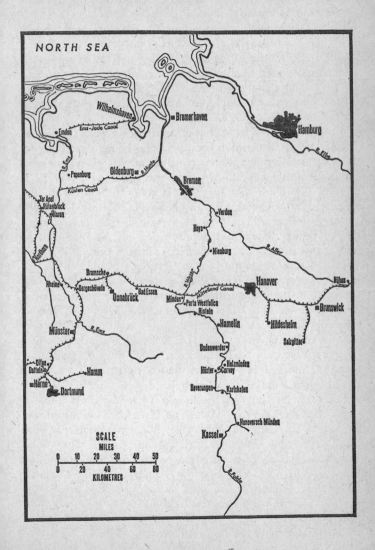

NORTH SEA

Wilhelmshaven

Bremerhaven

Hamburg

Emden
Ems-Jade Canal

R. Elbe

R. Ems

Papenburg
Oldenburg
R. Hunte
Bremen

Küsten Canal

Ter Apel
Rütenbrock
Haren

Verden

Hoya

Nienburg
R. Aller

Rheine

Bramsche
Bergeshövede
Osnabrück
Bad Essen
R. Weser
Mittelland Canal
Hanover
Rühen

Minden
Porta Westfalica
Rintein
Brunswick

R. Ems

Münster
Hamelin
Hildesheim

Olfen
Datteln

Bodenwerder

Salzgitter

Herne
Dortmund

Höxter
Corvey
Holzminden

Beverungen
Karlshafen

Hanoversch Münden

Kassel

R. Fulda

SCALE
MILES
0   10   20   30   40   50
0   20   40   60   80
KILOMETRES

or the countries of Eastern Europe. However, the relevant sections have been enlarged, and although the traffic is continuous there are no delays.

Contrary to what one might expect, the canal is extremely rural and offers many views over the low-lying Westphalian land. It crosses the Lippe and also the Ems on fine aqueducts which have been doubled during the enlarging process, and after passing close to Rheine it enters the Ems and becomes a river navigation, then an estuary, and finally a canal again for the last 9 kms. into Emden.

Moorings: DORTMUND has a large dock area. It produces one tenth of all German beer as well as being a steel city. A television tower with a revolving restaurant gives an excellent view of local industry and the canal which keeps it going. The *Henrichenburg Lift* is at the junction with the Rhine–Herne Canal, and any boatman interested in technical wonders will find it worth visiting the device, even if not going through it. The original lift was opened in 1898 and is a typical child of its Iron Age time, but a new one took its place in the 1960's.

At DATTELN a branch goes off eastward to HAMM (47 kms., 2 locks) but it is not a through route. 2 kms. further is the junction with the Wesel–Datteln Canal (q.v.) and lying is possible at the fork. At OLFEN there is a small, quiet harbour on the old arm of the canal, 4 kms. beyond the Lippe aqueduct. MÜNSTER has a harbour cut where one can pull in at the extreme end, not far from the town centre.

Münster, capital of Westphalia, has a famous place in history as the scene of the long-drawn-out negotiations to end the Thirty Years War. The Treaty of Münster was signed in 1648, and amongst other matters it established the independence of the Netherlands and Switzerland. The successful ending of the conference is said to have been due to an excellent Moselle wine (see Neumagen, on the Moselle).

Though almost annihilated during the Second World War, Münster has been rebuilt in all its Gothic glory, and the gables along the Prinzipalmarkt are perhaps as fine as when first erected in the 17th century. The 14th-century town hall has also been restored, and the panelled Friedenssaal with portraits of the delegates of 1648 is open to the public. The church of St Lambert has cages in which the bodies of Anabaptists were formerly exposed for the birds after they had been pinched to death with heated tongs.

BERGESHÖVEDE, the junction with the Mittelland Canal, has a quay by the chandlery and also a disused tug basin, but from this point onward there is no mooring except by the locks until PAPENBURG harbour (see *Inland Route, Channel–Baltic* for details, and also for moorings and navigation details between Papenburg and Emden).

The Left-Handed Canals. These rural waterways are owned by the *Genossenschaft der Linksemsischen Kanäle* – the Association of Canals on the Left Hand of the Ems. They are of similar dimensions to standard French canals, and are passable by yachts having a draught of 1 metre. They are in fact used by small barges engaged in local traffic. *Lock dues* are very small and are paid on entry.

Though still shown on maps, two of the three connections with the Dutch canal system are now derelict – though I passed through the Almelo–Nordhorn Canal in 1958 and the Alte Piccardie Canal in 1961. The remaining viable link is by the Haren–Rütenbrock Canal to Ter Apel in Holland. Altogether four canals are in the group :

(1) The Ems–Vechte Canal. From the Dortmund–Ems Canal at Hanekenfähr to the R. Vechte (not navigable) at Nordhorn. Length 20 kms. Locks 1 at Hanekenfähr tollhouse, normally open.

(2) The Süd–Nord Canal. From Nordhorn to Rütenbrock. Length 46 kms. Locks 7.

(3) The Haren–Rütenbrock Canal. From the Dortmund–Ems Canal at Haren to Rütenbrock. Length 14 kms. Locks 4.

(4) Such length of the Alte Piccardie Canal as may still be navigable. From Georgsdorf on the Süd–Nord Canal it ran originally to Coevorden in Holland, through 4 locks.

The Left-Handed Canals traverse a curious and strangely

deserted countryside of moor and fen and pastures. Except for Nordhorn there is nothing but the smallest hamlet in the vicinity and one has a strange feeling of being lost in some forgotten part of the world. The interest to the yachtsman is perhaps greatest if he is left-handed also, but these small canals form a useful link between the great barge routes of Germany and the many waterways of northern Holland. They are an ideal cruising ground for the businessman who wants to be certain that his secretary cannot find him – and really means it.

Mooring: Throughout, as the chances of being disturbed by other traffic is extremely slight. At Nordhorn one can stop by the lock which once led into the Almelo–Nordhorn Canal.

Mittelland Canal. From the Dortmund–Ems Canal at Bergeshövede to Rühen, where it passes into the German 'Democratic' Republic. Length 259 kms., Locks 2. There are side arms to Osnabrück (13 kms., 2 locks), to Linden (10 kms., 1 lock), Misburg (3 kms., no locks), Hildesheim (15 kms., 1 lock) and Salzgitter (18 kms., 2 locks).

The canal was built in the 1930's and has already been enlarged. Designed to carry traffic from the Ruhr to Berlin, it is the route by which Eastern European barges reach the Rhine. Traffic is considerable, and D.D.R., Polish and Czech flags may be met; but as the main interest of the Mittelland Canal to the yachtsman is as a means of reaching the Upper and Middle Weser the waterway is only described here as far as the junction at Minden.

The Mittelland Canal turns the end of a hill at Bergeshövede and then strikes across country on an astonishingly level course without either large cuttings or great meanders along a contour. In fact the distance between the lock at Münster (Dortmund–Ems Canal) and the first lock at Anderten is 205 kms. Even in Holland no such distance between two locks is to be found.

At first the route is through pinewoods and sandy heath with the Teutoburgerwald off to the right, the fatal forest in which Varus lost his Roman legions in A.D. 9. Eventually the canal emerges into a light and airy countryside of small farms with fruit orchards, Frisian cows, and occasionally a stork's nest on the chimney. Later it runs along the foot of the low wooded Wiehengebirge hills and comes at last to Minden. Here there are two descents to the Weser – by the single Schachtschleuse (shaft lock) at the western end of the aqueduct, north side; or by the two locks at the eastern end, south side. The first of these is a tourist attraction, and visitors actually pay to watch you. *Caution:* See that they get their money's worth of entertainment.

Beyond Minden there is no through route for yachts, but the frontier is still 157 kms. away and a boatman with time to spare can carry on across the aqueduct and visit Hanover out of loyalty to the crown, Brunswick for another look at Till Eulenspiegel (see *Elbe–Trave Canal*), Hildesheim for its cathedral and millenary rose-bush, and Salzgitter for motor engineering. Beyond the frontier the canal connects with the R. Elbe near Magdeburg by means of a vertical lift. See note 2 on p. 283.

Moorings: The only possible halts on the way to the R. Weser are at BRAMSCHE, where there is a quay and a small maintenance harbour, and BAD ESSEN, with a quay by the silo, and a widening of the waterway. This is a small health resort, interesting in that it has many village houses with carved and painted inscriptions on their exterior beams and gables. For MINDEN, see *River Weser*.

River Weser. The River Weser consists of three sections : the Lower Weser from the mouth up to Bremen (86 kms.), the Middle Weser from Bremen to Minden (159 kms.) and the Upper Weser from Minden to Hanoversch Münden (203 kms.), where the river divides into the R. Werra, not fully navigable, and the R. Fulda (see below). *Locks:* Middle Weser 7, Upper Weser 1. The river is tidal to the first lock (Hemelingen) 5 kms. above Bremen. There are no lock dues.

Navigation: For the Lower Weser downstream of Elsfleth see *Inland Route Channel–Baltic*. There are no problems on the rest of the tideway, the route to Bremen being comparatively narrow, and well marked. The Middle Weser is a typical modern river navigation with deep water and large, efficient locks. It is only on approaching Minden and crossing the conventional line into the Upper Weser that the navigation becomes more exacting.

From here, the river has considerable current, and for much of its course can flow as fast as the Rhine in its gorge section – that is to say, at 5 knots in a normal summer. Unlike the Rhine the course has no markers at all. The 'Talweg' or channel is maintained mainly by groynes and scouring, and all one needs to be certain of is precisely where this channel is. In fact, it is laid out according to a very simple rule : in the centre where the river is *comparatively* straight; about $\frac{1}{3}$L or $\frac{1}{3}$R on *moderate* bends, and quite against the shore on *decidedly* acute bends. The first hour or two of voyaging upstream will easily demonstrate the meanings of the three words in italics, and until the really very easy system is grasped, it is a good idea to station a pair of sharp eyes at the bow to watch for the training walls. The journey downstream should be taken as slowly as is feasible.

There are two points to consider about other traffic. Barges moving downstream may be hardly manoeuvrable if they are of the cold pressure type (see below). Regard them as floating, unmanned debris and give them adequate room. Upstream traffic will be plugging hard against a formidable current, and will set up a heavy wash, which should be allowed for when mooring.

A final curiosity of this intriguing and challenging waterway is the *Welle,* or wave. If the river becomes too shallow during a period of drought, barges loading at Hanoversch Münden have not enough water to run downstream. To meet this difficulty a wave is announced, and a flood of several hours' duration released from the Eder Dam. Skippers let almost the whole wave pass, and just before it tails off they set out in a flock to overtake it – or, more properly, just *not* to overtake it. By the time they have reached its front edge, they should be in the head-water of

Hamelin lock. By next morning the wave will have passed them again, and they can ride it once more to fetch the headwater of the first lock on the Middle Weser. For the boatman visiting the Weser – even by canoe – wave navigation can be a rare experience, but care should obviously be taken to go as slowly as possible in order not to outdistance the helpful flood. In some years no waves are released.

The Lower Weser is a typical estuary, but above Elsfleth it is a much narrower stream than one would expect of a river carrying a constant traffic of ocean shipping. It is this smallness which gives the approach to Bremen its particular charm, for liners pass close not only to your own boat but to the families lying in the sun on the sandy shores. At Vegesack the river becomes sophisticated, with sailing craft crisscrossing from side to side and smart restaurants flying their flags. Then comes an area of heavy shipbuilding before the cargo basins of Bremen open up on the port hand. Ahead are the first bridges, at Bremen itself.

The Middle Weser was not fully canalised until the 1960's and its large electric locks carry considerable traffic bound for the Mittelland Canal (q.v.) as well as a much smaller quantity continuing upstream of Minden. The country is flat and the banks are often high, but the river is rural and there appear to be more cows than humans living in the vicinity. The reason is the flooding in which the river used to indulge, so that no villages were built near to its banks unless they could be sited on rising ground. Only on approaching Minden does the country become more hilly, the woods and hamlets coming close to the river bank. There is a fly-over junction at Minden with connections between the Mittelland Canal and the river, the canal passing over the Weser on a long and massive aqueduct so that you may actually find Europaships passing above your own craft.

Already at Minden the slow-flowing and locked river is giving way to a swift and shallow stream of clear and clean water, the channel edged with groynes. This, the Upper Weser, continues for the next 200 kms., the only lock (at Hamelin) being put there to by-pass the ancient rights of a fish-weir belonging to a monastery long since vanished.

The Upper Weser is almost the last river in Europe to flow fast and virtually uncontrolled. Above Hamelin, its course is between forested hills (the Weserbergland) in which wild boar and deer abound, and because there is neither main road nor railway alongside its course the valley is one of the most peaceful to be found. Paddlewheel steamers still ply in summer, their graceful bright yellow hulls chugging doggedly around the tight bends of the stream. The current is too strong for heavily laden motorships, and what little traffic there is to Hamelin and above is usually hauled by tug. Downstream traffic often floats without a motor, yet actually travels rather faster than the current, and therefore has steerage way. The system is known as *mit kaltem Druck* (i.e. by cold pressure, as opposed to the hot pressure of steam). Opinions differ as to *why* a laden barge should move faster than the surrounding water. One theory is that the gradient of the Weser is such that the boat is actually sliding down a hill of water; another communicated to me by a physicist, is in terms of varying molecular attraction due to the immersion of the hull. The boatman is free to watch this extraordinary phenomenon for himself and propound his own explanation, marvelling that medieval boatmen ever discovered that one could voyage in this way.

For many years there has been talk of making the Upper Weser a locked river like the section below it, and even to cut a link via the R. Werra to the Rhine–Main–Danube waterway. However, the Iron Curtain has put an end to such schemes; and however much one might welcome the link one can only be glad that the river will probably remain for many decades, or even permanently, as a wild, un-polluted, and decidedly challenging stream.

Moorings: At BREMEN there are mooring stages between the third and fourth bridges. Because of their distance apart it is advisable to lie on a barge. The mooring is admirably placed, being close to all the interesting sights of the city. Old Bremen, much restored, is only about ½ sq. km. in area and the ramparts and moat, now a pleasant park with windmills, fortunately serve to keep the modern area at arm's length. Close to the fourth bridge (Weserbrücke) is the Schoorviertel, an area of one-time fishermen's houses rather Chelseafied, but with real charm. In the market the giant 15th-century statue of Roland (of the Chanson de Geste, and Rolandsbogen on the Rhine, q.v.) has almost the veneration of a local saint. The town hall has probably the best cellar of German wines in the world, all available to the public in an underground restaurant. Outside is a modern bronze of Bremen's four animal musicians. Architects will want to visit the Böttcherstrasse, erected all of a piece in the 1920's, and much better than the period might suggest.

VERDEN is just off the Weser but accessible by forking left into the R. Aller, 2 kms. above the upper end of Langwedel lock-cut. There is a W.S.A. harbour, which is better than the broken-down quay. (Permission should be obtained from the overseer.) Verden is a centre of horse-breeding. In summer, there is certain to be an inhabited stork's nest somewhere along the main street.

HOYA has a harbour with grassy banks, and NIENBURG provides a good quay immediately above the bridge. L. MINDEN has a large commercial harbour up a long cut leading off to starboard, but this is far from the town centre. Proceed up river for 2 kms. to a good quay with deep water just short of the road bridge. In Minden one may still sometimes see British soldiery, hang-overs of a war which was over before they were born. Some 10 kms. upstream is the PORTA WESTFALICA, the gash in the hills broken by the Weser waters after the last ice age, and still an impressive gap to sail through. Mooring here is poor, the only jetty being used by trip-boats, but anchoring is possible in the shadow of groynes. The eastern heights are disfigured with a television mast, but a path climbs to the hilltop on the western side, topped by a gigantic statue of Kaiser Wilhelm I, and a tower in honour of Bismarck – with an excellent view. RINTELN has a commercial harbour, R, just below the town, and also a good quay wall immediately below the bridge. There is no other mooring until HAMELIN (HAMELN), where one should

pass the barge lock and double back under the bridge into
the approach of the old single lock. There is also a commercial harbour, but the position is less stimulating.

Hamelin's claim to fame is its Pied Piper. He appeared
in 1284, and his impact was such that the town records
were afterwards dated as year 1, etc. 'after the disaster to
our children'. The event still provides an inexhaustible mine
of Ph.D. theses. Theories are many, and the only certain
fact is that the rat-catcher occupation was added later; but
the event is dramatised every Sunday morning in summer,
complete with rodents. A reference to the affair can be seen
carved on the Rattenfängerhaus of 1603, built in the 'Weser
Renaissance' style found throughout the upper valley.

BODENWERDER has a small harbour R downstream of the
town, and before the railway bridge. Local hero is Baron
von Münchhausen, cannon-ball riding raconteur. At HOLZ-
MINDEN the good harbour will probably be found silted, but
the town is edged with a good quay. CORVEY has a grass-
banked harbour, L, close to the former abbey from the 9th
century and later, whence the monk Ansgar went to evan-
gelise Scandinavia, and where the author of *Deutschland
über Alles,* a former librarian at Corvey, is buried. HÖXTER
has a quay wall in the stream beyond the bridge, L.
BEVERUNGEN has a jetty which can be used when steamers
are not due.

At KARLSHAFEN the entrance to the port basin of about
1700, surrounded by graceful houses of the period, has
regrettably been filled in, but there is an adequate quay
immediately below it. Karlshafen was built all of a piece in
excellent Landgravian style, and is now a resort. A fine view
of the geometrical town and the wooded bends of the river
is provided by the Huguenot tower on the hillside above.
The next village upstream is named Gewissenruh (Peace of
Conscience), recalling that the Landgraf Karl of Hessen who
founded Karlshafen opened his lands to the Huguenot
refugees.

There is no other bankside mooring for 40 kms. At
HANOVERSCH MÜNDEN fork right into the Fulda, pass the

lock, and back down to the point of the weir stream, where there is a reasonably good vertical wall. The town has hundreds of houses in half timber, many with curious symbolic carvings and biblical inscriptions. At the confluence of the R. Werra and R. Fulda stands the Weserstein with an inscription announcing the birth of the Weser. Local celebrities are Dr Eisenbart, 18th-century travelling doctor and noted quack, who died in the town; and Denis Papin, whose alleged steamboat was smashed by local Luddite boatmen in 1707. Or wasn't it? The scene is depicted in the Weser Renaissance town hall.

River Fulda. Navigable from Kassel to Hanoversch Münden. Length 27 kms. Locks 8.

This river is a gentle and pleasant continuation of the R. Weser. It presents no navigational problems, and provides an easy route to Kassel. It was hoped that the river could be developed as a link over to the R. Lahn and thence to the Rhine, and although the scheme has never been carried out it accounts for the exceptional size of the town lock in Kassel.

Mooring is possible along the bank, in almost complete absence of traffic. KASSEL has a commercial harbour below the city, but one can nose into the bank beyond the second bridge after the lock, in the Karlsaue Park, which has a lake and a ruined orangery. This is close to the centre of the town, which was one of the first to ban traffic from the main shopping area. Fairy-tale enthusiasts may enjoy the Museum of the Grimm Brothers. Both were professors of extreme erudition, and Jakob (d. 1863) is known in academic circles for his propounding of Grimm's Law, concerned with sound changes in related languages. About 8 kms. outside the city but accessible by tram is the vast Wilhelmshöhe Park, an early 18th-century fantasy of the Landgraf Karl which has everything from water jets to squirt elegant visitors to an artificial Roman aqueduct, grottoes, temples, and a colossal statue of Hercules 71 m. high. The great water staircase is turned on at week-ends, each step being a double waterfall.

The water takes 15 minutes to reach the bottom, whence it passes many other follies before reaching the lake by the residence where Napoleon III was held after the French defeat in the Franco-Prussian War of 1870. This palace contains the only wallpaper museum in the world, containing fine examples of Spanish leather wall-hangings and magnificent samples from the rococo period.

WATERWAYS FROM ANTWERP

ANTWERP is a considerable centre of inland shipping, and barge traffic and yachts can leave it in three directions; by the River Scheldt upstream toward Gent, or downstream toward Zeeland, or across the Campine in the direction of the province of Limburg. The Scheldt is dealt with separately, but in this section the various waterways accessible from its confluence with the River Rupel 16 kms. upstream of the Antwerp Royersluis dock entrance will be described in some detail.

River Rupel. From the Scheldt at Rupelmonde to Rumst. Length 16 kms., tidal.

The Rupel itself is short, commercial and somewhat dull, a river of brickyards, but it is the gateway to a number of more interesting waterways. First, and a mere 3 kms. from the confluence with the Scheldt is *The Brussels Ship Canal* or *Willebroek Canal.* Length 29 kms. Locks 3. Entered at Wintham Lock but with another entrance from the Rupel by a side lock at Willebroek on the opposite shore from Boom, this is a broad and at times stately waterway with occasional bankside factories and wharves. The sea-ships can go no further than the quays on the outskirts of the capital, before the first fixed bridge at Laeken, but the canal carries on into the city of Brussels.

Moorings: LAEKEN. Immediately before the first fixed bridge is the Brussels Royal Yacht Club. A tram-stop on the line to Brussels is nearby for those willing to risk crossing the traffic lanes of the busy and noisy road. Laeken is the site of the royal palace (not on view), and in the outlying

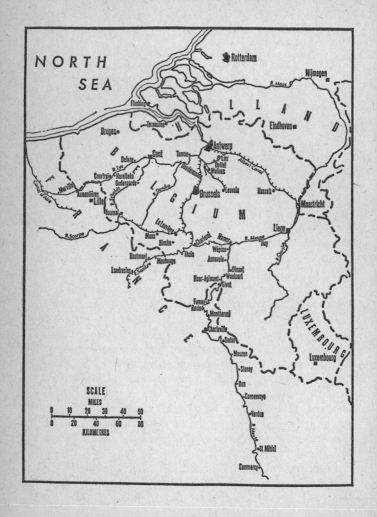

grounds are the rather decayed remains of the World Fair
of 1958, with the Atomium where one may penetrate
through stainless steel tubes into nine spheres, now exhibition rooms. Those unfamiliar with what an atom might (or
might not) be like if magnified 150 billion times should not
miss this strange entertainment, which is within 45 minutes'
walking distance of the Laeken mooring, or can be reached
from there by tram. The Atomium suffers from the fact
that its windows are inaccessible to cleaners, but is none the
less intriguing even if white-elephantine.

BRUSSELS is perhaps best visited from Laeken, although
the barge wharves further in have abundant mooring on
vertical quays. The city centre is only 1 km. distant from
them, but the canal scene is not one that would have inspired
artists of the Flemish School. Brussels is one of the duller
capital cities, though an excellent shopping centre. Its great
sight – and one of the finest in Europe – is the magnificent
Grand Place, imaginatively lit at night. The splendid city
hall (15th century) runs along one side and the others are
filled with the halls of the various trade guilds – No. 6 being
that of the Corporation of Boatmen – from the late 17th
century. The Maison du Roi contains an exhibition of
greatest interest to psychologists, the display consisting of
the innumerable suits of clothing given by the prudish or
lewdish to the famous urinating statue, carved in 1619,
which is close by the Grand Place. The Manneken Pis has
been an attraction to Brusselers for more than 350 years.

An unusual experience is an evening visit to the Toone
theatre in the Petite Rue des Bouchers, where marionettes
indulge in highly complicated rough and tumble drama.

At the lock of Molenbeek St Jean beyond the city centre
the canal becomes transmuted into the Canal de Charleroi.

Canal de Charleroi. Length 54 kms. Locks 10 and 1 inclined
plane. This canal is a masterpiece of modernisation, much
of the southern section having been entirely re-cut, a tunnel
eliminated, and the number of locks reduced by 28 – largely
as a result of the construction of the Ronquières inclined

9

plane, which climbs a 1 in 20 slope 1·4 km. long, carrying barges in Europaship-sized tanks each on 236 wheels. At the top is a tall viewing tower.

At Seneffe the Canal du Centre leads off to the right (see below), but the main route continues broad and magnificent to Charleroi. Landscaping of the canal has been excellently done, and the new large locks are notable for their flower-beds and the seats for those who like to watch barges.

Canal du Centre. From Seneffe to Mons, where it becomes the *Nimy–Blaton Canal* as far as the R. Dendre, and then the *Pommeroeul–Antoing Canal* from the Dendre to the R. Scheldt at Antoing. Total length 63 kms. Locks 8 and 4 vertical lifts. All this route is either already enlarged to Europaship dimensions or will be. For example, near Antoing 8 old locks have been by-passed by 2 new ones. From Blaton another link, the *Mons–Condé Canal* runs south-ward to the R. Scheldt at Condé. Length 18 kms. Locks 5 Belgian, 2 French. Customs at Condé. In spite of its name this canal does not run to Mons; that part of it having now been abandoned as it paralleled the Pommeroeul–Antoing Canal at a distance of only a few kilometres.

These canals are entirely in the area of the Belgian coal-fields and cannot be considered particularly attractive cruising waterways. Nevertheless, waterway enthusiasts will want to see the hydraulic canal lifts near LA LOUVIÈRE, and MONS is a hill town with many memories of the First World War. The town belfry gives a good outlook over the canals of the area, and on Trinity Sunday the bells ring for the annual procession and a fight between St George and a fearful dragon, the Lumeçon.

Though not itself on a canal, BINCHE is accessible from Mons (16 kms.), Charleroi (21 kms.) or Labuissière lock on the R. Sambre (10 kms.) and should not be missed by any boatman in the area at the beginning of Lent. Masked and in costume, the people dance fanatically in the streets and on Shrove Tuesday the 'Gilles' appear, dressed in huge hats of ostrich feathers, jigging in frenzy and bombarding the crowd with oranges. The day finishes with fireworks and general delirium. No adequate explanation of this curious festival has been found, though some of the costumes are curiously enough thought to reflect the conquest of Peru – Binche having of course been under Spanish domination in 1534.

The River Rupel abandons its identity above the small town of Rumst, the course dividing to become the R. Nete (to port) and the R. Dijle (to starboard).

River Nete. To Lier, where it becomes the *Nete Canal,* which leads through to the Albert Canal at Viersel. Length 25 kms. to Lier, and 10 kms. of canal to Viersel. Locks 2. *Caution:* The river section must only be run on a rising tide, otherwise there will not be enough water below the lock at Duffel, at the head of the tideway.

Though devoid of any good moorings LIER is one of the most charming towns of Brabant, crossed by a medieval canal with some picturesque merchants' houses from earlier centuries. A carillon plays in the 14th-century belfry, there is a peaceful *béguinage,* and the Zimmer tower contains a modern and extremely complicated astronomical clock, with figures which perform daily.

River Dijle. Upstream of its confluence with the R. Nete, the R. Dijle divides almost immediately into three at a point called the Zennegat. The right-hand channel is a minor tidal navigation, the *River Zenne,* which after about 7 kms. merely peters out.

The centre waterway is the *Canal de Louvain*. Length 31 kms. Locks 5. This comparatively straight canal was cut in 1750 under the Empress Maria Theresa of Austria (to which country the Belgian Netherlands then belonged) and runs to LOUVAIN only, ending in a canal basin at the edge of the city. Though lately famous more for student riots over the question of which language is to be used in its university founded as long ago as 1425, the city used to be renowned for its cloth. In 1914 it was sacked and the treasures of its library were burned. Destroyed again in 1944, Louvain is mostly of recent construction, but the city hall of the 15th century has survived.

The left-hand channel at the Zennegat is the *River Dijle* itself, navigable to Malines (Mechelen) and tidal to the lock at the edge of the city. Length 6 kms. Locks 1. Like the R. Nete, the R. Dijle should only be run on a rising tide, as the ebb falls away very rapidly.

Moorings: MALINES has good mooring throughout the town canal (though of course it can also be visited from the Canal de Louvain, which passed within ¾ km. of the centre). It was Margaret of Austria who, during her regency of the Netherlands (1507–30), built up the intellectual splendour of Malines and attracted to it such philosophers as Erasmus and Sir Thomas More. From the same period is the great church of St Rombaut, probably the finest in all Belgium, and certainly with the most notable carillon, on which concerts are regularly given – and actually heard, for Malines has little traffic. There is even a school for carilloneurs at Malines, which is Belgium's archiepiscopal see.

Albert Canal. From Antwerp docks to Liege. Length 129 kms. Locks 6, of Europaship dimensions.

Navigation: At Antwerp, enter the docks either behind coasters at the Royerssluis; or, if that is not available, by the Kattendijksluis or the Bonapartesluis a little further upstream, in which case turn left on clearing the lock and proceed straight ahead to pass down the long Kattendijk Dock and through a lifting bridge to reach the Lefebvre Dock into which the Royerssluis traffic also emerges. Turn hard right (or, if coming from the Royerssluis half right) and through two very large lifting bridges to the Straatsburg Dock.

At the first of these bridges a cantonnier will shout questions (in Flemish) and swing out a small box containing a numbered card, which should be taken out. The questions are : Name of the boat, and whither bound – to which the answer is *'Naar Luik'*, i.e. to Liege. *Caution:* Do not hold on to the box and pull the official into the dock.

Beyond the second bridge scores of barges are moored in the Straatsburg Dock against a jetty on the left. A halt must be made here to call at the Canal Office at the inner end of the jetty and hand in the numbered card, in return for which the clerk will deliver the papers which he has already prepared from the information phoned through by the cantonnier. It is important not to proceed without this permit, which is issued for a few pence and must be shown at the locks further ahead. A call must also be made at the toll office at the entrance to Liege, to show the papers. This office is on the right, a short way before the huge statue of King Albert (on the left) which marks the end of the canal and its junction with the course of the River Meuse.

Passage through the port of Antwerp is free, provided the ship is cleared into the canal within 24 hours. This gives ample time to visit the city (see p. 127) but if there at a week-end it is wise to maké sure that any swing-bridges to be passed will in fact be manned.

The Albert Canal was cut in the 1930's to provide a shorter and all-Belgian route from Antwerp to the industrial area of the Liege basin, and at the same time to serve as a somewhat optimistic extension of the Maginot Line. In recent years it has been enlarged and the traffic is heavy, but as there are one large lock and two smaller ones available at each step, there is rarely a delay of more than a few minutes. Starting from Antwerp in the morning one can make Liege the same evening.

The canal quickly clears Antwerp and strikes across the sandy heath of the Campine through a countryside of birch and pine, heather and evening primrose, and nightingales by the score. There is not a town or village on the route and only as it approaches Hasselt does the waterway show any signs of industry. The last three locks climb to the colliery area around Genk, but even here the pitheads are mostly seen only in the distance. Then the canal cuts through the ridge close to Maastricht and the Dutch frontier, passing through the deep cuttings of Vroenhoven and Kanne, the latter being cleft in the soft rock and reminding one of the Corinth Canal. Emerging to make contact with the Meuse at Petit Lanaye, the Albert Canal turns southward for the final 30 kms. into Liege.

There are a number of side links. Before the first lock out of Antwerp the *Dessel–Schoten Canal* with ten locks wanders away over the Campine, part of the former canal route from Maastricht to Antwerp. Next is the junction with the *Nete Canal* (see *River Nete*), then the *Bocholt–Herentals* and *Dessel–Kwaadmechelen* Canals. None of these are of any great interest except to those who wish to become lost in the wastes of the Campine. At the edge of Maastricht the short *Briegden–Neerharen Canal* leads into the old *Zuid Willems- vaart Canal*, which links Maastricht with Bocholt and the canals of the Dutch Campine. This is one way of reaching the Meuse at Maastricht, but by doing so one misses the grandeur of the Kanne cutting.

Moorings: It is difficult to find a night's halt out of the wash of the seemingly unending heavy traffic, but at HASSELT, a county town, a cut of 1 km. leads into the town harbour with good lying alongside barges. Otherwise quays subject to surge are available above the locks. For LIEGE see under *River Meuse*.

River Lys (*Leie*). From the Canal d'Aire to Gent. Length 128 kms. Locks 7 French, 6 Belgian.

The Lys runs parallel to the Upper Scheldt and provides a less heavily used connection to Belgium from the main Calais–Paris route. Its upper reaches are decidedly rural, but there is a heavily industrialised area where it enters the Lille basin and passes through Armentières into Belgium. Further ahead the river receives the continual addition of flax-retting effluent which makes it inky black in its lower reaches, and the only place of note on it is Courtrai (Kortrijk), from where it meanders over a farming countryside towards Deinze and Gent.

Moorings: In the upper reaches mooring to the bank is

certainly possible. At MERVILLE the river forks to make an island of part of the town, and there is a quay in the old river course below the lock, turning sharp left. At ARMEN-TIÈRES the town is to be by-passed by a new cut, but there is a reasonable quay in the town centre for anyone lured by the song about the Mademoiselle into thinking the town might be romantic, which it certainly is not.

In COURTRAI, moor in the backwater – which in fact is the original river course – nears the Tours de Broel, the one remaining fortified gateway from the 15th century which spans the stream. Courtrai was the scene of the Battle of the Golden Spurs in 1302, when the Flemish tradesmen un-horsed and slew thousands of French knights on richly accoutred chargers – one of the most undignified defeats of history. The original belfry clock is an intricate piece of machinery, but to see it one must travel to Dijon, to where it was removed by Philip the Hardy in 1382, after he had beaten the Flemings. At the downstream edge of the town there is a connection through to the Scheldt by the *Courtrai–Bossuit Canal,* with 11 locks and Belgium's only canal tunnel, 600 m. in length. Beyond Harelbeke – which smells fearfully of flax effluent – a side-branch leads through two locks to Roeslare. For the section beyond Deinze and through to Gent see *Intra-Coastal Route.*

River Scheldt (Escaut). From the Canal de St Quentin to the sea at Flushing. Length 325 kms., of which 172 are tide-way. Locks 16 French, 8 Belgian. Enlargement to Europa-ship dimensions is under way.

Navigation: Great areas of the Scheldt dry out quickly on a falling tide and to keep in the channel is essential. Sea charts should be used below Antwerp.

The French section of the Scheldt can hardly be described as a cruising waterway, being heavily used by traffic from the black country area of Valenciennes and (via the River Scarpe and the Canal de la Deule) from the mines of Douai, Lens and Lille. The Belgian reaches are somewhat more rural and from Tournai down to Gent the river passes through a Flemish countryside of woods and pastures and windswept farms. Without being spectacular the course is pleasant enough as a through route, and there is sufficient flow on the river to prevent its becoming blocked by coal dust. At Gent the Merelbeke lock is at the head of the tideway, and reasonably high water (Dover + 6 hrs.) should be present before one runs down to Antwerp. This section of the river is also under reconstruction, and the whole passage through the city is now by-passed by the southern section of the Gent Ring Canal.

The estuary is uneventful until above Antwerp the widening river opens out to a water-colour picture of Temse on the left bank before the junction with the River Rupel at Rupelmonde, from which point the Port of Antwerp stretches almost unbroken on the right bank as far as the Dutch frontier at Lillo, where there is a Belgian customs jetty from which a cutter may call on incoming craft. The river is now merging with the broad and usually ruffled or stormy waters of Zeeland, and the buoyage which begins at Antwerp marks the channel all the way to the sea.

Moorings: At TOURNAI the river runs through the town centre, and has a good vertical quay wall. Close to the magnificent cathedral built in the 12th to 14th centuries stands the oldest belfry in Belgium, from the same period. Carillon concerts are given on Sundays and holidays in the summer, and the bells are as well heard from the river as anywhere. Tournai has a carnival and floral procession in mid-June, and an annual procession on the Sunday nearest 8th September dates from the plague of the 11th century.

OUDENAARDE also has a quay near the centre. A small Flemish town with a Grand Place on which stands the 16th-century town hall and a Louis XIV fountain. Oudenaarde is mainly known from the decisive defeat inflicted there by the Duke of Marlborough upon the French, in 1708.

For details of GENT see under *Intra-Coastal Route*. To reach the Palais de Justice mooring fork left *before* the *Brusselserpoortsluis* lock and follow through the narrows behind the courts. DENDERMONDE (TERMONDE) has a wall

immediately upstream of the lock leading into the R. Dendre,
an alternative through route to the French coalfields but
with many more locks (36 on Belgian territory). There is a
rise and fall of several feet. TEMSE has a jetty above the
bridge but RUPELMONDE is not an easy place to stop. Apart
from being the birthplace of Mercator the cartographer
(d. 1594) it has no special interest for the boatman.

ANTWERP. The excellent Imalso yacht harbour has an
entrance lock available 2 hours either side of H.W. (Dover
+ 4 hrs.). There is every facility except reasonably easy
access to Antwerp, which unfortunately lies on the other
side of the river, and one may find it more convenient to
moor for a short time along the commercial river quays
(where there will certainly be plenty of wash) or in the
docks. Craft bound for the Albert Canal may spend up to
24 hours in the port without charge. The Bonaparte and
Willem Docks are the nearest to the city centre.

Antwerp has several faces. There is the main shopping
area and a seedy district near the docks where women in
diaphanous gowns lie in showcases. But the older city area,
much destroyed by the Spaniards in 1576, was rebuilt at the
time of Rubens (d. 1640), who is perhaps the most famous
citizen of Antwerp with Plantin the printer (d. 1589) in
second place. The houses of each are now museums. The
cathedral spire, 14th century, is visible far and wide over
the country, and a lift to the top makes it a good point from
which to see the docks and the river. The ancient fort of the
Steen on the waterfront contains a fine collection of models
of ships.

For TERNEUZEN see *Intra-Coastal Route,* and for FLUSHING
(VLISSINGEN) see *Inland Route, Channel–Baltic.*

River Meuse. Navigable from its junction at Troussey, south
of Commercy, with the Canal de la Marne au Rhin to the
Delta in Holland. Length : from Troussey to St Andries
(junction with the R. Waal course of the Rhine) 600 kms.
Locks 59 French, 17 Belgian and 11 Dutch.

Navigation: Under normal conditions there are no problems, but in the spring the river can flood after heavy rain or snow thaws, and if the locks are under water shipping may be held up for several days. Such hold-ups are limited to the gorge, where there is no room for the flood water to spread out. There is little current in the summer.

The Belgian Meuse and the first 2 kms. of the French river are built to 1,350-ton standards and large craft ply to the coal harbour at Givet. Beyond, the works are of standard French canal size. However, the river above Givet is not necessarily deep from side to side, and a course should be taken about 10 to 30 metres from the towpath side. Traffic is plentiful rather than heavy, much of it to and from the Solvay soda plant near Nancy, though the canalisation of the Moselle has now provided an alternative route.

Caution: In general, do not enter weir streams *below* the weirs where there may be rocks and little water. Going upstream the entrance to lock 58 (Trois Fontaines) is a bad one if the river is above normal. Coming down, great care must be taken not to miss the narrow entrances leading into the tunnels below lock 49 (Orzy) R, and lock 56 (Mouyon) L.

At Charleville, keep left at each of three junctions when going upstream. At the second turn the navigation is in the citadel moat and the deep lock causes difficult eddies when emptying. Lie off in the main stream until the gates are open and the passage clear.

Dues: The French section is free, but a fee of a few pence is demanded for the Belgian river. This must be paid at the *Bureau de la Navigation* at Monsin, which is on the starboard hand at the entrance to Liege, just before the end of the Albert Canal.

Customs: Dutch and Belgian on the long quay below the lock of Petit Lanaye. Belgian at the quay of Heer–Agimont; French at Givet – with no proper mooring facilities. Draw in on a barge. *Caution:* More people have gone on record in the last century and a half as having been frustrated at Givet that at any other customs post in the western world. Eat as much humble pie as necessary, or be prepared to cause an international incident.

The Meuse is a varied stream which flows through some of the most startling river scenery in Europe. Yachts often penetrate into the Belgian reaches, but few except those bound from Scandinavia to the Mediterranean have discovered the wild stretches of river in the French Ardennes, or the pleasant river towns of Lorraine. Maintained in excellent condition, the Meuse is within reach of craft based in southern England and can be combined with other waterways to make round trips with hardly a dull moment. Such dull moments as there may be are limited to the Dutch reaches, but these can be by-passed by taking the Albert Canal (q.v.) with a great saving of time. Being unattractive, the Dutch reaches will here receive little treatment.

The Rhine and Meuse (Maas, in Holland) become so involved with each other in their lower reaches that it is difficult to be sure which is which. The Dutch long ago gave up trying to identify them. However, the Meuse can be entered via the Hollandsch Diep, keeping to the right; and also at Woudrichem on the Waal (Rhine). Further up the Waal there is a connection through a lock at St Andries, and another by the Maas–Waal Canal which leaves the Rhine below Nijmegen. This link and the remainder of the Meuse up to Maasbracht is the main barge route to the Dutch coalfields around Sittard, and the traffic is more than the locks can easily handle. After waiting for two hours outside the Nijmegen lock I have turned around, made a detour of 200 kms. through Antwerp and reached Liege ahead of the craft which had been higher in the queue at the canal entrance. From this it can be assumed that only those engaged in research theses upon the family and social problems of frustrated bargees will find the Dutch Meuse route rewarding.

At Maasbracht the traffic takes the Juliana Canal which runs through the colliery land to rejoin the Meuse below Maastricht. From Nijmegen to Maastricht there are altogether 10 locks, and delays of up to several hours can be encountered at any of them. It is only on emerging into the river at Maastricht that life begins, but this town (which should certainly not be missed) is better reached by the

Albert Canal without loss of time or temper.

Above Maastricht the Meuse quickly passes into Belgian territory, converging with the Albert Canal a few hundred metres beyond the frontier at the lock of Petit Lanaye. As far as Liege the old navigation in the river course is hardly used, although it is accessible through a lock at Visé. At Liege the river becomes highly industrial, but picturesquely so, and the boatman will be astonished to see what transformations have been wrought upon the landscape since the Lancastrian John Cockerill introduced the first coke oven there (at Seraing) in 1823. However, the foundries and belching chimneys are soon left astern as the wooded river valley leads up through Huy to the confluence with the Sambre at Namur. Already the sides are steeper, with perpendicular crags dropping to the river, and the Meuse now turns one breath-taking bend after another, all the way to the French frontier at Givet. This is Belgium's finest piece of scenery, and the Belgians are very well aware of it. Between Namur and Agimont the banks are sprinkled – but not too thickly – with week-end cottages, country houses and splendid estates.

Across the French frontier the scenery becomes even more dramatic, but as the successful Frenchman can build a villa in Provence or keep his yacht on the Languedoc–Roussillon coast he leaves the Meuse to the fish and kites and the barges. In Belgium, riverside inns and restaurants abound. In France there are none. This strange disdain for the French Meuse is even shared by the navigation authority, which insists on calling it the 'Canal de l'Est, branche Nord'.

Through the gorge of the French Ardennes the river twists and curls so tightly that in two places lengthy loops are cut off by tunnels. The slopes, sometimes clad with impenetrable forest full of deer and wild boar, attain a height of 200–300 metres above the stream before at last, after 80 kms. of splendour, the river emerges into flatter land beyond Charleville-Mézières. Before Sedan the Canal des Ardennes leads off westward toward the Aisne and the Marne, while the Meuse continues through peaceful pasture land towards the ridges around Verdun, the crests of which are dotted with monuments of the world's greatest-ever slaughter. Across Lorraine, the river pounds become fewer, the canalised cuts longer, until beyond Commercy the waterway leaves the river altogether and climbs the final 5 locks in 6 kilometres to the junction with the main canal route from Paris to Strasbourg at Troussey.

Moorings: MAASTRICHT. The long wall in midstream connecting the two bridges is reserved for visiting yachts and is an excellent berth. Maastricht is an ancient and very un-Dutch city of the Netherlands, surrounded by moats and walls of every period from the 13th century onward. St Servaas cathedral, begun in the 10th century and recently restored after a disastrous fire, dominates the Vrijthof square. In the market stands a statue of J. P. Minkelers (1748–1824), who heated coal dust in a shot-gun and later lit Louvian university by gaslight. There are intriguing walks to be had on the ramparts near the river, and outside the town one can penetrate (with a guide) into the maze of subterranean quarry galleries under the hill of St Peter, the diggings from Roman times onward having furnished the stone to build Maastricht. Similar quarries exist at Valkenburg (11 kms.), a 'popular' resort in which some galleries are painted black and fitted out to simulate a coal mine of the nearby Sittard coalfields. Maastricht also provides the opportunity at 24 hours' notice to buy limitless stores out of bond before reaching Belgium or France. (The Belgians may seal a proportion at the frontier.)

LIEGE (LUIK). Preferably in the branch canal, a dead-end on the starboard hand before the city centre, failing which on any vacant quay wall. A good berth can be found in the yacht port on the left bank below the Pont Albert I, where heavy traffic roars past on a high level; this mooring and the branch canal are both safe from wash. If you like Birmingham you might also fancy Liege. But the city at least makes something of its river, and the view from the citadel is splendid, even if there are 407 steps to climb. Beyond the Pont Albert I the River Ourthe comes in, R, and makes a possible side-trip of 5 kms. through two locks in the suburbs. A further 125 kms. are available to canoeists.

CHOKIER. Moor at the long quay under the trees, L. In contrast to the tar-laden walls in Liege city, this mooring is clean, and clear of the channel.

HUY (HOEI) has deep water at the quay immediately above or below the road bridge, R. A good shopping stop, Huy has an airy market square and a 19th-century citadel full of grisly memories of the Second World War. From across the river a cable car takes off to fly high over the valley and town to the hill of La Sarte, and gives an excellent opportunity to photograph your own boat. Huy, like all the other towns of any size as far upstream as Commercy, is one medieval horse-hauled day's barge journey upstream of the previous one, in this case Liege.

NAMUR (NAMEN). Draw in at the quay L just above the main road bridge (second bridge up from the lock of Grands Malades), or perhaps turn into the Sambre just beyond this quay and draw in on the starboard hand when through the first or second bridge. Namur has been the scene of many sieges and bombardments, but the citadel, fortified in turn by Coehorn and Vauban, is now a mixture of playground, barracks, museum and band arena. It is reached by a cable-lift. At Easter, there is often a Passion play at Jambes, across the main river. The Meuse cliffs at Marche-les-Dames, below the city, are where King Albert fell to his death when climbing the rocks in 1934. For DAVE and WÈPION, anchor off the Château de Dave. Both places are renowned for their strawberries. PROFONDEVILLE has a quay L just above the canoe club barge. The village is shaken by traffic, but the ascent of the tall cliffs opposite gives a fine view (not a free one) of the country and river.

ANNEVOIE has no quay. Anchor above the bridge. A short walk up a side valley leads to the chateau with gardens by Le Nôtre, and an elaborate system of hydraulic *jeux d'eau*. On the forest ridge, a platform on stilts enables one to see the Meuse in seven sections separated by the hills of the Ardennes.

At DINANT, there is an excellent quay and steps R by the flowerbeds, and upstream of the trip-boats. Belgium's greatest river resort is overloaded with its two tripper products – ginger-bread and pressed copper – but nevertheless its appearance from the river is never to be forgotten, the over-bulbous spire of the church ballooning out below the vast bulk of the citadel where Charles de Gaulle first hit the high heroic by scaling the rock and tearing down the German flag. Two cable-lifts conduct to an exhibit of dummies in '14-'18 uniforms slaughtering each other. Dinant's citadel easily wins the prize for gruesome exhibitionism, but the ridge of Mont Fat and gardens are beautiful in lilac time. The 'La Merveilleuse' cave is notable for the purity and translucence of its groups of stalactites. On the southern edge of the town the riverside pinnacle of the Rocher Bayard marks where this magical horse of the Chanson de Geste made his final exit. From Dinant one can take a train to Houyet and make the descent of the wild River Lesse either in hired and fairly tough kayaks, or, if more sedate by nature, in a large punt propelled down the rapids by a native. *Caution:* Hold tight over the two weirs. Another excursion is to the vast caverns of Han-sur-Lesse, which provide two hours of strange experiences ending with a subterranean voyage and gunfire. A steamer also runs during the summer between Namur and Dinant, and local craft ply between Dinant and Anseremme.

ANSEREMME. Small craft can enter the Lesse and moor to the bank beyond the Pont St Jean. Otherwise, round the top of the lock, underneath the railway bridge – a safe mooring but very noisy when the ore trains clank overhead in the night. WAULSORT has a yacht quay by the ferryman's house R. Water is available at this quiet and perfect mooring.

At the HEERAGIMONT customs quay there is fuelling and chandlery. In GIVET the only possible point is alongside the wall L below the road bridge and Givet was designed to give its defenders endless opportunity for sniping and, is dominated by the remains of the Charlemont, once a vast fortress complete with streets of shops. Like most French ruins it is partly inhabited by the army, partly by night-ingales. To reach the top and explore the relics, walk straight past soldiers and act dumb if questioned.

For AUBRIVES, on emerging from the Ham tunnel and lock-cut turn left and moor in the reeds against the bank L above the weir. At FUMAY, pass the town, curve right round to the back of it (3 kms.) and find the vertical wall just above lock 52 (Uf), which is within a kilometre of the town centre. The town itself is a somewhat nondescript place of small foundries, and the same applies to most towns short of Charleville – but from across the weir there is a woodland walk round the crest of the great loop of the Meuse with a splendid view to the river far below. *Caution:* The accursed baron and his hellhounds hunt in the air by night.

Approaching REVIN leave the lock to port and run up to the quay R. On no account proceed beyond the road bridge. Alternatively stop in the basin above the lock, with per-mission from the lock-keeper. MONTHERMÉ has deep water along the meadow, L, just above the bridge, and CHÂTEAU REGNAULT has satisfactory mooring alongside at a village quay when stopping to visit the Four Sons of Aymon, rocky peaks of slate. On the one nearest the river is a statue of Aymon, Reynaud and his brothers, and their magical steed Bayard. From the point of view of mooring, these romantic outcrops are less easily visited by bus from Monthermé (4 kms.).

CHARLEVILLE is badly provided. There is not a single serviceable mooring alongside. The best point is on a barge beyond the second railway bridge, opposite the moat leading to lock 42 (Mézières). Whereas Mézières is dull, its attached twin has the magnificent Louis XIII Place Ducale in mellow stone and brick, with the statue of the Duke of Gonzagues who created it, and after whom the town is named.

At SEDAN go through the lock (37) and turn down the weir stream R before the next bridge. There is a reasonable quay with rings a short way down on the starboard hand, opposite the bathing establishment. The mere name of Sedan still makes French generals shudder, for it is synonymous with

River Lahn at Dietkirchen

Wesel-Datteln Canal

A lock on the River Doubs

The Rhine in December

River Ill at La Petite France, Strasbourg

Old style lock, Dortmund-Ems Canal

Canal de la Marne au Rhin at Lutzelbourg

The Belgian Meuse at Freyr

Canal du Nivernais

River Saône at Tournus

Crossing the Loire. Digoin aqueduct on the Canal lateral

Pouilly tunnel, Canal de Bourgogne

Four-step lock, St. Roch, Canal du Midi

A rolling bridge, Göta Canal

defeat – in 1870 and again in 1940. Standing in the shadow of an immense medieval château-fortress which survives as a curious relic of the era of strongpoint warfare, Sedan is primarily a city of weavers, and as such it is a good place for picking up fabric bargains. For miles upstream the hillsides are spotted with the useless gun-slits of the Maginot Line bunkers. Mooring in the picturesque cut at MOUZON is not practicable because of drawing-off. Moor either at the tail of the lock, in the weir stream; or beyond the town on the port side under the trees. STENAY has an old port, entered between the pillars of a vanished bridge a short way before the lock (31) and on the port hand. This is an excellent mooring, free from wash. At DUN, pass the lock (28) and double back round the point to moor under the trees on the promontory. The village is overlooked by a 16th-century hilltop church giving a view across the Argonnes forest. CONSENVOYE has deep water against the bank L, below the entry to the lock-cut, which makes mooring easy – but the design of the lock is so idiotic that the name will stay implanted in your memory.

VERDUN has the best mooring on all the French Meuse – and no wonder, as it was a gift after 1914–18 from the City of London. Draw alongside by the Officers' Club, exactly opposite the steps leading to the 'They Shall Not Pass' memorial. Verdun has many sombre memories and once did a great trade in manufacturing eunuchs for sale to Moorish sultans. The modern town is synonymous with the great battle and for those who like war relics and preserved bones by the million' this is undoubtedly the place. Speciality, sugared almonds.

AMBLY has a basin, somewhat silted and weedy, and ST MIHIEL has a silo quay L. Otherwise the best point is against the steep grassy bank, R, about 150 metres above the bridge, but leave the stern hanging out. At the entrance to the town the river is flanked by a row of rocky bluffs, along the top of which a track forms a pleasant evening walk where one may find the Pasque flower, *Anemone pulsatilla*.

At COMMERCY the only facility is in the entrance to the

maintenance basin, $1\frac{1}{2}$ kms. above the lock (6), but the basin may be somewhat silted. Commercy has a Worshipful Company of Madeleine-Makers, and seems to thrive on their confections. There is even a madeleine festival in June. The speciality is said to have been begun by a girl who came to the rescue of the Duke of Lorraine in 1755, when the cook walked out during a party. At the canal junction 10 kms. ahead an interesting side-trip is to turn to the right for 1 km. (no locks) to look down from the aqueduct of the Canal de la Marne au Rhin upon the rural River Meuse, 600 kms. upstream of where the barges queue to enter it at the busy lock of St Andries.

River Sambre. From the Canal de la Sambre à l'Oise at Landrecies, to the Meuse at Namur. Length 148 kms. Locks 9 French, 19 Belgian.

Navigation: There are no difficulties except that the Sambre has a tendency to flooding. The river drains a large area, and after heavy rain the passage of the narrow bridges at Lobbes and Thuin can become difficult because of the current. At times navigation is suspended altogether because the water is too high for barges to pass under most of the bridges.

This river, which was explored by R. L. Stevenson in a canoe and is the scene of much of his first book *An Inland Voyage,* is a curious mixture. For the first 15 kms. it winds over the meadows as though uncertain where to go, hardly touching any civilisation as it skirts the Forêt de Mormal. Then it enters the area of foundries and passes beside the casting halls of Hautmont to Maubeuge and the glass-making centre of Boussois. Heavy industry lines the banks for most of the way to the frontier at Erquelinnes, where France and Belgium both have their customs posts. Throwing off its smoky atmosphere the Sambre then decides to become a country river again, flowing past faded old villages of the Thudinie and skirting Lobbes to pass by Thuin and the ruined Abbey of Aulne before reverting to an even greater bout of industry through Charleroi. The pits and foundries continue most of the way to Namur, but only in patches separated by long meanders between wooded cliffs. Finally the river sweeps on a double curve through Namur itself, passing beneath the walls of the citadel to its confluence with the Meuse.

Moorings: In the upper reaches mooring on the steep meadow banks is easy. MAUBERGE has a good quay on either side below the lock. Greatly destroyed in two world wars, Maubeuge has been rebuilt in modern style and it also has a zoo. Distorting mirrors on the wall remind the boatman that this is a glass-making area. THUIN has a long quay at the foot of the terraced cliff on which stands the town belfry. Many Belgian barges are registered to this traditional town of shippers, yet it is a town of only five thousand inhabitants. Half of Thuin constitutes the port area, whilst the rest is clustered above the terraces and reached by flights of steps. Water jousting takes place in the summer, the boats being hauled from the towpath. On the third Sunday in May the remarkable March of St Roch occurs, a ten-mile circuit performed by men in military uniforms of various periods in commemoration of a victory in 1654 when the Thuin teenagers routed the besieging French.

CHARLEROI offers no good mooring in the town centre, but there is a possible pull in above the lock, in the weir stream. The King Charles of Charleroi was Charles II of Spain (1661–1700), during whose reign the town was first established. It has since become the centre of Belgian bargee life, and the river is lined with craft waiting to load at the mines and foundries. There is even a floating chapel. Nevertheless the town is deadly dull, and such a rain of dust and dirt falls from the sky that Charleroi with its choking atmosphere is best left speedily astern.

At the upstream edge of Charleroi the Canal de Charleroi leads off northward to Brussels. Below here the river is filthy, and locksides and ladders are coated with sticky tar. It is best not to land at all.

At NAMUR there is good mooring at the quay opposite the citadel. For further details see *River Meuse.*

THROUGH ROUTES, BELGIUM TO THE
RIVER SEINE

There are several routes from Belgium across northern France toward Paris, but without question the most scenically magnificent is by way of the River Meuse (q.v.) through the Ardennes gorge to Pont-à-Bar, 12 kilometres short of Sedan and above Lock No. 40, Dom-le-Mesnil. At this point the Canal des Ardennes runs off on the starboard side and eventually leads through to a choice of routes – the R. Aisne and R. Oise, or by Reims to the R. Marne – both of which lead to the R. Seine.

The waterways concerned are here dealt with in the order in which they are encountered from the R. Meuse.

Canal des Ardennes. From the R. Meuse at Pont-à-Bar to the Canal latéral à l'Aisne at Vieux-les-Asfeld. Length 61 kms. Locks 44. There is a side-branch to Vouziers, 12 kms. and 4 locks.

The canal climbs slowly through long pounds across farmland to the summit length, which passes through the small town of Le Chesne before plunging down one of the longest flights of locks in France (27 locks in 9 kms.). There can be few prettier descents than this one, the canal twisting and turning down a valley of limestone farms with sheep and cows grazing in the meadows, before levelling off to longer pounds of several kilometres as it follows the meandering brook of the Aisne to Rethel and wandering pleasantly onward to its end. Traffic is moderate. Mooring is at the bank, or at occasional silo quays along the route.

Nothing more than a change in the colour of the paint on the lock rails marks the transition to the next waterway.

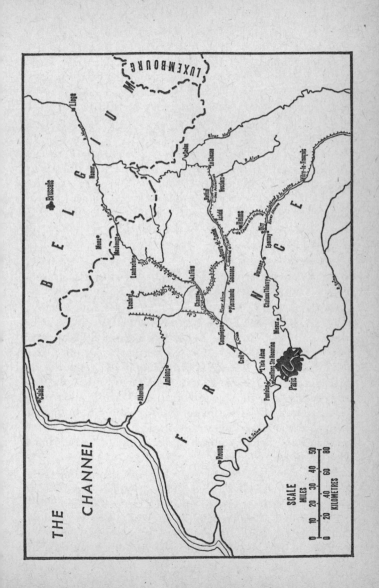

Canal latéral à l'Aisne. From the western end of the Canal des Ardennes to the R. Aisne at Condé. Length 51 kms. Locks 8.

As can be seen from the small number of locks, this canal has long pounds (one is 20 kms.). It leads peacefully along the gentle fall of the river valley, for most of the distance flanked by the copsy waste of waterlogged land between a flooding river and a canal which is so typical of French waterways. Featureless but dreamy it leads into the river 14 kms. upstream of Soissons.

The canal has two important connections. At Berry-au-Bac the Canal de l'Aisne à la Marne (see below) leads by Reims to the R. Marne (q.v.) and at Bourg-et-Comin the Canal de l'Oise à l'Aisne provides a connection for the Channel ports traffic to the Canal latéral à l'Oise near Chauny. There are 13 locks and a tunnel of $3\frac{1}{2}$ kms. on this link of 48 kms.

River Aisne. Navigable from Condé-sur-Aisne to its confluence with the R. Oise at Compiègne. Length 56 kms. Locks 7.

The Aisne is part of the route by which barges from the Meuse can reach the Oise, but it does not carry the Channel ports traffic, which cuts off a corner by taking the Canal de l'Oise à l'Aisne. There is little shipping and the river is distinguished by its clear and unpolluted water, the fish being visible over the side of your boat. Small hamlets come to the water's edge, the houses gay with bright gardens. It is perhaps the most English of all the French rivers, and a pleasant one in which to ease off for a day or two during a long voyage.

Moorings: The only place of consequence upon the Aisne is SOISSONS, blessed with a considerable length of good quay in the town centre R. The town war memorial depicts all the heroes of Soissons, ancient and modern, and among them Clovis, King of the Franks (d. 511), who is seen in the incident of the Soissons Vase, which was the result of a quarrel over the share-out of war booty. An ancient and ecclesiastical city which has suffered much in two World Wars, Soissons nevertheless can be proud of its cathedral, built from the 12th century onward, and excellently reconstructed after being shot almost to the ground in the 20th century.

In spite of its grand name, LE FRANCPORT is an almost non-existent hamlet, but the bridge is a mere ½ km. from the Armistice Clearing. It may be possible to make fast against the bank, but the river's edge is stony, and to visit the clearing is probably easier from Compiègne. (See below.)

River Oise. Navigable from the junction with the Canal latéral à l'Oise at Janville to its confluence with the R. Seine at Conflans Ste. Honorine. Length 104 kms. Locks 7.

Navigation: The locks are by-passed in flood time by dropping the weir barrages and marking the navigable passes by signs. This can make an enormous difference to the time of passage. I normally reckon 2 to 2½ days from Compiègne to the Seine, but I have run it in 6 hours on an April flood – one hour of which was spent at anchor waiting for the fog to lift and reveal the weir-passage.

The river is a rural one with only limited patches of industry, especially around Pontoise and Creil. Part of the main barge route from the Channel ports to Paris and also (via the R. Aisne) a connection to Antwerp, it carries considerable traffic, and is unfortunately almost devoid of moorings.

Moorings: One is almost certain to wish to stop during the ascent or descent of a river of this length, and in general the best system – though not in flood-time – is to join the anglers in the peaceful water of the weir streams, either above or below a barrage, and anchor or moor against the bank. Otherwise there is good quay accommodation L by the town bridge at COMPIÈGNE, though one may have to lie alongside a barge for lack of free space.

Compiègne is a pleasant town which has somehow escaped being totally destroyed. To one side of the main street is the palace, rebuilt by Louis XV, and by good fortune Napoleon was so enamoured of it that he occupied it himself. Its use as a headquarters during the First World War caused it to be bombarded, but restoration has brought it back to Son-et-Lumière graciousness. One can view the royal apartments, but engineering enthusiasts are more likely to want to visit the Musée de la Voiture, with its ancient motors and stately coaches for the great. There is a steam bus, an early Paris omnibus, and a range of early vehicles down to the cycle without pedals invented by Freiherr von Drais, and even sedan chairs (which have no connection with Sedan).

The ornamental park extends eastward until it becomes imperceptibly transformed into the Forest of Compiègne, which stretches from the R. Aisne to the castle of Pierrefonds. Although the Armistice Clearing of 1918 is almost on the bank of the Aisne the lack of good moorings on that river makes it easier to visit the site from Compiègne, by bus or on foot (7 kms. through the woods, 10 kms. by the towpath of the Aisne to Le Francport bridge).

This is a sight which should not be missed. The spurs of railway laid for artillery wagons are still there, and one can almost picture the scene when the German envoys stepped from their sealed and shuttered coach into the dripping, foggy, November woodland. A replica of the Wagon-Lits dining car is there too, but under cover, and the table for the discussions which preceded the Armistice is all set. It is a curiously moving scene of great historic interest, though one may regret the adjacent row of what-the-butler-saw devices where children can view some of the more ghastly and bloody scenes of the phenomenal four-year slaughter.

Pierrefonds is also within bus distance, a vast and splendid medieval castle complete with walls and keep and bastions, raised by Viollet-le-Duc in the 19th century from the ruins of the original.

The best chance of a mooring at L'ISLE ADAM is in the reeds R between the lock and the road bridge, the padding of the vegetation giving protection from barge-wash. At PONTOISE, there is a quay R. Talbot, the 'Scourge of France' (see *R. Dordogne*), took the town in 1437, the English soldiers advancing in a snow storm and wrapped in white sheets – or so it is alleged. The museum contains a stuffed leg of Catherine de Medici (pickled 1589).

For CONFLANS STE HONORINE – see *River Seine*.

ALTERNATIVE ROUTE FROM BERRY-AU-BAC

Canal de l'Aisne à la Marne. From the Canal latéral à l'Aisne at Berry-au-Bac to the Canal latéral à la Marne at Condé-sur-Marne. Length 58 kms. Locks 24.

This canal crosses the watershed between the Aisne and Marne valleys. It is not spectacular, but it offers wide views over the smooth, chalky and undulating plains around Reims. There is a tunnel of 2 kms. at the summit level, where care should be taken not to follow a barge too closely, because the flow of water through the tunnel toward the locks which lead to the Marne valley may be sufficient to carry you forward into the ship ahead, which will be moving more slowly. A charge for *not* being towed is levied.

Moorings: There are several loading bays on the canal, but the only halt of interest is at REIMS, where there is good berthing in the commercial port outside the town, and better placed if less good conditions in the old port almost in the town centre and six bridges beyond the commercial basin.

Everything that could be said in praise of the great gothic cathedral on one of the earliest Christian sites of France has already been said. Charles VIII in 1484 declared it to be noble above all the churches of France. The baptistery where St Remi (Remigius) baptised Clovis, King of the Franks, in 496 and thus nominally converted the Franks to being a Christian people, can still be seen. Discovered during the diggings for the restoration of the cathedral after its bombardment during the First World War, it is sited in the remnants of a former Roman baths. After Clovis, the Franks entered the communal font in groups of 300 at a time. Not far from the town lock (No. 10, Fléchambault) is the basilica erected in 1896 for the 14th centenary of this event and

dedicated to Ste Clotilde, the Christian wife of Clovis. The
then archbishop of Reims sought to acquire relics of all the
saints who had 'played a part in French history', and in fact
the crypt contains bits and pieces of more than one thousand.
Canal latéral à la Marne. From Vitry-le-François to the R.
Marne at Dizy. The whole length is 66 kms. with 15 locks,
but we are here concerned only with the length between
Condé and Dizy, 18 kms. and 4 locks.

The canal is a typical lateral canal, the meandering river
continually coming close and then veering off again. It flows
to the foot of the slopes where the fizzy wine still known by
the name of the area – Champagne – was first produced.

River Marne. Navigable from Epernay (3½ kms. above the
canal entrance) to the R. Seine at Charenton, 9 kms. upstream of the centre of Paris. Length 182 kms. Locks 18.

The Marne is a good cruising ground in its own right, and
was the first French river to have a fleet of hire craft based
on it. The country through which it flows is that of Champagne and Brie, and the gentle curving course of the river
as it flows between low hills dotted with woodland is somewhat reminiscent of parts of the Thames valley, though the
several memorials visible on the ridges remind one also that
this was the scene of the vital Battle of the Marne. Although
part of the main route for barges between Paris and the R.
Rhine at Strasbourg, the traffic is not heavy. The barrages
are often couchés (laid flat) in times of flood, when one may
shoot past those locks which are not on the long canal sections downstream of Meaux. There are two tunnels on canal
cuts which short-circuit bends in the river, but they are only
about 300 and 600 m. in length respectively.

Moorings: In general, on the river bank, and sometimes
behind islands. At EPERNAY (turn left on leaving the canal)
a factory quay provides the opportunity to see how the wine
is made which so unaccountably has become a status symbol
at weddings in Britain. At DORMANS there is mooring on
the steep bank R above the bridge, opposite the town, but
CHÂTEAU THIERRY has a long and well-built quay R with a

good depth of water. A town of biscuit-making, and the birthplace of Jean de La Fontaine (1621–95) and perhaps of some of his fables, it is overlooked by the remains of the feudal castle, now converted into a pleasant park with walks and bastions. The town market is a good place to stock up with Brie cheese.

In the backwater R 2 kms. above the Trilport railway bridge, is the POINCY base of *Saint Line Cruisers,* where mooring space is usually available with every facility. MEAUX has a somewhat awkward loading jetty R, just below the right-angle turn into the entrance of the Chalifert cut. The town ramparts still survive on the landward side and provide a good view of the cathedral (12th century onwards), with its episcopal palace and the gardens by Le Nôtre. The palace has an inclined plane which served to enable a crippled bishop (Cardinal Briçonnet, appointed 1516) to reach his rooms. Near Trilport itself is St Fiacre, scene of a pilgrimage on 30th August. St Fiacre is said to have been son of a Scottish or Irish king, and to have evangelised the area about the year 630. Growing vegetables for the poor he ended up as patron saint of gardeners – but not of cabbies, for the fiacre takes its name from the Paris Hôtel de St Fiacre, where they were first introduced (c. 1650).

ALTERNATIVE ROUTE FROM THE BELGIAN MEUSE

Another possibility is to take the R. Sambre (q.v.) from Namur into France, where it runs to its end at Landrecies and becomes transformed into the Canal de la Sambre à l'Oise.

Canal de la Sambre à l'Oise. Joining the R. Sambre with the La Fère branch of the Canal de St Quentin, which here runs down the valley of the R. Oise. Length 67 kms. Locks 38.

The canal rises through only 3 locks in 12 kms. to reach the summit pound, and then begins to drop quickly to the valley of the Noirrieu brook, which joins the R. Oise near

Lock 19 of the descent. Passing through nowhere at all the canal is rural and unspectacular until just short of its end.

Canal de St Quentin. From the R. Scheldt (q.v.) at Cambrai to the Canal latéral à l'Oise at Chauny. Length 92 kms. Locks 35 and a tunnel of $5\frac{3}{4}$ kms. The La Fère branch is 4 kms. long without locks, and joins the main line 7 kms. from the end, at the foot of the Lock No. 31.

This is an uninteresting piece of canal, with heavy traffic. It is continued as the Oise lateral canal.

Canal latéral à l'Oise. From Chauny to the R. Oise at Janville, 7 kms. upstream of Compiègne. Length 34 kms. Locks 4.

Part of the main barge-route from the Channel ports to Paris, this canal has been reconstructed to Europaship dimensions and carries heavy traffic through a rather flat countryside with scattered patches of industry. Below Janville the route joins the first route described above, at the confluence with the R. Aisne.

CALAIS TO PARIS

It is possible to take a yacht from the Channel to the River Seine without a voyage down the coast from Cap Gris Nez to Le Havre along an open shore very short of harbours which can be entered at any state of tide. The canal route to Paris is a voyage of about 470 kms. with a total of 38 locks (37 of them large) between the sea and the Place de la Concorde. For early risers the journey should not take more than 7 days, but much depends on the traffic, for the canals concerned include some of the most heavily used in France.

Most of the route is now able to take 600-ton vessels, and work has continually gone ahead to by-pass awkward towns and reduce the number of locks. There are two modern tunnels on the Canal du Nord, a new canal which cuts off most of the heavily locked Canal de St Quentin, but those who feel deprived of the experience of several hours underground in a long train of towed barges can still take the alternative route through Cambrai and enjoy the thrills of the Grand Souterrain de Bellicourt, 5·67 kms. in length.

Although a useful link between Paris and the Channel ports (except Boulogne, which has no connection with the canal system), the canals pass through the least interesting area of all France, much of it beset with collieries and smoke. For this reason the route will not be described in great detail, but it can be assumed that adequate quaysides are to be found all the way.

ST OMER is the only place before the River Oise which can be considered much more than a French Wigan, and there one can be in comfort at the quay in the old navigation,

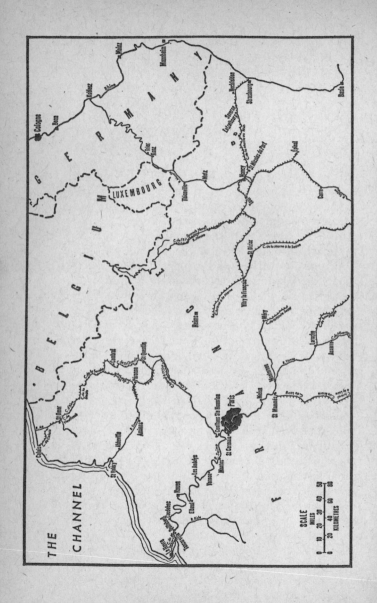

which branches away from the new by-pass 2 kms. short of
the city. Just beyond St Omer is the only vertical lift in
France, the *Ascenseur des Fontinettes,* which was paralleled
by 5 locks for use when it was under repair. This is a fascinating piece of Iron Age engineering worthy of inspection
by any waterways enthusiast, but its dimensions were those
of the standard French barge, and during the recent enlargement of the canal it was replaced by a deep lock for larger
vessels.

The whole route is made up as follows :

> Canal de Calais (see *Intra-Coastal Waterway*)
> R. Aa (do.)
> Canal de Neuffossé
> Canal d'Aire
> Canal de la Deûle
> Canal de la Sensée
> Canal du Nord
> Canal Latéral à l'Oise (see *Through Routes, Belgium
>   to R. Seine*)
> R. Oise (do.)
> R. Seine (q.v.)

The Canal du Nord shares 20 kms. of its course with the
River Somme (q.v.), which provides an alternative outlet to
the sea and avoids all the more heavily industrialised
stretches of the route above.

RIVER SOMME

From the Canal de St Quentin to St Simon, or the Canal du Nord at Péronne, to the sea at St Valéry-sur-Somme. Length: from St Simon, 157 kms. with 25 locks: from Péronne 120 kms. and 19 locks.

Inevitably remembered by name on account of the prolonged battle which took place in the valley during the First World War, the Somme is a quiet river which flows somewhat half-heartedly toward the sea. Its gentle gradient means that much of its course is through marshes, and it is certainly a river for duck-shooters. Two cathedral cities, Amiens and Abbeville, are on its course, and at the latter the navigation decides to stop meandering and proceed as a ship canal straight to the tide lock at St Valéry, 14 kms. distant.

Moorings: From Péronne, where the constant flow of barges diverges northward along the Canal du Nord, the Somme has extremely little traffic and one can moor almost anywhere. At AMIENS there is an excellent quay and a most picturesque one at the Place Parmentier, where on Tuesday, Thursday and Saturday morning the market gardeners in curious long boats with a raised ramp at the end bring their produce by water to unload directly to the market under the trees. The Palais de Justice is built on the spot where the Roman officer Martinus (later St Martin of Tours) divided his cloak in two to share it with a beggar. Traces of Roman temples have been found in the city.

The cathedral was presented in the 13th century with the anterior half of the alleged skull of John the Baptist, with the result that the place became a centre of pilgrimage. The choir stalls are regarded as the finest collection of wood carving in France, and were executed in the early 16th century.

ABBEVILLE has docks capable of handling coasters, reached by turning sharp right after passing the town lock. It is not a city of great interest, and its most famous possession was lost in the bombardment of 1940. This was a stuffed lizard some 1½ m. long, presumably an *ex voto* but alleged to have lived in the church (St Vulfran's) and nourished itself on the wax of the candles and the oil in the lamps.

The 'Vow of Abbeville' taken by Louis XIII in 1638 was decreed to be celebrated annually by a procession in all the churches in France. Though the custom has in general lapsed, some churches still carry out the instruction on the Feast of the Assumption. The original vow was taken after Louis XIII had declared war upon Spain.

ST VALÉRY has possible mooring at the quay (tidal) below the lock. It is the town from which William of Normandy set out to conquer England, and a stained-glass window in the small chapel on the hill recalls his praying for fine weather for his fleet. The spring which once was a bathing pool for gay pagan nymphs later become the Fountain of Fidelity. Departing boatmen would drink from it with their spouses, and St Valéry was said personally to guarantee mutual fidelity provided both drank from the same cup. Yachtsmen can no doubt join in the practice and test the theory.

RIVER SEINE

Navigable from Méry to the sea at Le Havre. Length 543 kms. Locks 33, of which the first 14 kms. and 6 locks down to Marcilly are not river but the Canal de la Haute Seine. (The numbers shown on the bank are kilometres counted from the junction with the Canal de St Martin above the Île St Luis in Paris.)

Navigation: Although in the lower estuary there is at least 8 m. of water even at lowest tides, it is sensible to make the run up to Rouen on the flood, because in places the ebb can have a formidable current.

Caution: In the lower tidal reaches a bore (Le Mascaret) runs up on spring tides and should not be encountered at anchor in a small boat, even if the Marscaret is no longer what it once was. Originally a severe tidal bore of several successive waves, it was a danger to shipping and sank 105 ships in 22 years. The dredging and dyking of the route for large vessels has robbed it of its terrors, yet it should still be treated with respect. The bore is not a solid wall of water, or a wave, but a sort of fast-moving low-angled slope where the tide travelling upstream overpowers the ebb moving down. It is an interesting sight, for watching the water's edge one can see that the tide is reversed instantaneously (an unpleasant experience, no doubt, if one is moored to a jetty) and within the next half minute the level may rise by 1 metre. The rise then continues, with such effect that the entire range from low to high water can occur within about 1½ hours. This should be borne in mind if going ashore even for a few minutes to buy a loaf of bread, and care must

obviously be taken not to let any part of the boat get underneath a beam on a jetty. Lines should never be left tight.

Between Rouen and the sea there are numerous and
active ferries which function also after dark but are well lit.
The river up to Rouen can be run by night or day on a single
tide.

The Seine has particularly heavy traffic between Conflans
and St Mammés, and considerable shipping all along its
length. Coasters can penetrate right up to Paris. The locks
are modern and efficient – and long waits are uncommon.
There are no special difficulties, but an unusual feature is
that ships do not slow down. Sailing dinghies, fishing punts,
bankside anglers, moored barges and scullers have to take
what is coming to them – which may be a 2,000 or 3,000-ton
pusher driving at full speed and making a massive wash. It
is a Darwinian river, upon which only the fittest survive.
The remainder go elsewhere.

One result is that some highly neurotic anglers and
hysterical stewards of sailing clubs will seek to vent their
repressed hatred upon the first yacht to appear in their
sights. Above Paris, anglers will sometimes work themselves
up into paroxysms of fury, but their imprecations should be
disregarded and their fist shakings interpreted as curious
gestures of welcome and answered with smiles and waving
of the hands in greeting. When sailing-club officials drive
close across the bow of your boat to try to make you stop,
you can safely adopt the response of the barges – which is, to
look the other way and accelerate. At the same time, courtesy to fishermen in punts or tethered dinghies and special
consideration for scullers and sailing-school novices will so
astonish people that you will be hailed with surprised expressions of thanks. That the river is really a free-for-all
dog-fight can best be judged from the fact that water-skiing
and sculling are allowed in the same reaches, and that the
authorities actually permit the lunacy of a 24-hour race for
speed-boats through the Paris bridges where the wash is
certain to damage any craft whose owners have not speedily
removed them. Not even the night is peaceful in the city, for

vast floating greenhouses carrying late night dinner-dancers sweep up and down the central area. In more than twenty years the only place where I have had people flung out of their bunks is in the centre of Paris.

Waterways connecting with the Seine are, from the sea upwards, the R. Risle (15 kms. tidal), the Canal de Tancarville (a 25-km. length of dreary and oily docks canal leading to refineries and basins at Harfleur and le Havre, with outlet to the sea), the R. Oise (q.v.), the Canal St Denis, the Canal St Martin, the Canal du Loing (leading to the Canal du Centre) and the R. Yonne (q.v.).

The Seine is one of the most meandering of European rivers – the distance from Paris to Rouen is 240 kms. by river but only 140 by road – and for most of its length it traverses an undulating and rich farming country with here and there a patch of forest. Its gradient from Paris onward is so slight (the locks are far apart) that it has negligible current under ordinary circumstances, and so has plenty of time to wander about and in times past to move its actual bed.

Because the Seine is connected to every corner of the country except Brittany and the west by its tributaries and canals, the river carries more traffic than any other French waterway, and below Paris some of the units are extremely large. The run from the sea up to Paris is a favourite one with British yachtsmen, though many from the Thames cross northern France by canal and only reach the Seine at Conflans Ste Honorine. For practical purposes the river is used as a cruising ground or as a through route (to the Mediterranean) between its confluence with the R. Yonne at Montereau, and the entrance to the Canal de Tancarville, which leads into the docks at le Havre, and as boatmen from Britain usually voyage first in an upstream direction the Seine will here be described in that order.

The tideway, which extends to above Rouen, is surprisingly peaceful and devoid of industry, its course consisting of long, tightly curving loops as the stream is continually flung from side to side by the limestone wolds through which it tries to cut its way. Remarkably few towns large or small are set on its banks, and its rural course is between thickly wooded hills and chalky cliffs.

Immediately above Poses lock at the head of the tideway, the river sweeps majestically round long curves at the foot of steep limestone cliffs, sometimes wooded but occasionally with sheer faces of brilliant white set back some distance from the water. Twice – at Petit Andelys and La Roche Guyon – it flows at the foot of what once were formidable castle fortresses, the ruins of which are reminiscent of the Rhine gorge and yet on account of their greyish stone are softer and less ferocious. Still rural and without main road or rail along most of its valley, the river leads up through one wide loop after another and past quiet waterside hamlets to the residential villas of the reach above Mantes, before passing the lock at Carriéres to become little more than an open sewer all the way to Suresnes, at the inner edge of Paris itself. The pollution and stench for 60 kms. are almost beyond imagination, and it is not surprising if for once no fishermen are to be seen.

From its junction with the R. Oise at Conflans Ste Honorine to Sèvres and St Germain the river is bordered by a semi-industrial suburban sprawl which is drab and often messy, particularly now that a universal licence seems to have been granted to reinforce the banks against erosion by tipping refuse down them – an activity which is much welcomed by rats. Yet even the stench is worth enduring, for from the Statue of Liberty onward the famous and incomparable sights of Paris itself are spread along both banks of the river all the way to the Île St Louis. The traverse of Paris is something never to be forgotten, and from a boat one sees all the best sights and none of the worst – if perhaps one can except the extraordinary slum village of makeshift African shacks up beyond the lock of Port a l'Anglais.

After a shorter and less depressing stretch of suburbs the Seine runs between wooded hills near Morsang and Boissise-le-Roi, where splendid mansions and tasteful modern summer residences set an air of great elegance which continues to beyond the modern lock of La Cave. The only town lying fairly astride the water is Melun, where guards in watchtower cabins look down upon the prison blocks and the convicts in turn look down wistfully upon the passing boats. Then the river skirts the magnificent forest of Fontainebleau before becoming more modest and prosaic as it approaches Montereau and its junction with the R. Yonne. Already much of the traffic has left the river, and as the Seine narrows toward its dead end 80 kms. distant it is almost entirely a waterway of canal cuts with only the rarest whiff of free-flowing country river.

Moorings: It is an extraordinary fact that the whole river, from end to end, is almost devoid of places where a boat can draw in. Bankside mooring is impossible because of the wash of passing craft. One can nose cautiously up behind some of the many islands at the side of the navigation channel and come to anchor, but otherwise the only opportunity in most localities is to draw alongside a moored barge, after asking permission and discovering when it is leaving. It may also be possible with permission to lie above some of the locks, but these positions can be subject to considerable wash.

TANCARVILLE has only the pilings outside the lock. One lies more easily in the canal, and if waiting for the tide there may be a chance to examine Europe's longest suspension bridge, opened in 1959. The bridge charges a toll even for pedestrians, so take some small change if you intend to walk across for the view of the estuary; the distance from end to end is about $1\frac{1}{2}$ kms. and a slot-machine at the Tancarville end provides an English tape-account of the construction. Near the lock there is a ruined castle which goes back to the 10th century, but the rocky bluff which used to project into the river was partly dynamited by the *Ponts et Chaussées* in 1904 in the interests of navigation – a pity, because until then it was one of the favourite haunts of the giant Gargantua, who used to sit upon it and bathe his gargantuan feet in the Seine.

QUILLEBEUF has a long straight wall, with all the domestic shops alongside and $4\frac{1}{2}$ m. of water at H.W. springs, and at

CAUDEBEC there is a modern quay in the centre of the water-front. A pleasant riverside resort such as one might find on the Rhine, Caudebec was much destroyed in 1944, but the church of Notre Dame begun during the English occupation (1426) has survived, together with a few of the older houses. About 1 km. upstream R is the prominent memorial to the crew of the flying-boat *Latham 47*, which left in 1928 on its maiden flight to search in the Arctic for the survivors of the Italian airship *Nobile*, in the course of which it disappeared.

Stopping is otherwise not easy until ROUEN, which has an excellent length of quayside (about 4 kms.). Customs must be cleared at the office by the jetty on the right, just inside the first dock basin on the port hand (Bassin St Gervais, km. 245). The most convenient mooring for the city centre is on the port hand after the third road bridge, close below the tip of the island with ornamental trees. From here, the cathedral is a mere 200 metres. Rouen is a large city, about ⅓ million population. The British no longer burn young ladies in the market-place, though the spot where they did so in 1431 is marked for your inspection. The cathedral (15th century) is the centre point of the town, but another notable sight is the great 16th-century clock set in an arch over the street (Rue du Gros Horloge) between the Joan of Arc monument and the cathedral.

There is only one possible mooring between Rouen and Poses lock at the head of the tideway – which should be run on the flood tide. This is ELBEUF, where there is a long public quay L between the two bridges.

Beyond the first lock the problem of mooring is slightly easier. At PETIT ANDELYS there is a really good yacht harbour R just below the suspension bridge. On the spur of cliff immediately above is the ruined Château Gaillard, which was erected by Richard Coeur de Lion in 1196 to control the Seine highway. Although considered impregnable it was stormed by the French only eight years after. Later the castle was the scene of the strangling of Queen Marguerite of Burgundy, charged by her jealous husband Louis X (Louis the Quarrelsome) with adultery. *Caution:* Midnight wailing of ghosts of washerwomen who laundered the smalls of the English soldiery are said sometimes to disturb the boatman's sleep.

The neighbourhood is another haunt of Gargantua. The rock known as the 'Tête à l'Homme' was one of his resting places and the Gravois, a menhir on the road to Vernon, is known to be merely a pebble which he took out of his sandal.

At VERNON the only possibility is at the sailing-club lawn in front of the chateau R immediately below the ruined arches of the old bridge. LA ROCHE GUYON has a somewhat exposed piled quay R. Above, and at the entrance to a magnificent reach of white limestone bluffs with cliff-top walks, the ruins of the triple-walled 11th-century fortress tower over the later chateau at its foot. PORT MARIA, 2 kms. below Mantes R is a marina in a backwater, with all facilities, but there is also a creek R 200 m. below the bridge of MANTES, the cathedral of which dates from the 12th century and was partly built with a legacy from William the Conqueror, who fell off his horse in Mantes (which he had sacked) and was fatally injured. He was later buried at Caen, but not before the son of the owner of the ground had successfully stopped the funeral by raising the Clameur de Haro.

Although there is a quay at CONFLANS STE HONORINE it is certain to be occupied by dozens of the hundreds of barges awaiting loading orders, but drawing in on these craft is satisfactory. The barge capital of France, Conflans has an annual 'pardon' and waterborne procession in June. The life of the town is entirely centred upon barges and its Museum of Inland Navigation in the chateau next to the church of St Maclou on top of the ridge is an excellent example of how well a specialised museum can be organised. No boatman should miss this unique institution, with its exhibits of chain-towage and early methods of mechanical propulsion. The town also has the unusual feature of a floating church and boatman's social centre, which one may visit upon asking. Good worn clothing, misfits and similar items will always be received with gratitude by this boat, the *Je Sers*.

There is an annual pilgrimage on 27th February, when crowds arrive from the scattered localities which share the same 3rd-century saint, Honorine.

St Germain and Marly-le-Roi are both close to the river, but unless you care to nose up into the weir stream L, behind the island below BOUGIVAL lock, or into the end of the outfall from the higher weir immediately to the left of the lower gates, they are best visited from a more adequate mooring higher up, or by metro from the centre of Paris. St Germain was formerly a massive medieval fortress which slowly evolved into a magnificent royal residence. Henry IV raised the place to great splendour and equipped it with ingenious hydraulics which operated mythological characters in grottoes and finished by sousing the spectators with jets. Unfortunately these glories are departed, and the hey-day of a carefree monarchy is now more obvious in the gardens. Among those who lived in the castle (and died there) was England's King James II. Marly was the site of the huge but inefficient Machine de Marly operated by the slight current of the Seine, which pumped water to a reservoir on the hill-top to operate a series of waterfalls, connecting 52 marble basins down the slope. Louis XIV had a pavilion at the head of the terrace, twelve week-ending favourites chosen from a list of supposedly interesting talkers occupying others. Little is left except to the imagination of any boatman who cares to walk up the length of the *tapis vert,* a lawn which replaced the great cascade, and see such pieces of the complex as have been restored. Another possible mooring for visiting these wonders is on the long quay wall, L, at the approach to SURESNES lock. Otherwise proceed into Paris, the centre of which is only 12 kms. ahead.

PARIS has good quays through much of its length, but for a safe mooring with night watchman and the chance of having a telephone put on board for any who think the world will come to a halt unless they are available on the line, the *Port de Plaisance* run by the Touring Club de France is by any standards first class. After a short free period, the charge per day begins modestly and climbs an increasing slope, so

that anyone tending merely to live in the port is discouraged.
The port is between the Pont Alexandre III and the Pont de
la Concorde R, and could not possibly be better placed. The
quay is far below the road level and trees shut off most of
the sound of traffic. The only disadvantage (which applies
to all other Paris berths) is the wash set up by the large glass
Noah's Ark craft which run dinner trips at night and can
throw your crockery and any sleepers in upper bunks to the
floor.

To attempt to describe Paris in the scope of this book is
impossible. It is an excellent city for a good row by dinghy,
and one can even take a yacht on a round-the-lighthouse trip
(46 kms. 17 locks) by entering the Canal de St Martin a
short way above the Île St Louis, R, and cutting through
darkest Paris to emerge again into the Seine opposite the
Île St Denis. Even without this trip you will experience Paris
more intimately from your boat than in any other way.
There is hardly a building of note that is not within strolling
distance of your berth, and if a diet of works of art is required
the *Venus de Milo* and the *Mona Lisa* are almost at your
elbow.

Upstream the moorings are deplorable, but there is a quay
R at MELUN, on the south side of the island in the town. This
is the best mooring from which to visit Vaux-le-Vicomte,
a 17th-century palace-mansion with ornamental gardens by
Le Nôtre. Still privately owned, the gardens are not open
every day, and careful enquiry should be made at Melun or
at Paris before undertaking the journey of 6 kms. Although
the river passes along the edge of the Forest of Fontainebleau there is no possibility of stopping to visit the palace a
few kilometres distant. Only at MONTEREAU is there at last
a good quayside, but this is in the R. Yonne (q.v.).

FROM THE MEUSE AND MOSELLE TO THE RHINE

The Canal de la Marne au Rhin is the main waterway connecting the Paris basin with the R. Rhine at Strasbourg. Its whole length from Vitry-le-François is 313 kms. with 154 locks and one inclined plane, but the section which here concerns us is from the junction with the R. Meuse (q.v.) or Canal de l'Est, branche Nord, to Strasbourg. The length of this connection is 222 kms. and there are 72 locks and 1 inclined plane.

The canal is the main east–west waterway across France and carries sufficient traffic to be kept in excellent condition and modernised. Recent years have seen the suppression of short flights of locks and their replacement by paired deeper ones with side chambers to save water, and the building of the inclined plane in the Zorn valley to eliminate the long flight of locks east of the Vosges summit tunnel. This last improvement alone is reckoned to save a barge $1\frac{1}{2}$ days on its voyage.

The waterway also serves as a link between others. At Vitry-le-François it has a junction with the Canal latéral à la Marne and also with the Canal de la Marne à la Saône, a favourite route to the south of France for yachtsmen who do not like other traffic. Further east it serves to connect the north (Meuse) and south branches of the Canal de l'Est (q.v.), the latter having a junction at Nancy as well as one at Toul. Next, on the edge of Nancy itself, the canal connects with the R. Moselle through Frouard lock, and on the summit level of the Vosges the Saar Collieries Canal leads off northward toward the R. Saar and Germany. There is no through route to the R. Moselle at Konz, upstream of Trier, for the lower reaches of the Saar are not navigable, so the Collieries Canal (or Canal des Houillères de la Sarre) is in fact the only route by which Saarland-registered barges can reach their German home port of Saarbrücken. For this reason, Saar craft have all to be of French standard dimensions, but they have the special status of counting as French for loading purposes when in France, and as German when in Germany.

Scenically the canal varies greatly. The first 10 kms. from Troussey junction are along a single-level pound ending in the Foug tunnel ($\frac{3}{4}$ km.) between the Meuse and Moselle basins. Then begins the flight of 14 electric locks down to Toul, a flight which I have on one occasion passed in $2\frac{1}{2}$ hours, on another in $1\frac{1}{2}$ days – for much depends on the fortune of the traffic. At Toul the waterway becomes a lateral canal to the R. Moselle but at Liverdun it passes under the town in another tunnel ($\frac{1}{4}$ km.) and leaps the river on a fine aqueduct broad enough for two-way traffic. A pound of 18 kms. then leads to Nancy, following closely the R. Moselle until that river curves away suddenly northward at Frouard (see *R. Moselle*). (See note 1 on p. 283.)

Next comes the passage of Nancy and then a slow climb up the back of the Vosges mountains until through a final deep lock the canal reaches its summit pound of 30 kms. which ends in two tunnels in quick succession, the first a mere $\frac{1}{2}$ km. in length but the second being more than $2\frac{1}{4}$ kms. long and calling for resolute and concentrated steering. The connection with the Saar is west of the tunnels, and consists of 63 kms. of canal with 27 locks followed by 15 kms. and 3 locks in the actual river. This is a very industrialised waterway, but Saarbrücken itself is pleasantly situated astride the river and is a fair sample of a rebuilt town of considerable wealth. For nearly 11 kms. above the town the Franco-German frontier is down the centre of the stream.

It is beyond the Vosges that the Canal de la Marne au Rhin suddenly becomes one of the most attractive in France, a waterway which invites the boatman to linger. First it drops down the steep, pine-wooded and almost Alpine valley of the R. Zorn, where trout flash in the sunlight. The villages are Alsatian, the red sandstone crags are often topped with the remains of castles of tough knights, and one has continually to convince oneself that this is still France. At Saverne the broad plain of the Rhine begins, and the canal cuts across the fertile fields of maize and tobacco and vegetables, with storks prodding in the ditches for frogs or sitting regally on their nests on town hall or church. Two or three hours beyond Saverne the great spire of Strasbourg cathedral can be seen in the distance, and after cutting through the outskirts of the capital of Alsace the last lock is passed only 100 m. before the junction with the R. Ill, where a turn to the right will lead one to the very heart of the city. Ahead at the same junction lie the docks, the locks to the R. Rhine, and the way to Germany, Switzerland, or the canal through the Jura toward the R. Rhone (see *Canal du Rhône au Rhin*).

Moorings: At TOUL there is a good basin at the Porte de France, immediately below Lock 25. This is convenient for walking into the town centre, about 1 km., but an even better mooring is in the deserted and grass-banked St Mansuy basin beyond Lock 26. This is a quiet corner, and only a short way from the Porte de Metz, the massive gateway which gives access to the older and more picturesque part of the city.

St Mansuy was the first bishop of Toul (4th century), but the cathedral is St Stephen's (St Etienne), completed in the 16th century but sadly damaged in 1940. In the adjacent episcopal palace, now ruined, Joan of Arc was tried and aquitted of breach of promise of marriage, but the name of her husband *manqué* is not known. The best view of the cathedral is to be had from the bridge over the R. Moselle, or from a boat in the adjacent Canal de l'Est.

LIVERDUN has a small basin and quay R immediately after the first bridge beyond the tunnel. A flight of steps leads up to the older town on the hilltop which dominates a double bow of the river. NANCY has mooring at quaysides for a

distance of several kilometres but the most satisfactory one
for convenience is the St Catherine's basin, the third sizeable
widening after a prolonged curve through a quarter circle
to the left. Although it is primarily a coaling basin and one
where barges lie waiting for cargoes, there is usually room
along the end wall by the bridge. From here the Place
Stanislas is about 600 m. distant.

Sight-seeing alone could occupy a day or two at Nancy,
which is one of the most elegant cities of all France, having
been capital of the Duchy of Lorraine. It was greatly em-
bellished by Stanislas Leszczinski, an unthroned King of
Poland who was also father-in-law of Louis XV. The square
named after him is one of the finest in Europe, and is now
reprieved from use as a car park. Its gilded fountains
and wrought-iron grilles with splendid gilded hanging lamps
are still a delight and so is the former Governmental Palace
with its rounded and colonnaded Place de la Carrière,
approached through an Arc de Triomphe. Adjacent is the
park of La Pépinière, still kept up in the grand style and
with an 'English Garden' of a kind never seen in England.

At ST NICOLAS-DU-PORT there is good lying at the foot of
Lock 23, before the passage through the Solvay soda plant.
Presumably every boatman should stop there, for the great
basilica in an otherwise not very notable canal village was
built c. 1500 to contain a finger of St Nicholas of Myra,
original Santa Claus and 3rd-century bishop, a former desert
monk who was eventually to become patron saint of scholars,
Lorrainers, little children, girls ripe for marriage – and inland
waterways boatmen.

The summit pound of the Vosges contains a number of
minor basins, and mooring is also possible at a quay between
the two tunnels of Niderviller and Arzviller, but the best
stopping point is further ahead at LUTZELBOURG, where it is
possible to draw out of the fairway into a widening which
serves as a harbour for loading timber from the Vosges
forests. This mooring is in the second basin at Lutzelbourg
and a mere 100 m. or so before the next lock after the village
centre. There is excellent trout fishing in the R. Zorn, and

inns where they are on the menu. Itta, wife of the Count of Lutzelbourg, ran a school for witches at the bourg itself – the ruins of which stand on a crag above the canal – but in the year 1120 the bewitchings stopped when the local people built a chapel of St Michael on the same spot.

The best mooring at SAVERNE is probably just above the town lock on the quay R, the wall of which shows many Roman stones. The broad water where the canal cuts straight across the avenue of the palace reconstructed by Cardinal Rohan (see Strasbourg) is somewhat silted at the edge, but mooring on the palace side may be possible for any boatman who does not mind being floodlit as part of the evening Son-et-Lumière spectacle which tells the story of the kings and queens and clerics of splendour who have lived there. Saverne has several workshops of Alsatian marquetry, a storks' nest in the main street, a cardinal's rose-garden, and outside the town centre a footprint of Charlemagne's horse on the Roche du Saut de Prince Charles, and a chapel of St Vitus, where those stricken with his dance used in the Middle Ages to gyrate round the altar in the hope of being cured. There are pleasant walks up to the two Geroldseck castles and to the Haut Barr, near which is a reconstituted Chappe visual semaphore telegraph in working order.

By HOCHFELDEN bridge there is a disused quay R, with a good depth of water. *Caution:* Beware imprudent but appreciative motorists. I once caused a head-on collision here between two cars, and drivers of which both said, '*Ah, quel beau bateau*' as they looked at my craft lying at the quay, but never saw the vehicle coming the other way. The road was blocked for four hours and one somersaulting car landed upside down by our stern, inconsiderately fouling our warps.

For the excellent possibilities of mooring in STRASBOURG see *River Rhine*.

ACROSS FRANCE – NORTH TO SOUTH

From Holland, Belgium, or the French Channel ports of Calais, St Valéry and Le Havre, one can reach the Mediterranean by inland waterways. The Rivers Rhine, Moselle, Meuse, Sambre and Seine which give access to the canals leading southward are all treated separately in this book, but according to which of these rivers is the starting point of the voyage there remains a choice of canal routes, all of which converge upon the R. Saône, which in turn leads to the R. Rhone and so to the Mediterranean. Four of these canals will be dealt with in detail because I happen to consider them the most attractive, and know them intimately from ten years of voyaging through them. But for those who wish to compare the choices the details are as follows :

Locks to Chalon-sur-Saône

	from canal entrance	from Paris
Canal du Loing	151	158
Canal de Bourgogne (q.v.)	194	220
Canal du Nivernais (q.v.)	194	222
Canal de la Marne à la Saône	117	148
Canal de l'Est, branche Sud (q.v.)	124	248
Canal du Rhône au Rhin (q.v.)	116	310

. The two last are more suitable for craft heading south from Scandinavia, Germany and the Low Countries, long lengths of the heavily locked Canal de la Marne au Rhin

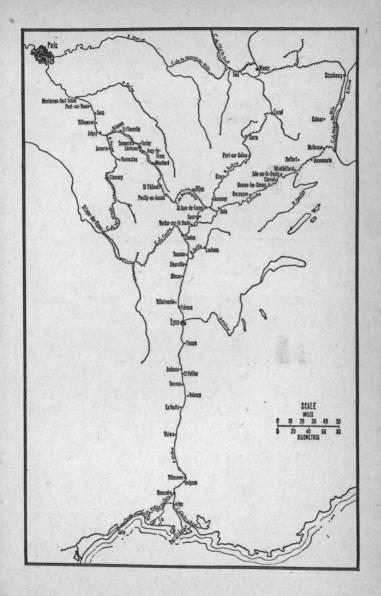

Paris

R. Marne

C. de la Marne au Rhin

C. de la Marne au Rhin

Toul Nancy

Strasbourg

R. Seine

R. Rhine

Montereau-faut-Yonne
Pont-sur-Yonne

Sens

Epinal

Villeneuve

Joigny

Migennes
St Florentin

Colmar

C. du Rhône au Rhin

Tonnerre
Lezinnes

Tanlay

Auxerre

Ancy-le-
Franc

Cora

Mulhouse

Vermenton

Montbard

Port-sur-Saône

Belfort

Dannemarie

Clamecy

R. Saône

Gray

St Thibault

Dijon

Isle-sur-le-Doubs
Clerval

Montbéliard

Pouilly-en-Auxois

Baume-les-Dames

Besançon

R. Doubs

St Jean-de-Losne

C. du Centre

Seurre

Dôle

R. Doubs

Verdun-sur-le-Doubs

R. Doubs

St Léger-des-Tours

C. du Centre

Chalon

Louhans

Tournus

R. Seille

Fleurville

Mâcon

Villefranche

Trévoux

R. Saône

Lyon

Vienne

R. Saône

Audance

St Vallier

Tournon

Valence

La Voulte

R. Rhône

SCALE
MILES
0 10 20 30 40 50
0   20   40   60   80
KILOMETRES

Viviers

Villeneuve

Avignon

Beaucaire

Arles

Sète

Port St Louis

R. Rhône

being involved in reaching them from the Seine. The number of locks on any route cannot be taken as a precise guide to the time of passage, because much depends on the density of traffic and the opportunity of overtaking. Thus on the Canal de Bourgogne there is only one pound lengthy enough for a cruiser to make up on a laden barge and overtake it, but on the other hand barges are so rare (2 or 3 a day) that the chance of catching up another craft is very slight indeed. The Canal du Nivernais also has very little traffic until it reaches the Canal latéral à la Loire, but from there onward the route is heavily used, though with some opportunities of overtaking. Each route has advantages and disadvantages for those in a hurry; but those less pressed for time can take their choice according to the scenery, in which case there can be little doubt that from Paris the Canal de Bourgogne route is the one to select.

River Yonne. Navigable from Auxerre to its confluence with the R. Seine at Montereau-faut-Yonne. Length 108 kms. Locks 26.

Navigation: The locks take 4 to 6 barges, and the paddle-gear is so simple that one can only be amazed that it has not been adopted as standard. However, very few locks are fully mechanised, and the majority are of the *cuvette* type, basins with sloping sides against which one cannot make fast but can easily damage a propeller It is advisable either to lie outside a barge, or else to hold the stern securely within the short straight-walled recess by the gates.

The Yonne is one of the most beautiful of French rivers, and as a cruising waterway it is ideal – particularly in spring and autumn, when the colours of the woods on the limestone hills are at their best. Traffic is generally not heavy, but as the Yonne towns are in an area which produces maize and millet and wheat, the harvest period is one when many more boats ply along it. Nearly all are empty when going up, full when coming down.

The river is one of the routes from the Channel to the

Mediterranean, as it connects both with the Canal de Bourgogne (q.v.) at Laroche, and the Canal du Nivernais (q.v.) at Auxerre, so that one may reach the R. Saône at either St Jean-de-Losne or at Chalon. Those in a hurry should be able to run up it in one day, but its attractions are such that one could spend several over the same trip.

As most craft will first encounter the Yonne at its confluence, the river is here described from Montereau upward.

Moorings: Bankside mooring is easy along many of the rural stretches of river. At MONTEREAU there is a good quay R, immediately beyond the bridge at the confluence. The town is industrial and dull, but Napoleon addicts will find a handsome equestrian statue of the Emperor almost hidden by trees on the point between the two rivers.

Regrettably, PONT-SUR-YONNE, with its half bridge reminiscent of Avignon, has no facility whatsoever. At SENS there is a stone quay R just short of the old bridge. The cathedral exhibits the gown of Thomas à Becket, from the time when he took refuge there. VILLENEUVE also has a quay R just below the bridge. There is a covered market and the town has two turreted gateways from its days as a royal seat. At ARMEAU there are some public landing stages under the trees R on the bend about 1 km. above the lock, and JOIGNY has a proper quay R just below the rather noisy main road bridge. The main interest of the town is historical, the vanished chateau having been where St Vincent de Paul was tutor to the family of the Commander of the Royal Galleys. The final mooring is at the town quay L between the two bridges at AUXERRE, one of the most ecclesiastical of Burgundian cities, with three notable churches apart from the cathedral (13th to 16th centuries). One of them, the abbey church of St Germain, was founded in the 6th century over the tomb of St Germain l'Auxerrois, who was forcibly christianised by the bishop he intended to murder, and whom in due course he succeeded as bishop.

A trip-boat runs on the Yonne, from Sens.

180   THE WATERWAYS

Canal de Bourgogne. From the R. Yonne at Laroche to the
R. Saône at St Jean-de-Losne. Length 242 km. Locks 189.
Height above water level, 3·4 m.

This waterway is one of the prettiest routes from northern
France to the River Saône and thence to the Mediterranean.
As a cruising ground it is pleasant and easy, for it is avoided
by most of the barges because of its large number of locks.
The canal is mostly clean and the water clear and good
for bathing. It is a favourite with fishermen, and a pot
dropped over the side of the boat at night is likely to bring
up some crayfish.

The locks are particularly easy to work, having ground
sluices and only one paddle on each gate, which opens with
a curious bent iron crank which operates very much like
the traditional English balance beam and only requires to
be leaned upon with sufficient weight. The ladders are not
in the pens but on the downstream side of the gates, but
as the rise in each lock is only some 3 m. or less it should be
possible to reach the lock-side off any but a very low boat.

The western ascent is up the wide valley of the R.
Armançon, past a number of Burgundian villages of great
beauty, their pale grey houses of local stone being roofed
with deep red tiles. Sometimes there are crags and one may
see buzzards and ospreys over the river, which is usually
close beside the canal. After the first 60 locks the route turns
more southward and climbs steeply through a pastureland
reminiscent of Worcestershire, the next 40 locks being in
quick succession and involving some hard work. Flattening
off again to its only pound of 10 kms. the canal passes St
Thibault before making a second rapid ascent to the summit.
By now the boatman is 378 m. (or about 1,250 ft.) above
the sea.

The watershed tunnel is not only one of the longest in
France, but is exceptionally low. The approach to either
end is by a long trench cut in the rock, and narrow enough
for one to become accustomed to the constriction before
plunging under Pouilly hill. The portals are deceptive, for
only a few yards inside them the ceiling drops about 1 m.

lower and it is easy to clip the corner of the cabin top on the sharply curving roof. Some steersmen may find the bare power wires a few inches above their heads rather terrifying, but it is quite possible that these are only live when the tug is passing through on its twice daily journeys in either direction.

This tug is compulsory for barges, which have to pay to use it. By that peculiar logic found only in France yachts have to pay for *not* using it (about £3 in 1974). The tug itself is an interesting piece of machinery, being a genuine chain-ship, which hauls a heavy chain up from the canal bed at the bow and passes it through its works like an earthworm to void it at the stern. Power is supplied trolley-bus fashion by pulleys picking up from a pair of overhead lines, and as these wires run down the centre of the tunnel and both cuttings it is easy to mount a staff at the bow and steer by running down the tramwires. There is no light in the tunnel and not much ventilation, and altogether the experience is one that should not be missed and certainly will not be forgotten.

Perhaps the most impressive sight on all the canal is from the canal basin at Vandenesse, below Lock 8 on the eastern side, where the view opens to the hill on which stands the impressive medieval castle of Châteauneuf. At night this chateau, brilliantly floodlit, seems to float in the sky above the dim outline of the rolling Burgundian countryside.

Beyond the summit the canal drops sharply and is flanked for a while by the noise and bustle of the main Paris to Marseille motorway, but soon turns northward to descend the valley of the Ouche, a little stream which winds along a valley of meadows where the cowbells toll as the cattle plod home at milking time. The hillsides are at times densely wooded, with outcrops of grey limetone cliffs which become more dramatic toward Dijon. There are no towns, but a number of villages of mellowed stone, usually with a quietly elegant manor belonging to some local family not yet taxed out of existence.

At Dijon the canal reaches the wide plain of the R. Saône, and cuts straight across the rich farming land toward the river, 30 kms. and 20 locks distant.

From Pont de Pany to Dijon the lockhouses are square buildings of stone with semicircular dormer windows. They are extremely elegant, though not such desirable residences as one might suppose, having neither electricity nor water except from a well.

Commercial traffic is very light – only 2 or 3 barges a day cross the divide – but between Dijon and the Saône there is rather more. When taking the canal from east to west it is worth realising that the barges tend to spend the night at St Jean de Losne and leave early in the morning in order to be at the next lock at opening time (6.30 a.m. in the summer). Any laden barge will therefore leave St Jean by six o'clock, and one wishing to be ahead of his fellows will probably moor a short way up the canal to leave by 5.45. It is wise to leave by 5.30 and pass the whole lot in order to be first in the queue, for there will be no other chance of overtaking before Dijon – or, if a barge is going further, before the summit. This will make all the difference between making Dijon at midday or late in the evening, and may put the summit within two days' reach instead of at least three.

On the Canal de Bourgogne the lock-keepers have orders to empty a lock immediately after passing an up-comer. On the ascent all locks should be ready, but on the descent none of them. A cycle or a crew member running ahead is invaluable.

Moorings: There is just enough commercial traffic to make bankside mooring imprudent. On the western side, immediately after the first lock, there is a port basin at LAROCHE, a noisy railway junction with plenty of din at night. A quieter one is 2 locks further up at BRIENON. A good grass-banked basin off the canal is provided at ST FLORENTIN, the centre for marketing the famous cheese of that name, and there is an adequate loading basin at CHARREY. TON-NERRE has a long and shaded quay between the two locks.

Across the Armançon, split into several streams, the town once sacked by King Edward III rises up a hill to the church of St Pierre, 14th to 16th centuries. Below, a spring of bluish water known as the Fosse Dionne gushes out of the cliff and is surrounded by a horse-shoe shaped washery still in use, the older houses clustered round it. The hall of the hospital founded by Margaret of Burgundy in 1293 is a fine building of immense size, and on its floor is an ingenious trace made by an astronomer monk, a spot of sunlight at noon striking a calendar line. Hidden behind the altar and below ground level is a fine pieta tomb of the 15th century. Tonnerre is also famous for the ambisexual mysteries of the Chevalier d'Eon.

There is a bank at TANLAY from which one can visit the chateau with its elegant 16th-century gatehouse reached by a bridge. The village is one of the prettiest on the canal, much of it being built of trimmed greyish stone. Three other adequate moorings are available at LÉZINNES (rather malodorous), ANCY-LE-FRANC – which also has a notable Renaissance chateau open to the public – and RAVIÈRES, before MONTBARD, where the best mooring is against the grassy bank of the basin above Lock 65. Rats also like this bank, but it is close to the pleasant stone-built up-and-down town which spreads on both sides of the R. Brenne.

The Comte de Buffon (1707–1788) (statue in the Place Buffon) converted the castle into a scientific garden. It is now a pleasant park, with gay formal flower-beds set in the usual uncut French lawns. His laboratory and study where he wrote most of his vast *Histoire Naturelle* in 36 volumes, shamelessly cribbed by Oliver Goldsmith for his *Animated Nature,* are on view. The park contains a statue of his colleague and fellow Montbardian, Louis Daubenton (1716–1799) the anatomist. The sheep at his feet are Merinos, which he introduced to France. 6 kms. outside the town is the excellently restored but sadly vacant range of buildings of the Cistercian abbey of Fontenay, which contains a fine tomb of an early bishop of Norwich. The abbey owns a flourishing trout farm in the valley, where the boatman may catch his own trout — which are so numerous it would be difficult to miss.

PONT ROYAL is not the grand place that it sounds, but at least it has a basin for mooring. So has POUILLY-EN-AUXOIS, where barges have to stop to form up in convoy for the tunnel. Between the two it is possible to pull in on the corner by the washery at the edge of ST THIBAULT, where the vast church (12th century onward) is on the site where the saint founded an abbey about the year 1000. It was once the object of a pilgrimage imposed on penitents.

On the eastern side there are canal basins at VANDENESSE, PONT DE L'OUCHE, PONT DE PANY, PLOMBIÈRES (where fuel can be obtained) and a pleasant port with a wooded island at DIJON. From the bus stop nearby the lines 5, 6 and 7 run regularly into the centre of the city, renowned for its gastro-nomic specialities, ranging from mustard to gingerbread, sugared almonds and *cassis* (a sort of liqueur). Dijon still has the clock stolen from Courtrai (see R. Lys) but the clock-jack has been provided over the years with a wife and a boy and girl, all of whom play appropriate roles in striking the bells. The city itself is a busy and pleasant one, curiously un-French in some of its surviving buildings from former times, which are more reminiscent of Alsace or Franconia.

There is a final basin at ST JEAN-DE-LOSNE. For details of this town see *River Saône*.

Canal du Nivernais. From the R. Yonne at Auxerre to the R. Loire at St Leger-des-Vignes. Length 174 kms. Locks 116. Depth limited to 1.5 m. in parts.

A fleet of hire cruisers is based on the summit pound: *Saint Line Cruisers*, Rue de la Montagne, La Collancelle, 58-Corbigny.

This canal is probably the least frequented of all the waterways leading from the R. Seine and its tributaries toward the R. Saône and the Rhone valley. Scenically it is also one of the most delightful, the course following the valley of the R. Yonne for the first 96 kms. and either flanking the river itself or making use of the stream for navigation. The countryside is one of rolling pasture and vineyards, with sometimes tall chalky cliffs as at Saussois. Several villages with manors are spread along its route, but the only town is Clamecy, the last point at which navigation is in the flowing river. After turning sharply away from the Yonne beyond Corbigny the canal climbs 24 locks in quick succession to the summit pound, where three short tunnels joined by a deep cutting lead to the beginning of the descent toward the R. Loire. The waterway forms a succession of loops as it drops down through the beech woods, following the twisting course of the R. Aron, until it straightens out, picks up some slight barge traffic, and heads for the Loire valley to end in the river.

The R. Loire is here navigable in an upstream direction for 2 kms., to afford a crossing into the side branch of the Canal lateral à la Loire, which in turn leads to the Canal du Centre. Turn sharp left at the junction, proceed up through the town bridge and enter the lock to starboard.

Moorings: Traffic being almost non-existent except for pleasure craft, mooring at the bank is possible almost anywhere. For AUXERRE see *R. Yonne.* VERMENTON, at the end of a side arm (4 kms. 2 locks) leading off the main canal above Lock 71 Manoir, is a small town on the River Cure from which one can visit the limestone caves of Arcy-sur-Cure (9 kms.). These, however, are not quite what they were. In the 18th century, it was a matter of status to have an artificial grotto, and as the Arcy caves were within cartage distance of Paris they were pillaged mercilessly for the grotto of the Trainon at Versailles. It is still the custom for local wedding processions to pass through the caves, which also have a festival on August 17th. A plaque at the entrance to Arcy states that the town is 200,000 years old – which it may well be.

From the quay of CLAMECY, once a centre of lumber-rafting, a visit can be made to Vezelay (23 kms.) a hilltop town whose ramparts contain the remains of the abbey which from the 12th century was a great place of pilgrimage as the repository of the remains of St Mary Magdalene. It was also on one of the main tracks to Compostella. However, it suffered a decline when a further set of remains of St Mary Magdalene turned up at St Maximin in Provence. The basilica of Ste Madeleine at Vezelay dates from the 12th century and was brilliantly restored in the 19th by Viollet-le-Duc. There St Bernard of Clairvaux preached the Second Crusade to Louis VII and an alleged audience of 100,000 knights and nobles packed on the slope of the hill. There also Thomas à Becket pronounced (from a safe distance) the sentence of excommunication on King Henry II.

Canal de l'Est – branche Sud. From the Canal de la Marne au Rhin at Toul or Nancy to the River Saône at Corre. (For Branche Nord see *River Meuse*.) Length 147 kms. Locks 99. Dimensions are standard French, though the depth of 2·20 is by no means to be counted upon throughout the canal.

Navigation: Much of the northern half of the canal is shallow and rocky at the edges. There is a tendency for laden barges to plough down the centre regardless. A Nelson touch may be needed to make them shift over.

Caution: There is a speed limit of 7 kms./hr. in the summit pound, which is strictly enforced by phoning through the time at which a boat passed Lock 1N or 1S. It is not always easy to run as slowly as this, particularly if there is a wind, but one can contrive to stop for grocery shopping at Les Forges or to hide in the wood about 1½ kms. down from Lock 1N. This is the standard practice among barge skippers. Do not be tempted to think the limit does not matter; I have personally taken to a bank in Épinal the skipper of a German yacht sent to collect 600 frs. (about £55) to pay the fine before being allowed to proceed.

This waterway owes its existence to the Franco-Prussian war of 1867, which gave Alsace and much of the Canal du Rhône au Rhin to Germany, with the result that a new eastern route to the Saône had to be cut if French ships were to keep out of enemy territory. It is the quickest and most convenient route to the Mediterranean for craft

coming either up the Moselle or up the Meuse. If coming
from the east (Strasbourg, or the R. Saar) there is a short
cut from the foot of Lock 25 of the Canal de la Marne au
Rhin outside Nancy, which leads 10 kms. over the divide,
with 18 locks, to join the Canal de l'Est just above Lock
46N. The saving in distance is 54 kms. but there are 6
more locks; more important, this route misses the very
pleasant river sections of the Moselle. (See note 1 on p. 283.)

Shortly after leaving the first lock (53N) in Toul the
main line of the Canal de l'Est enters the Moselle, which
even here is wide and deep and stately, flowing clear and
clean between wooded hills, a haunt of fishermen and
bathers. After 20 kms. the river is abandoned (except as a
feeder) and the waterway climbs doggedly through locks 1
to 3 kms. apart, passing through no place of any consequence.
Yet the canal is not dull. There are some beautiful woodland stretches, and several striking moments such as when,
above Lock 43N, the course crosses the Moselle on an
aqueduct. There is little industry, and most of the villages
can provide a good evening meal.

The northern ascent of the canal reaches the summit by
a final burst of 17 locks in less than 5 kms. Above Lock
15N a cut of 3 kms. leads off on the port hand to cross the
Moselle on another aqueduct and run to Épinal.

The southern slope of the canal is much more attractive,
for after the long and winding summit pound through the
pastures of Lorraine it drops quickly down the Void de
Girancourt into the golden valley of the Coney, running
beside this river through beechwoods and gradually levelling
out as it approaches the Saône at Lock 46S.

Moorings: None at all along the main line of canal.
Overnighting is outside locks, with an early-morning
departure to keep out of the way of traffic. However, the
side branch has no locks and leads quickly to ÉPINAL, where
there is a sizeable inland port with good quays and clean
water from the river. Épinal is situated on both banks of
the Moselle, a surprisingly large river even at this point
and long ago navigable for horse-hauled barges. In the

15th century the city was a free state but later was in-
corporated in Lorraine and finally in France. Once a strong
walled town it was destroyed in various wars, and modern
Épinal is mostly from the period after 1945. However, the
promenades along the Moselle have a spa-like quality, and
outside the town the pine and beech woods stretch away
into the Vosges, which reach a height of 1,400 m. The
arcaded town of Remiremont and the mountain lakes of
Gerardmer and Longemer are also within striking distance,
and in May the mountain sides are golden with wild
daffodils.

Épinal has long been the centre of an unusual industry,
devising and printing strip cartoons and comic illustrations
in colour, many of them dealing with such sacred subjects
as Napoleon and Puss-in-Boots.

Canal du Rhône au Rhin. From the Rhine 14 kms. downstream of the Swiss port of Basle to the Saône at Symphorien. Length 236 kms. Locks 114.

Navigation: A yacht leaving Strasbourg on a Sunday
should have a free run all the way, because the loaders
do not operate on Saturdays and the nearest barge heading south will have left already on Friday afternoon or
early Saturday morning and be well ahead. French customs
are cleared at Niffer lock, where the waterway leaves the
Grand Canal d'Alsace. There are no problems until after
Lock No. 7, oddly enough the *fifth* lock beyond the watershed. There the canal enters the Allan, which runs swiftly.

Caution: Do not miss the exit into the next cut, which
is extremely hard to see until the very last moment. Below
Lock No. 17 (i.e. the 15th) the crossing of the Doubs is impassable for barges when the river is running fast. Aim
well upstream fearing nothing, but keep within 30 m. of
the one-time bridge for tow-horses and on no account drop
downstream of the direct line between the canal entrances
on either side of the river.

Lock No. 27 (Papeteries) is where the river run begins.
The Doubs drains much of the Jura mountains, and after

heavy rain will make 4–5 knots. A diagram on the lock-
side shows the shoals in the next reach – or at least the
positions of them when the diagram was made. Below the
lock change to R aiming directly from the lock-cut toward
the bank to starboard at a point 150 m. distant. Keep
within 15–20 m. of this bank all the way through three
pounds until the stop-lock and cut leading to No. 30 (Plaine
de Pompierre).

Caution: All weirs until Lock 49 are fixed stone spillways
with no superstructure. From upstream, especially if the
water is ruffled by breeze, it is remarkably difficult to see
the weirs at all and a very sharp watch must be kept not
to miss the lock, which is set right in the corner of the weir
and without any cut either above or below. Unless your
craft has plenty of power and is easily manoeuvred, do not
approach the lock from the upstream side until the gates
are open and the lock vacant, or you may find yourself
being carried over the weir and annoy your underwriters.

The navigation was constructed at a period when small
underwater obstacles could be removed, but not large ones.
The result is that a few sizeable rocks about as large as a
billiard table have been left *in situ* and – which is more
important – right in the fairway. It is wise to miss these,
and the simplest way is to give half a franc to each lock-
keeper in the river sections, and ask him whether and
where there are any obstructions in the next reach. The
following sailing directions will also meet the need.

Below No. 31 (Pompierre) a large, flat rock lies inshore
R at the foot of the tall white cliffs where the river curves
to port. Keep 20–25 m. from the shore, R, and remember
that the current is washing you over toward the rock.

Leaving the cut at the foot of No. 34 (Branne) make
diagonally for the bank L and hold the course 10–15 m.
from this shore until leaving No. 37 (Crucifix). Keep 12 m.
out until the small chalets L, then move over and be sure
to be 20 m. out when passing the fir trees. Hold this until
the bend begins to straighten out for the next lock, then
edge in to 15 m.

Caution: Do not exaggerate; if you stand out more than 25 m. you will hit a shoal.

From 500 m. above No. 38 (Raie-aux-Chèvres) keep 15 m. from the bank L in all river sections until the foot of No. 40 (Baumerousse). There, keep to the centre until the railway has closed the river bank R. Then at once run 10 m. from the shore R until past the village of Esnans away to port, and when half way round this bend move out to 15 m. from the same shore. Hold this distance all the way to the entrance to the cut for No. 48 (Chaleze) only deviating to take the central arch of Laissey bridge (below No. 44). The reach beyond this bridge is buoyed.

Resume the river below No. 48, and cross to the bank L, by aiming for the bend of the bank to port. At Besançon, do not miss the tunnel entrance but wait for the signal to enter.

Below No. 52 (Velotte) keep to the left half of the centre arch of the bridge. The distance of 15–20 m. from the bank can be held in all the remaining river sections, the course changing from L to R after the short Thoraise tunnel. After the lock (No. 56, Thoraise), aim straight out into the river and cross to within 12 m. of the point of the bend.

The Rhine–Rhone Canal is scenically by far the most attractive route to the Mediterranean. Although navigationally the most difficult it is not so tricky that a steersman with sense and experience cannot manage it unaided, even if the barges use pilots on the 120 kms. for which the course is in the somewhat capricious bed of the River Doubs.

Begun under Napoleon, the waterway was opened in 1833, since when it has undergone some changes, particularly in the Alsatian section. Already the entrance lock at Niffer leads to a 12-km. cut enlarged to Europaship dimensions, which crosses the Rhine plain toward the new port of Mulhouse, beyond which the canal carries on in its original size, although an enlargement right through to the Saône is on the menu of the French Government. Considering the vast works involved it seems almost inconceivable that the new waterway could ever be cut — but that is certainly to underestimate the determination of French canal engineers.

The distance from Mulhouse to the summit at the Belfort Gap is only 34 kms. but the locks are fairly thick on the ground and there are 12 in the final 2 kms. of ascent. The watershed pound is a mere 5 kms. in length and at the further side the canal begins to drop through much longer pounds to the valley of the River Allan, which it first enters and then crosses on an aqueduct. Only 11 locks from the summit the canal passes the edge of Montbéliard, and from there onward the scenery is superb. At first the course is through a narrow trough cut at the edge of the Allan, then it crosses the River Doubs at water level to follow its valley, curving round the wooded hillside to L'Isle-sur-le-Doubs, where it decides to take the plunge and become a river navigation.

No words can do justice to the gorge of the Doubs, with its splendid limestone cliffs and wooded hillsides rising for hundreds of feet to subalpine meadows from which the sound of cowbells tinkles down to the river below. Continually one feels that nothing could be more beautiful, and yet each bend leads to some other view as fine if not better. Besançon is passed by tunnelling right beneath its citadel, and then the river slackens off as it approaches Dole by way of a stately avenue of pollarded trees. There the Doubs takes its bow, and 16 kms. of more mundane canal lead quickly to the junction with the Saône only 4 kms. upstream of the entry of the Canal de Bourgogne.

Moorings: MULHOUSE has a useful basin in the town centre, just beyond the short tunnel near the railway station. There is water enough alongside, and the berth is very convenient for shopping. Mulhouse is large, wealthy and rather modern, the centre of the textile industry but also a good base for side-trips into the high southern Vosges. Bombs and slum clearance have removed much of the old

town, but the market still has character and the canal itself
has real elegance where it passes Dutch-fashion down the
middle of the street. The 16th-century town hall is alleged
to be built on the site of the mill from which Mulhouse
takes its name, but this is more likely to have been on the
River Ill. On one side of the building is the 'Klupperstei',
a stone mask with its tongue protruded and a chain connecting the ear-lobes. Gossips and rumour-mongers were
obliged to ride round the town on the back of an ass with
this 25-pound weight hung round their necks.

DANNEMARIE has a grass-bank mooring beyond Lock No.
17, port side, on the bend. The village is $\frac{3}{4}$ km. up the road
on the same side. At VALDIEU there is good mooring in the
maintenance basin below the bridges and summit lock.
Express trains rush past occasionally in the night on the
main line from Calais and Paris to Basle. At the summit
and near the Café du Canal a feeder stream cascades into
the canal, just above the top lock. Waterways enthusiasts
can spend a pleasant summer's day walking along it and
following it across an aqueduct to its source. Below ALLENJOIE
there is good undisturbed berthing beneath the pines at the
junction with the Belfort branch (15 kms. 11 locks to the
end) and 5 locks further there is water enough alongside
the low quay in MONTBÉLIARD basin, port side and usefully
opposite a wine wholesaler's warehouse where stocks can
be laid in, blended to taste. The town is a centre of motor
manufacture and nonconformity.

COLOMBIER–FONTAINE has a factory quay immediately
after the lifting-bridge, but sleep will be intermittent because
the economics of this foundry seem to necessitate dropping
piles of tin trays from the top of a high tower at alternate
hours between midnight and 6 a.m. At L'ISLE-SUR-LE-DOUBS
pass the lock and draw in on the concrete wall 200 m. ahead,
starboard side. The main part of this little town is spread
between the canal and the river, the older houses actually
being perched along both shores of the Doubs, which here
is split by an island as the name implies. These houses face
the stream and are a picturesque jumble of loggias and

balconies, with direct gravity lavatories thrust out over the stream.

At CLERVAL, stop in the lock-cut about 100 m. short of Lock No. 32, and at BAUME-LES-DAMES against the outside bank at·the point of the lock-cut leading to the stop-lock 40-bis, or by the maintenance boats 750 m. down the cut. As the name implies, there was once a notable convent here, the one at which Ottilia (St Odile, d. 720) was a blind novice and received her sight: A legend recounts that the place was menaced by a terrible monster, incubated by a toad from a cock's egg – a strange parentage indeed. Every nun who looked at the creature fell dead, but one girl eventually had the resource not to look at it, but to approach with her eyes closed and holding a mirror. The monster succumbed to the fatal stare of its own reflection. The French Revolution annihilated the convent too.

BESANÇON has an excellent mooring, the best since Mulhouse. Pass the tunnel and the lock at its further end to turn right immediately on emerging; there is deep water all along the stone quay leading toward the spill-over weir. The university city of Besançon has all the marks of a capital, which it was (of the Franche-Comté). Earlier it was the Roman Vesontio. From its days of great prosperity before its capture by Louis XIV many splendid buildings of wealthy merchants remain, with court-yards and flamboyant staircases, but there is also a Roman triumphal arch (the Porte Noire). Victo Hugo's birthplace (b. 1802) is in the town, and so is the house of the Lumière brothers (b. 1860's) who invented colour photography. The cathedral of St Jean has an elaborate astronomical clock with moving figures and dials for such esoteric data as high tide in Guadaloupe. The city is almost encircled by the river and is topped by a vast Vauban citadel which has outlying forts on hills all round. The ascent is well worth the grind, and from the top there is a wide view over the Swiss Jura mountains and down to your own quarterdeck. A row by dinghy round the town is also an energetic entertainment.

From Besançon it is a haul of half a day to DOLE, with

bank mooring in the old port at the foot of the hill on which stands the ancient town tightly squashed around its fine church but washing its feet in the tannery canal, a most picturesque waterway (not navigable except by dinghy) which flows past a row of very quaint houses which open out to it at water level for ease of washing the tanned goods. This part of Dole dates from the rebuilding after the sacking and burning of the town in 1479 – a further onslaught in 1636 being repulsed. One of the tanneries was operated by a retired Napoleonic sergeant-major whose son was born in the house in 1822 and as Louis Pasteur made an un-equalled succession of discoveries connected with fermen-tation, crystal structure, bacterial diseases and vaccination. The house is now a Pasteur museum, and contains many exhibits connected with his researches.

Dole provides the last reasonable mooring on the water-way. St Symphorien is almost non-existent. If stopping for the night move down to St Jean-de-Losne (see *River Saône*).

Rhinau and Colmar branches. The Canal du Rhône au Rhin as now existing is truncated, much of the original northern section which led from Mulhouse to Strasbourg through 45 locks being now by-passed by the Grand Canal d'Alsace with only 7 locks. However, two detached sections have been retained for local traffic, but both limbs now connect with the Rhine instead of with the original line of canal. The one branch leads from Strasbourg at the Bassin d'Austerlitz and runs a straight and unspectacular course from Lock 86 to Lock 75, then swings away through a new cut to join the G.C.A. at Rhinau lock. The other is of more interest to yachtsmen; it leaves the G.C.A. at the foot of Vogelgrün lock, curves away westward and strikes the old canal just below Lock 62. Beyond Lock 63 the main canal is abandoned but it is open as far as the junction with the Colmar branch, a delightful rural cut which heads across the Alsatian plain straight for the Vosges and after 13 kms. and only one lock ends in the commercial harbour of COLMAR, a basin somewhat tainted with sewage but used by barges and an excellent mooring from which to take excursions up into the forests and high summits of the Vosges.

Colmar is typically Alsatian, a town of half-timbered houses gay with ornamentation and flowers and roofs of coloured glazed tiles, set in a land of storks, *Gewürztraminer, choucroute garni* and Münster cheese. Its most famous possession is the Unterlinden Museum (once a convent) with its cloisters in red standstone from the 13th century and the great polyptich of the Isenheim altar by Matthias Grünewald, painted in 1576 for the convent of the 'Antonites' who tended those sick of 'St Anthony's Fire', an ulcer-producing disease not yet positively identified. The church of St Martin contains Martin Schongauer's *Madonna in the Rosebush,* 1473.

Within reach of Colmar are many villages of special interest — and of excellent Alsatian wines. Ribeauvillé still boasts an annual gathering of minstrels on the first Sunday in September. Riquewihr is a great centre of vintners. At Türckheim the night watchman with horn and lantern sings his curfew at the street corners.

River Saône. The longest navigable river in France, the Saône is part of the waterway from the North Sea or Channel to the Mediterranean, all six routes across northern France converging upon it. Navigation is from Corre to the Rhone at Lyon. Length 375 kms. Locks 29. The first 16 are of standard size, but beyond Gray they become gradually larger. A very few are electrified.

Navigation: Strangely, the Saône becomes more difficult in its lower reaches. This is because the lesser gradient causes shoals, and in order to keep the stream within reasonable bounds it is supplied from Macon onwards with plenty of underwater groynes and walls, which betray their position better in summer than in spring because of the weed growing on them. Steering a safe course is easy if the level is high enough to cover all these dangers with 2 metres of water, or low enough to leave them protruding. More usually the condition of the river is between these extremes, and as some of the obstacles reach half way across the bed it is wise to acquire (at Chalon-sur-Saône) the very large-scale and excellent 70-page chart *La Saône* published by René Salagnac, which covers the whole river and is used by the bargemen, or the *Guide de la Saône* published by Giraud-Rivoire of Lyon.

Because of the reduced gradient, the level in the lower reaches rises considerably after heavy rain. The needles of most weirs below St Jean-de-Losne are then drawn and the staging removed over part of the length. Ships can pass through the gap instead of using the lock, which is in any event under water. When these conditions apply a prominent signboard and arrow is displayed at the point of the lock-cut, and green-and-white signal boards are placed at either side of the navigable pass. There may be a drop of ¼ metre through the gap in the weir, but it is nothing to be alarmed about.

One of the most beautiful of rural rivers, the Saône shares with the Rhone the fate of being hurried through by boatmen with no time to stop. Its attraction is more in the unspoiled pastoral setting of its upper reaches, the river meandering through a wide valley of copses and pasture, past villages of great age, redolent with cow manure. In spring it provides one of the pleasantest voyages in Europe, and the whole journey is charmingly described in P. G. Hamerton's *The Saône, a Summer Voyage*, published in 1887. From the illustrations one can see that the river has hardly changed since then. Even the moorings are the same.

Below Auxonne (km. 145) the hills recede and the plain broadens out to become less interesting. The gradient drops away (there are 15 locks in the first 100 kms. below Corre, but pounds of 50 and 60 kms. lower down) and the interest is more in the places through which the river passes.

The Saône is a fisherman's river, and every device is used from eel nets, seine nets and drop-nets for friture, to crayfish pots, trots, individual lines and even small-bore shooting from the bow of a punt. Many of the fishermen are professional but in the summer their numbers are swelled by thousands who come to camp by the bank and fish from dawn to after dark. Among such numbers there are certain to be a few who become neurotic at the sight of a boat or who will foolishly cast their lines across your bow.

Moorings: At CORRE on the river bank L round the bend below the canal entrance lock. Beyond Corre there is only one alongside mooring for the 99 kms. to Gray. It is inadvisable to stop in a lock-cut because of drawing off by passing barges, but one can usually pull in on the bank in the upper end of the by-passed weir streams, where there is always plenty of water. The one good halt on these upper reaches is at PORT-SUR-SAONE (km. 37), at the further end of the grass-banked basin opposite the navigation office, by the first bridge beyond the town centre. GRAY (km. 99) has a long and low stone quay below the lock, R. Long warps are needed to reach the rings. The town is a double one, the more modern being along the river and the older one perched on the hilltop and reached by a flight of steps. The square at the summit is usually deserted, and the 15th-century church and the Renaissance town hall with its smart roof of coloured glazed tiles look down upon nobody. The castle (now a museum) gives a fine view of the Saône below. A small trip-boat, the *Val de Saône,* runs from Gray.

At AUXONNE (km. 144) bring up on the wall L beneath the rampart immediately upstream of the road bridge – but leave room for barges using the inshore bridge arch. The town has a Bonaparte museum, for it was at Auxonne that Napoleon spent a year in training as a young officer.

ST JEAN-DE-LOSNE (km. 162) has the basin of the Canal de Bourgogne, a good place to moor if the stay is protracted. Otherwise draw in against the wall R immediately below the road bridge. Do not attempt to enter the old mooring basin below, which is filled with mud. This traditional town of bargemen was sometimes known as *Belle Défense,* on account of its remarkable resistance, recalled on a monument by the bridge. In 1636 it was a frontier town, and the citizens aided by only 150 soldiers withstood a siege by sixty thousand troops of the Holy Roman Empire, and drove them off.

At SEURRE (km. 189) the old bridge has been removed but its abutments are obvious, upstream of the new one. There is good mooring alongside the wall L at the lower end – the position clearly marked by the names of barges which have moored there painted on the stonework. The quay wall 1 km. further down is not satisfactory because of drawing off. VERDUN-SUR-LE-DOUBS (km. 208) offers no possibility of alongside moorings in the Saône, but there is a good stage (without shore access) about 500 m. up the Doubs and right in the village. At CHALON -SUR-SAONE (km. 234) there is ample mooring on the wall, perhaps of necessity alongside barges, between the two town bridges, R. Chalon has been a town of boatmen since Roman times, and has a busy modern port basin. The massive river quay was built by Emiland Gauthey (d. 1806), himself a Chalonais who also laid out the Canal du Centre. It was here that Joseph Nicéphore Niépce (d. 1833) succeeded in 1822 in taking a photograph with a *camera obscura*; the museum has his apparatus and other exhibits of local interest, including water-transport. In the early autumn there is an antique fair as well as a festival of the river with fireworks.

TOURNUS (km. 264) has a quay R beneath and just above the first bridge. The gravel port further down is messy and inconvenient – and so is the quay after heavy rain. Nearby a magnificent assemblage of ecclesiastical buildings surrounds the superb romanesque cathedral of St Philibert from the 10th to 12th centuries.

FLEURVILLE (km. 278) has a pontoon by the inn below the bridge, R. The inn is an excellent place for eels, crayfish and friture de la Saône (a sort of fresh-water whitebait). Across the river is the disused entrance lock of the abandoned Canal de Pont de Vaux.

MACON (km. 295) has a long quay R, but it may sometimes be under water. On the open space above it there is usually a large and busy market. There is also a so-called Port de Plaisance in an old gravel working a few kilometres

above the town R, but it is too far from the shops and the
town itself to be of much use. It serves mainly as a base for
local sailing dinghies. The town itself is not particularly
striking, largely because the natives foolishly burned all
their churches – some of them notable ones – in their hysteria
at the time of the Revolution of 1789. However, it is much
the best mooring from which to visit a number of nearby
places of note. Famous vineyards abound, and such villages
as Pouilly and Fuissé are unspoiled and built of the rather
Cotswold-type stone of the area. Close to them and visible
from the river is the sharp rocky scarp of Solutré, where
our progenitors (Solutrian man) drove wild animals over
the precipice to their deaths some fifteen thousand years
ago. Further north the remains of the abbey of Cluny are
a poignant relic of the vast religious institution which was
the pride of the middle ages. The abbey church was the
largest in the western world after St Peter's in Rome, and
even what little is left of it provides an impressive example
of what monastic building could achieve around the turn of
the 11th century. The institution survived almost intact to
1789, when of course it was wrecked. In some respects its
modern counterpart is found in Taizé, only 10 kms. distant,
where the modern Church of Reconciliation run by the
protestant Taizé Community is a pioneer venture in ecu-
menical living.

Mooring is possible at ST ROMAIN DES ÎLES (km. 309) at
the Port Jean Savoyet immediately below the bridge R.
Most places designated 'port' on the chart may indeed have
been a stopping point for horse-drawn craft in the middle
ages, but nowadays are more likely to be a heap of stones
from a decayed quayside.

VILLEFRANCHE (km. 335) has a genuine harbour R with
quay and ladders. The only facilities are coal dust and an
exceedingly scruffy pub, but it provides a safe berth if fog
or night is falling. However, TRÉVOUX (km. 344) has a quay
L on the bend and almost under the suspension bridge.
One of the most attractive moorings on all the river, this
is a favourite overnighting halt for barges. The town seems

to have been poured down the hillside on the bend in the river, and is the first place to exhale a real whiff of the south. Its pantile roofs at a low angle are Mediterranean, and they are best seen from the remnants of the feudal castle keep above. The council chamber or Parliament from the days when Trévoux was capital of the free principality of Dombes, was built in the 17th century and has a very fine painted ceiling. Old faded houses and alleys and flights of steps abound. *Caution:* After dark the name of the Rue Casse-Cou should be taken seriously.

LYON. Moorings can be found through the town, but best of all is the Port de Plaisance (km. 371) by the Pont Bonaparte, which has minimal facilities but offers one the chance to check the motor and buy fuel supplies before descending the Rhone. This mooring is right opposite the floodlit Cathedral of St Jean (11th to 15th centuries) and the hill crowned by the great basilica of Fourvière.

Lyon really consists of three cities. The Roman and medieval one is partly clustered on the slopes of the Four-vière hill west of the Saône, whilst the 18th- and 19th-century city fills the point of the space between the Saône and Rhone, which for some 4 kms. run parallel and only a few hundred metres apart. The modern industrial sprawl is mostly situated east of the Rhone and has nothing to commend it.

The old city is superb and calls for exploring. It is rich in Roman remains, including the amphitheatre in which occurred the fearful torturing of Christians in A.D. 177 when St Pothinus and the young Blandina were killed before the crowd. Twenty years later eighteen thousand other Christians were massacred at Lyon. The lower slopes of the hill are a jumble of Gothic and Renaissance houses both rich and poor. A mountain railway leads from the square opposite the Port de Plaisance to the Roman area, and another to the summit of Fourvière, topped by the remarkable basilica erected after the Franco-Prussian war of 1870 by the Arch-bishop of Lyon, who had vowed to build a great church if the Germans did not reach Lyon. It contains a miraculous

statue alleged to protect the city from pests, epidemics and
Prussians, and the interior of the church has the history of
Lyon set out in vast mural mosaics. From the pinnacle of
the basilica, there is an unforgettable view over the three-
city area, offering what is probably the nearest to an aerial
photograph of your own boat that you will ever be able to
take. *Caution:* The hill of Fourvière can also be climbed by
a stairway of more than 600 steps, but weak hearts travel
better in the mountain railway.

The town between the two rivers also has some interesting
corners, particularly where another funicular climbs to the
hill of the Croix Rousse. Here there was no room for streets
enough, so the area is riddled with vaulted alleys known
as *traboules*, which are characteristic of Lyon. This is also
the site of the Gallic town, the amphitheatre of which has
been excavated, but at the foot of the hill lies the more
modern shopping area which ranks as one of the best in
France. *Caution:* Bearing in mind that Lyon has an age-
old reputation for its silks, the skipper should not be either
surprised or churlish when he finds that the ladies aboard
have spent all the ship's husbandry money on Lyon fabrics.

River Seille. Navigable for 40 kms. from its confluence with
the Saône, 5 kms. below Tournus, up to Louhans. The
entrance is on the port hand going down the Saône and is
just short of a wood. The second opening is the correct one,
and leads to the lock at La Truchère. The first is merely the
outfall from the weir and mill.

Locks 4. 35·6 m. × 5·17 m.

Draught 1·55 m. in locks, but deep water elsewhere
throughout.

Headroom 4·7 m.

No permit is needed, except the lock-keeper's blessing.

Navigation is easy, with little current. The only shallows
are where the tail-cuts and weir streams rejoin below the
locks, but the laden barges keep them reasonably well
ploughed. The first three locks are extremely stiff to operate
and patience is needed. The third is unmanned, and a

windlass handle must be picked up at the previous lock.

The Seille is normally used only by two small gravel barges. As each knows where the other one is, a barge-master may leave his craft in the lock over the week-end while he goes to a pub at La Truchère, from which he can however be extracted by the lock-keeper's son, who probably knows which pub he is in. For the same reason a barge is never expecting to meet a strange vessel, so care should be taken to blow off before any blind corner.

One of the most beautiful cruising waters in all France, this charming river is rarely visited because yachtsmen are in such a hurry to reach the Mediterranean. It is more like the Upper Thames than any other river, its mills and long weirs reminiscent of those in the Chilterns. In spring the meadows are bright with snakes-head lily and cowslips, and the copses and meadows are the haunt of egret, night heron, and little bittern. Between La Truchère and Louhans the stream meanders without actually touching any place, but the hilltop village of Cuisery is only a few minutes' walk from the mooring above Lock 2.

Moorings: Throughout, on firm grassy banks. At LOUHANS the river forks and very small craft may draw into the bank in the right-hand fork and on the starboard side. But deeper water is available where rings are set in the ground beyond the gravel quay and on the port hand, outside a builder's yard just before the confluence.

Louhans is a town with a long main street preserved under an Order of State, its double row of arcaded houses and shops of different dates being classified as a historical monument. The Hôtel-Dieu of the 18th century, with a relief of the Samaritan over the door from the garden, is maintained by the nursing order of St Martha. Its most priceless possession is a collection of chemist's jars and glassware ranged in handsome wooden racks of the 18th century, and housed in the original dispensary. The con-tainers, from Moorish times onward, can be seen by anyone bold enough to apply at the modern Maternity Ward of the hospital and persuasive enough to be led through into the older wing, which is still an old people's home or hospice, with modern comfort but an old-world atmosphere of a happy community. One does not need to be a ceramics enthusiast to enjoy this unusual excursion.

River Rhone. From Lyon to Port St Louis. Length 323 kms. Locks or more (according to progress in the canalisation of the river). The depth varies within wide limits according to the rainfall in Burgundy and Lorraine, and the thaw or freeze in the Swiss and French Alps.

Navigation: The Rhone is partially buoyed, in that red starboard hand buoys mark the outer edge of the channel on that side, R. At least, they do in theory, but they are no substitute for intelligent navigation. The buoys are often swept off station, and I have even passed one lodged in the top of a tree by the winter floods.

The river is a blue-flag stream, but it is the custom for some of the Rhone ships to blink either their red or their green navigation light as a signal that they wish to be met on that side, whether the rule of the road or not. Answer the flashing green with your blue flag to show have got the message.

There is no charge for using the huge locks, but pleasure craft are not always locked immediately, and may have to face a delay (maximum 3 hrs.) while waiting for commercial craft to arrive.

Caution: Do not let children fool about on deck. If anyone falls overboard it may be impossible to retrieve them, and the river is no place for even the strongest swimmers, except in the locked sections.

Special Instructions: Some places need special care. The lock-cut of the first lock below Lyon (Pierre Bénite, or the Holy Stone) is long and uneventful, but at its end the Rhone sweeps in, for the first time, unbridled and magnificent and yet a sight to make the stoutest heart fail, for the course immediately ahead is seen to be dotted with a host of rocks (les Pierres de Ternay) and markers. Fear nothing, but run within 10 to 20 m. of the bank R, leaving all the black-and-white marks and rocks to port. Then breathe again and settle down to enjoy the experience of a lifetime.

Approaching Les Roches de Condrieu at km. 41 there is a very sharp bend to the right with the current setting hard to the shore L and rebounding as strong whirlpools. This bend is best taken under full power and about 20 metres from the retaining wall. Then cut past the jetty and straight over to the opposite shore above Condrieu bridge.

At the end of the long cut below St Pierre lock the Rhone sweeps in from the right. The curve after the junction is one of the fastest and most turbulent on all the river. Keep well to the left, and if a ship is coming up cut as close to it as prudent.

Above Arles, at km. 275, the channel changes sides. Keep close to the bank R, until 150 m. short of the yellow lozenge (not very conspic.) on the longitudinal training wall in the stream, L. Aim immediately for this sign and pass within 10 m. of it.

The Rhone is certainly impressive, but boatmen can safely disregard the wilder stories of its velocity. It is a river to which the Pilkington rule applies. This can be stated as follows :

The true speed of a river is one half the figure given in a yachtsman's published log, one third of the figure which the same yachtsman states in a boating journal, or one quarter of the figure alleged by him at the Members' Bar.

More precisely, under fairly average conditions a boat travelling at 9 knots will make 1 km. in about 9 minutes when forging upstream in the uncanalised sections of the Rhone above Avignon and St Vallier, except in certain exceptionally swift passages where the progress will drop to 1 km. in 15 minutes.

Going downstream the boat should not be driven flat out, but just fast enough to give good steerage way and keep a useful margin of power in hand for whirlpools and shoreward-setting currents, which may attain several knots. Covering the ground at the rate of 2½ to 3 minutes for a kilometre is quite fast enough, and much less exacting for the steersman, who will have to concentrate very hard for several hours at a time without a moment's inattention.

Before descending the Rhone, it is essential to enquire of the *Ponts et Chaussées* in Lyon, or of the *Port de Plaisance* (see *R. Saône*) to be sure that the depth is adequate in the uncanalised sections. It is also vital to consider the matter of pilotage.

Pilotage: On the Rhone, pilotage is expensive, just because the canalisation of the river is bringing forward the day when pilots will no more be needed – by which time they must all be able to retire into an affluent society of ex-pilots. In 1965, the pilotage fee for a run of 1½ days was about £12 plus expenses. By 1974 the same distance was charged at £50. There is therefore a strong inducement not to take a pilot, or perhaps to share one between several yachts. This latter procedure is naturally very unpopular with the pilots, and following yachts should not be surprised if the course is laid within feet of deadly rocks which will side with the pilot and teach the parsimonious a lesson.

Another idea is to follow a barge. This is strongly to be discouraged, for two reasons. Rhone barges are exceptionally powerful and speedy, and it is not really very sensible to expect a sailing boat with an auxiliary motor capable of 5 knots to keep on the tail of a ship travelling at 12 or 15 knots. There is also a possibility that a barge may swing round and stop at a private jetty, leaving the following boat guideless in a swift and tricky river.

But the great disadvantage of pilotage, apart from the money thrown away, is that one is haunted by the feeling that even to stop to buy milk and bread will cost another pound or two of the man's time. Stopping just to enjoy the scenery is out of the question, and the descent of one of Europe's grandest rivers becomes a nightmare voyage in which the places flash past like single frames of a movie, and all the owner can do is to pretend to enjoy the fact that he is not even being allowed to steer his own boat. In fact, the majority of yachtsmen descending the river seem to be in breathless haste to reach the pastures of the Côte d'Azur – where it is they themselves that will be milked by extremely experienced harbour-men and beachcombers – but others who are not so easily persuaded of the delights of Cannes and Monte Carlo are sure to regret running the entire Rhone in one single exhausting beat with at most a night's stop in the 'garage' of a hydro-electric works.

The Rhone can be run without a pilot, and I have myself made the trip several times. But it would be foolish to attempt it without plenty of experience of rivers such as the Rhine or Weser in their faster reaches. To have pottered about in the Thames or Hamble tideways is not enough. The Rhone runs twice as fast as their maximum ebbs, its sharp curves cause whirlpools of great strength, and the bed has plenty of shoals, groynes and underwater rocks lying close to the actual channel. A good rough chart is available from the *Port de Plaisance* in Lyon, and this is invaluable for crossing over at the right points and for showing those places such as Vienne where the channel is not on the outside of the bend as one might reasonably expect. The most necessary part of a steersman's equipment, however, is the ability to make out from the appearance of the surface ahead of him where the deep water is, and where are the rocks and shallows. No exact guide can be given here, except to stress that the English saying 'still waters run deep' is the surest way to shipwreck. On the Rhone, as on the Rhine, still waters overlie shallows. If in doubt keep your nerve and make for the roughest water – remembering that a shipwreck in the Rhone is likely to be a total loss.

Probably the best arrangement for those who want to take the journey gently but safely is to pick up a pilot at Lyon to run to St Vallier, or wherever the first stretch of unbridled river ends; then proceed at leisure through the next 110 kms. of deep, locked water, take another pilot from St Pierre lock to Avignon, proceed alone in dead water to Tarascon or Beaucaire, use pilotage again to Arles (a mere 16 kms. but with an awkward section above Arles), then take either the Canal d'Arles à Bouc, or proceed by the Thirds Rule down the now much gentler and slower river

to Port St Louis. This will cut the expense and give the
opportunity to look around.

Any boatman who has not experienced the uncontrolled
reaches of the Rhone should hurry to do so before the whole
river has been finally tamed by the immense barrages of the
Compagnie du Rhone. However medieval life may be in a
small French country town, there is no doubt about the scale
and enterprise of French engineering. Within the last quarter
of the 20th century, the whole of the Rhone from Lyon at
least to Arles is likely to have been converted into a succession of gigantic reservoirs, each with a hydro-electric
station and a lock at its lower end. The rapids and whirlpools will all have vanished, the groynes been hauled out
by grabs, and the valley transformed – as half of it has
already been – into the bed of a wide, deep, slow-moving
body of water in which even the most foolish yachtsman or
bargemaster could not possibly come to grief.

Wild life on the Rhone can be interesting. There are few
duck, but I have seen ospreys along the reaches by the Tour
de l'Hers and Aramon, and purple herons above Ardoise.
Marsh harriers and kites occur all along the valley and
below Arles there is just a chance of seeing flamingoes flying
over the river – their favourite haunt on the Étang de
Vaccarès being only 5 kms. distant over the right bank.
Along these lower reaches all the birds of the Camargue
may occasionally be seen, though on the whole the river
here is more notable for its lack of birds of any kind.

Moorings: In some places the flow is strong enough to
keep the screw of a moored boat turning continually. Apart
from the unpleasant dreams caused by the endless whining
of the gearbox, it may be bad for the bearings if lubrication
only occurs when the engine is running. A stilson wrench on
the shaft is an easy means of stopping the rotation.

At VIENNE (km. 29) there is good mooring alongside, below
the second bridge, L. It is a hurrying, bustling town, which
can be reached in safety by a tunnel under the terrifying
main road on the river bank. Vienne has remarkable
Roman remains including the temple of Augustus and Livia,

standing very confidently as though it had only recently been built. The theatre, which was the scene of the terrible tortures of the Christian community under Marcus Aurelius, was closed when Constantine became emperor, but in modern times it is often the setting for open-air plays. The splendid cathedral of St Maurice also recalls a martyr, a soldier of the Theban Legion. Downstream of the moorings a curious obelisk standing on an arched base and just visible from the river, is the alleged tomb of Pontius Pilate, who is said to have drowned himself in the Rhone, but there is no inscription on the stonework.

At LES ROCHES-DE-CONDRIEU (km. 41) one can make fast alongside the trestle jetty upstream of the bridge, L, to shop at Condrieu across the river, but at ANDANCE (km. 69) the only chance is alongside a barge, R, if any, and with permission. The channel runs within 10 m. of the river wall, so wash is likely to be heavy. At ST VALLIER (km. 75) one is already in the peace of the head water of the next lock, and there is mooring below the quay wall by the bridge L, in a somewhat dusty and noisy position beside a main road. St Vallier is an uninspiring town, only redeemed by the excellent dinner to be had at the Hôtel des Voyageurs.

TOURNON (km. 91) has a yacht harbour, R, before the bridge. Sound the depth carefully upon entering. It may be as low as 0·80 m. at low river level. Tournon's simple but stolid castle from the 15th century stands proudly on a rocky knoll above the quay, and has a wide view across the Rhone to Tain-L'Hermitage with its famous vineyards. Near the yacht harbour is a statue to Marc Seguin, the inventor of the tube boiler and constructor of France's first suspension bridges, including those over the Rhone. Tournon has also preserved a narrow-gauge railway which runs far into the country, usually at summer week-ends.

At km. 98 the weir stream leads off to the right, and about 500 m. down it is a public quay L, in front of a row of trimmed acacia trees. The village is LA ROCHE-DE-GLUN, and it is interesting to see that the present normal water level is considerably higher than the mark in the village street for the great flood of 1840. There are inns and restaurants, and the village still has a crenellated gateway, but unfortunately its once pleasant aspect has been spoiled by building a very uninspired block of flats in front of the church. However, many of the houses are built of courses of Rhone cobbles which in itself gives the place a real riverside character. The former castle of robber barons was razed by St Louis in the 13th century.

VALENCE (km. 110) provides a long quay, L, beyond the bridges. The older part of the town is clustered untidily around the cathedral of St Apollinairis, but the chief attraction is the park which spills down the hillside, and above it the broad expanse of the Champ de Mars. Across the river the brilliant white castle of Crussol, built in the 12th century, is so weathered and ruined that one cannot distinguish at a distance how much of the mass is fortress and how much the rocky spur which serves as its foundation.

At LA VOULTE (km. 128) there is a convenient and unobstructed wall beyond the road bridge, R. The wall slopes slightly, but the mooring is excellent and there is always a depth of at least 3 m. alongside. La Voulte is perhaps the easiest and most convenient shopping stop on all the Rhone, the shops being all within two minutes' walk of the mooring. Some days there is a market under the plane trees by the river wall. At the inner end of the Rue Rampon, beside the old fountain in the wall, an archway leads to steps and alleys which wind up to the summit of the rock on which a castle dominates the whole town. La Voulte is a cosy, comfortable place without too much road traffic, and one is easily tempted to sit for half a day at Chez Maurice or one of the other unpretentious establishments near the Rhone.

At LE POUZIN there is a quay R, immediately upstream of the km. 133 mark. The town is small and somewhat dusty and industrial but it lies at the foot of fine limestone cliffs giving a chance of pleasant rambles with views over the Rhone toward the high mountains of the Drome. CRUAS (km. 145) has a slightly sloping stretch of quay wall, and the village is about 1 km. distant up the lane. Cruas has a romanesque abbey church from the 11th century, and on the cliff behind the town is a 12-century chapel of refuge (from Rhone floods and marauding armies) later so altered by the addition of defences that it more resembles a fort. Unfortunately a large cement works is now established at Cruas, and the little town is slowly becoming a uniform and ghostly grey.

VIVIERS (km. 165) has a quay wall in the old port, providing an excellent mooring in still water, away from the river traffic. Turn right about 2 kms. below Châteauneuf lock, into the weir stream arm of the river. The old port is only a short way inside, R, and there is plenty of water. Viviers is an excellent specimen of a French town which seems to be unaffected by modernity. A cathedral city from the 5th century onward, it has a curious fortified ecclesiastical enclave perched on a knoll, from which there is a startling view over the faded pantile roofs of the cramped houses. At the edge of the town a Roman bridge still spans the R. Escoutaye. A rocky bluff beside the Rhone has a statue of St Michael slaying a (German) dragon, erected in thankfulness that the Viviers bridge was bombed by the British, with the loss to inhabitants limited to one cracked denture, instead of by the Americans, who missed the bridge of Pont St Esprit lower down the river, but nearly demolished the town itself. (Maybe a different version is given to visitors from the United States.) This steep hill is well worth the tough ascent to see the view of the famous Donzère gorge, now flooded by the barrage.

ST PIERRE (km. 187) is likely to be a stop-over point, though mooring is only possible on the piles at the foot of the lock, L. Ask permission of the lock-keeper. This is not an easy mooring, and is subject to wash, surges, and curses from bargemen.

The lock was opened in 1952 as the first to be built on the Rhone, and it had the second deepest fall in all the world, being exceeded by only one on the Tennessee system. It is interesting to time the descent and discover that locking down some 26 m. or more takes no longer than to pass a standard French canal lock.

The André Blondel power station produces more than 2 milliards of kilowatt-hours annually, but it is not shown to visitors. However, from the lock one can burrow under the motorway to St Pierre village by a culvert, and follow the lane which winds up about 5 kms. to Barry, a weird 'troglodytic village' now deserted but containing scores of cavedwellings from Gallo-Roman to late medieval times, and even a chapel cut out of the soft rock. From the castle ruins above, the view extends to Mt Ventoux, snow-clad in spring, and in clear weather to the French Alps.

La Bollène, also reached from the lock of St Pierre, is a tight circular old town of narrow streets, surrounded by hideous modern expansion for the Rhone valley industries. There is a monument to Louis Pasteur and the sheep and pigs for which he did so much.

The next mooring downstream is at the quay of the commercial port of L'ARDOISE (km. 214), a place of no other attractions at all. This is the last halting point until AVIGNON (km. 241), which has now been bypassed by the Villeneuve lock and cut. To reach it, pass the lock and proceed down to the railway viaduct before turning left and back up the dead arm to the long and modern quay beside the town wall. The vast assemblage of splendid buildings climbing up to the summit of the Rocher des Doms gives an overpowering impression of wealthy and aristocratic armed self-confidence, ready to defy heretic and orthodox alike. It was in 1309 that Clement V abandoned Rome and established the papal see at Avignon instead. Six other popes, all from the Languedoc, succeeded him there, one of whom (Benedict XII, 1334-42) began the magnificent palace, for which he is tactfully alleged to have received the money from an aged Jewish woman whom, as a lad, he cured of flea-bites.

There is a curious sundial laid out in the garden on top of the bluff. Standing at the appropriate point for the date, one becomes a gnomon and reads the hour by one's own shadow.

The city lives partly on its visitors, but the entertainment is select and there is the chance of a good concert, or an exhibition, or perhaps a recherché play at a pocket theatre. One can also dine in an open square into which the restaurants push their tables, serving through the traffic, or sit in the gardens above the river and watch the ferry which is propelled merely by the force of the river striking the bow at an angle. The famous Pont d'Avignon alleged to have been constructed in the 12th century by a shepherd lad, later to become St Benezet, can be visited for a small charge. *Caution:* Do not dance upon it and bring down the remaining arches.

The bridge originally had nineteen arches equipped with ice-breakers, and the master builder is alleged to have died at nineteen, before it was finished. He was buried in a chapel over the fourth arch. Over the centuries various arches collapsed, and the ones now surviving were rebuilt by Pope Clement VI, but in the seventeenth century all attempts to keep pace with the depredations of the river were abandoned.

Across the river, Villeneuve was once a smart place to live if one was a cardinal. Today it is a delightful and forgotten village with a steep street of vine-clad houses gay with miniature gardens, its noble past proclaimed by such monastic remains as the Revolution allowed to stand, and the 13th-century Tower of Philip the Fair which once commanded the approach to the Pont d'Avignon – which at that time was on the frontier between France and the Holy Roman Empire. Above the town stand the massive medieval bastions and wall of the Fort St André, so stout and impregnable that they have the appearance of being built for a film set.

Below Tarascon lock pass under the bridges, turn the point of the long ait to starboard, and leave the tip of the spit 50 m. upstream. Cut over to the further shore, R, and keep within 10 m. of the bank for the short run up to the former entrance of the Canal du Rhone à Sete at BEAUCAIRE (km. 268).

Caution: Take the entrance carefully, as it may silt. The deeper water is close to the promontory, starboard hand. Once inside, take the centre and moor on the grassy bank to starboard, just short of the lock. Do not attempt the entry unless the level of the Rhone is above normal. It is prudent to enquire of the Tarrascon lock-keeper.

Tarascon can be reached by walking over the bridge, which leaps the Rhone just beside the massive fortress castle of René the Good, the poetry-loving Duke of Anjou who was father-in-law of King Henry VI of England. The castle keeps its feet cool in the river, but it has also been a prison. Close to the end of the bridge is the church in which St Martha is said to be buried, the sister of Mary and Lazarus. She is claimed also to have defeated the local dragon, the fearful hominivorous Tarasque, an effigy of which can be seen, and on certain festive occasions actually met under way in the streets. *Caution:* These animals are dangerous.

Beaucaire also has a tall castle keep of the same period, standing in a public garden and giving a view over the Alpilles hills, blue with rosemary in early summer. A walk in these hills can make a whole-day excursion, and leads eventually to the curious town of Les Baux, where dwellings of several eras have succeeded each other, partly cut in the soft rock and partly built among the ruins of their pre- decessors. The town is also immortalised by giving its name to the reddish ore known as bauxite, from which the chemist Henri Deville (d. 1881) under the patronage of the Emperor Napoleon III succeeded in producing aluminium.

At ARLES (km. 283) if taking the Canal d'Arles à Bouc, lock through and moor on the bank in the basin inside. Otherwise at the quay wall, L, immediately before the second bridge. The R bank is subject to wash, and is used by barges fuelling. The compact city has an astonishing assemblage of Roman remains of surprising size — the arena at one time contained a town of several hundred houses. The ancient cemetery of Les Aliscamps (The Champs Elysées) is a peaceful and strangely moving place, even if its many chapels are ruined and the stone coffins of Christian merchants from the earliest centuries A.D. have been despoiled or rearranged. It is said to have been begun by St Trophimus, a disciple of St Paul. As far up as Lyon, the bodies of the wealthy were formerly consigned to the Rhone in wooden coffins along with some money for the watermen of Trinquetaille (opposite Arles) whose job it was to intercept them in the current and land them for burial.

On the canal to Bouc, the double-bascule bridge painted by van Gogh is $2\frac{1}{2}$ kms. along the towpath. Arles is also the place from which to make an excursion to the bleak salt-marshes of the Camargue where flamingoes, egrets, stilts, rollers, bee-eaters and other unusual birds can be seen. Wild bulls are fortunately in fenced enclosures, but the Camargue ponies are more accessible. A single road, kept rough to deter most motorists, crosses the whole expanse to Les Saintes Maries, and gives an adequate view of the wild life. Serious naturalists wishing to wander off to the side can purchase a permit in Arles, valid only for the day.

Navigation ends at PORT ST LOUIS DU RHONE (km. 323) a minor commercial port. There is mooring along the quay at the lock approach, L, but better facilities in the basin beyond the lock. Ask permission of the keeper. The lock leads to a straight cut with no mooring facilities, which ends in the Gulf of Fos, 5 kms. distant. Customs are cleared beyond the lock.

ACROSS FRANCE – EAST TO WEST

Canal du Rhône à Sète. From the R. Rhone at Beaucaire to the terminus of the Canal du Midi at Sète. Length 98 kms. Locks 2 – but since the construction of St Gilles lock the entrance is no longer at Beaucaire but some kilometres down the Petit Rhone. Fork right above Arles.

Navigation: Care should be taken at the water cross-roads at Carnon and Palavas, where differences in level between the sea on one side and the salt-marshes on the other can cause a very strong cross current which may not be obvious in the dark until the ship plunges to one side and strikes the bridge or wall.

Caution: Unattended nets may sometimes be left across the water at night, particularly near the fishing hamlets cramped on the dykes through the lagoons.

The canal provides an internal connection with the Canal du Midi, and so forms part of the inland route from Northern Europe to the Emerald Coast and the Costa Brava. For half its length it skirts the marshes of the Camargue before becoming a course dyked off from the salt-marshes and lagoons which stretch most of the way from Aigues Mortes to Sète. The waterway is perhaps seen at its best if run at night, especially between Aigues Mortes and Frontignan. There are no obstructions, for the railway swing-bridge at Aigues Mortes is left open at night and there is no need to stop until the road lifting-bridge at Frontignan, 7 kms. from Sète. Sunset or dawn over the salt lagoons have a beauty all of their own, and at night the rather shoddy or over-pretentious developments of the Lanquedoc coast, 1 km.

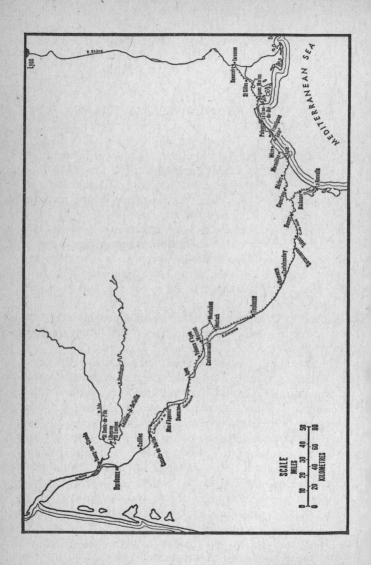

MEDITERRANEAN SEA

Lyon

R. Rhône

Bordeaux

SCALE

MILES
0   10   20   30   40   50

KILOMETRES
0   20   40   60   80

distant, become a blaze of tinsel lighting, even the roller-
coaster at Carnon Plage taking on a fascinating form in the
darkness. Here and there the canal teems with fish which
rush ahead of the boat or alongside it, their motion stirring
the water to phosphorescence and forming a shoal of brilliant pale blue arrows so that the ship seems to move in a
cushion of ghostly azure.

To arrive at Aigues Mortes by night is also a delight, the
floodlit Tour de Constance standing out against the dark
sky. But the canal is interesting by day also, and west of
Palavas one may see great flights of rosy flamingoes over
the salt-marshes, and the flats alongside the waterway are
favourite stalking ground for the flocks of black-winged
stilts, easily recognisable by their absurdly long and pink
legs. Between Aigues Mortes and St Gilles the fauna of the
Camargue roams freely up to the bank, wild ponies and
bulls peering at the boatman with mild curiosity. Rollers
and bee-eaters and hoopoes flutter among the scrub and
white egrets are in attendance on the bulls as though their
hosts were African elephants.

Beyond the seaside resort of Palavas-les-Flots on the
nearby shore, the deserted former cathedral of Maguelone
stands forlorn in a group of pines on what once was an
island. Sacked by the Saracens in the 8th century, it was
rebuilt and fortified, but as the population had left the
inhospitable marshes it never really recovered its status.

There are two outlets to the sea by side branches. At
Aigues Mortes it is possible to turn left to Le Grau du Roi
(the Roi being St Louis), a somewhat fish-and-chip seaside
resort with an exit between two moles but no mooring facilities at all, except alongside sardine boats. The swing-bridge
in the town opens only occasionally, and not at all on
Sundays. The outlet at Palavas is obstructed by two fixed
bridges with headroom limited to about 2·5 m., but is otherwise suitable for small craft. The La Peyrade branch to
Sète docks is now filled in.

Moorings: For Beaucaire and St Gilles turn right beyond
St Gilles lock.

At BEAUCAIRE there is a good basin. The town has narrow alleys, with houses in some of which cattle are still kept on the ground floor. From the tall tower of the 13th-century castle set in a pleasant park, there is a magnificent view across the Rhone to Tarascon and the rosemary-covered range of the Alpilles hills.

ST GILLES has a long quay between the two bridges. The façade of the somewhat ruined abbey church of the late 12th century is famous for its carpings in Languedoc style, notably the kiss of Judas. It was here that Pierre de Castelnau was murdered, an event which unleashed the full fury of the persecution of the Albigensians in the 13th century. There is a small quay by the bridge of PONT D'ARLES near Bellegarde, but AIGUES MORTES has a good and shady quay-side by the loading ramp just outside the town walls and before the railway bridge. This town, with an entire rectangle of walls round which one can walk, was actually on the sea when it was built in the 13th century as the base port from which, in 1248, St Louis (Louis IX) and a vast army of nobles embarked upon the Seventh Crusade.

At PALAVAS there is a good quay at the maintenance depot beyond the quayside, on the right. FRONTIGNAN has hundreds of metres of quayside, both before and after the lifting-bridge. The smell betrays the town as a refinery area, but it is also the centre of manufacture of a sweet amber-coloured dessert wine. The vintners' co-operative can be visited; and wines can be tasted and loaded aboard at a blending establishment just short of the road bridge and on the right.

For mooring at SÈTE see *Canal du Midi.*

Canal du Midi. From Sète to Toulouse. Length 240 kms. Locks 65, and 13 on the La Nouvelle branch. These are not of standard French size but are both broader (5·5 m.) and shorter (30·0 m.). (The 13 on the La Nouvelle branch are slightly wider.) Draught 1·80 m. Height of lowest bridge, 3·50 m. in the centre.

Note: The bridges are of many different shapes and some

of them cut in more quickly from the apex than do others.
The three lowest are (in increasing order of restriction) at
Carcassonne lock, the road bridge at Colombiers on the long
pound, and the more westerly of the two bridges at Capestang, also on the long pound. Both these last can be avoided
by taking the La Nouvelle entrance (see below) the lowest
bridge on that line being at Truilhas lock, 0·9 km. short of
the junction, the limitation being easily overcome if
necessary by dropping the level in the very short pound concerned. Another possibly very low bridge is the one to the
west of Ariége lock between Agde and Béziers, the water
level here being affected by the level of the River Orb. In
the case of a beamy boat with high superstructure a diagram
of its cross-section should be sent to the chief engineer of
the canal at 2, Port St Etienne, Toulouse, for checking.

Navigation: From the Canal du Rhône à Sète the entry
into the Bassin de Thau is unobstructed and available at any
time, but the entrance from the port itself is crossed by a
number of swing-bridges between the sea and the Bassin,
which open either at set times or when a cargo ship is passing. Enquire of the bridge-keeper at the first bridge.

After the final railway bridge (good mooring to starboard except in a northerly wind), keep straight ahead,
leaving the point on the port hand at least 200 m. distant
and passing outside the buoy off its tip. There is then deep
water throughout the salt lake.

Caution: The Bassin de Thau is famous for its mussel and
oyster fisheries, which involve driving wooden piles and old
railway lines into many acres of the lake, especially on the
northern side. Do not attempt to cross in the dark. The lake
can mount a heavy sea, and at Mèze there is actually a lifeboat stationed. The sheet of water lies in the area of the
Mistral and Tramontana winds, either of which can carry
the mate's washing line away, and if a northerly wind is
blowing it is wise to stay as close to the northern shore as
the piles will allow; similarly, if the wind is from the south,
keep close to that shore. In a westerly gale stay in port.
French Chart No. 5729 is useful but not essential.

The entry to the canal is immediately to the right of Les Onglous lighthouse at the far end. *Caution:* All the way to Bagnas lock (6 kms.) the canal is crossed by eel-nets, the owners of which may need waking with a polite hoot.

All locks are oval, which means that the fenders fore and aft need to be really thick. The ladders are on the gates, downstream side, which means that one cannot climb to the lock-side when the boat is in the pen. The lock-winder has to be put ashore earlier or made to climb the gate. Altogether the Canal du Midi locks are excellent for bringing into use those long-forgotten muscles in many parts of the body.

Hire craft: Blue Line Cruisers (France) Ltd. has an excellent fleet of very well-maintained and modern craft based on Castelnaudary, with alternative facilities of beginning or ending the trip at Marseillan if so desired. The craft are of several sizes, and well suited to the Midi canals. Address : 11 Castelnaudary.

To join the Atlantic with the Mediterranean by a waterway which would avoid both the currents and the pirates of the Gibraltar Strait was for long a dream of rulers and engineers alike. When at last the 'Canal Royal' was constructed it was not the first watershed canal but was certainly the first to join two seas – whence its alternative name, the *Canal des Deux Mers.*

This famous canal was opened to traffic in 1681 and has hardly been changed since that time. In an edict of 1666, Louis XIV declared that this piece of work would indeed be worthy of his patronage, and 'capable of perpetuating through the centuries to come the memory of its author and reflecting the grandeur, liberality and happiness of his reign'. By author he meant himself, and not Pierre-Paul Riquet, Sieur de Bonrepos (d. 1680), who thought up, designed, laid out and constructed the whole of the Canal du Midi, with the help of his engineer Andreossy. Yet in declaring it to be something that would astonish people for centuries, the monarch was certainly right.

Although crossing one of the driest areas of France, the Canal du Midi has never been short of water because Riquet cut a feeder stream 65 kms. long to bring water from the turbulent trout stream of the Alzau in the rain-drenched Montagne Noire. The waterway originally linked the Mediterranean at the specially constructed canal terminus town of Sète with the Atlantic by way of the Garonne, which it entered at Toulouse. The Garonne itself is no longer navigable so far upstream, and the navigation between Toulouse and Castets is by way of the Canal Lateral à la Garone (q.v.).

Crossing the Languedoc and starting from the hot shore of the Mediterranean, the Canal du Midi is a waterway of the sunny south, warm enough for cruising in April and October and very rarely frezing. Built in a period of royal magnificence its detail is often elegant, and it is not in a neurotic hurry to reach its destination. For much of its way it tends to follow contours for as long as possible before jumping to another level. One such pound is 54 kms. in length. Because of the great heat in summer, almost the whole course of the Canal du Midi is planted with plane trees for shade and some groups of these are the originals from the 17th century.

The canal has many remarkable engineering details — the aqueducts by Vauban, the feeder streams, the flood-lock of the Libron, staircase locks, a round lock, siphons, and some very attractive if difficult bridges.

From east to west the scenery changes. At first the canal crosses the great salt lake of the Bassin de Thau with its little ports glinting in the sun, then cuts over the brackish saline flats to the first lock (Bagnas), where at once it assumes a stately tree-lined appearance and passes through Prades lock (normally open through) to spend 1 km. in the River Hérault before reaching the round lock of Agde with an outlet to the sea through Le Grau d'Agde (see below). At Béziers it begins to cross drier country and beyond the great staircase lock of Fonseranes the long pound leads on for a day's voyage through a pleasant farming landscape, with occasional views across to the Pyrenees, which are within easy driving range.

Immediately above the flight of locks the canal enters a long avenue of cypresses, and you may be alarmed at grating sounds apparently emanating from the motor. In fact it is merely the combined noise or love-call of thousands of cicadas. If none alight on the deck you will have an opportunity to see these pleasant insects of the sunny south if you visit the Oppidum of Enserune, where they can be found sitting in bunches on the stems of the pines. Beyond Carcassonne and Castelnaudary the canal climbs more steeply to the summit level, beginning its descent again only 51 kms. short of Toulouse – and ending with a moated tour round the edge of the city to reach Riquet's very fine port basin of the Ponts Jumeaux.

Moorings: It is possible to moor against the bank almost anywhere along the canal, though naturally one should only do so without obstructing the channel. Certain villages such as Homps, Trèbes and Bram have proper quays. At SÈTE one can moor throughout the town, but especially in the basin opposite the railway station, or just short of the final two bridges. Alternatively beyond the railway bridge, starboard side. All are good quay walls. Sète was originally built all of a piece to serve as the canal terminus, and even the main jetties are part of the energetic works put in hand by Riquet in the late 17th century. The town is set at the foot of Mt St Clair, and occupies a narrow strip of land between the sea and the Bassin de Thau. The vista along the canal to the colourful sardine port is delightful, and the whole town has a tang of fish about it.

As Sète is also the major port for importing Algerian wine for blending into standard and well-known brands, a whiff of aperitif drifts over the town as well. Above the fish quays there is a long range of sea-food restaurants ranging from very expensive to cheap but excellent. In summer the town canal is the scene of water jousting tournaments – a sport found throughout this part of the Languedoc, and on no account to be missed. One can usually be certain of seeing the jousts on the Sunday nearest 29th June, on Bastille Day (14th July), the Monday nearest 25th August, and the first Sunday in September. Each of the boats carries not only the jouster on his platform but ten oarsmen and two musicians who play a curious air contemporary with the founding of Sète.

BOUZIGUES is a charming little Mediterranean-style port in the Bassin de Thau, but mooring is possible only for very small craft. MÈZE can provide a good berth alongside, just inside the mole and near the shower for bathers. Much the most picturesque of the Thau ports, Mèze has a mussel-boat harbour as well as the main basin. All the industry can be seen here as the boats come in, and there is good bathing on a sandy beach by the mole. Those who have never floated on a salt lake will find it a pleasant entertainment, and a shower (provided free) is advisable afterwards. In summer there is a strange custom concerned with the tauromachy so widespread around the Mediterranean. A giant bull with sixteen legs (there are eight men inside) is led round the town, roaring fearfully with the aid of a resined rope attached to a tympanum.

MARSEILLAN harbour, further west, is fitted out as a marina. It is useful as a night stop, but the town cannot compare with its neighbour Mèze, for there is no fishing activity based on the port, which originally was more used by wine lighters. At AGDE, pass through the round lock and moor at the quay immediately beyond. It is also possible by using the side entrance of the lock to drop down to the level of the River Hérault below the mill weir, but as the lock has a tendency to silt outside the axes of use it is important to keep the boat lying immediately opposite the side-exit gates, and in a straight line across the lock. At the end of the cut turn downstream through the centre arch of the town bridge, and swing round to bring up just below the cathedral, at a point where there are some trees on the quay-side. Be on the watch for stones and perambulators against the wall if the water is low, and preferably leave the stern

hanging out. For sheer beauty of position this is a mooring
never forgotten.

Agde is an extremely ancient little town, founded by
Phocaean traders from the Aegean, and the museum has
many interesting items from its earliest centuries. The existing fortified cathedral from the 12th century is the third to
exist on the site, and its appearance hints at the fact that the
port was often attacked by moors and other raiders. Agde
is another place where water-jousting occurs, and the boats
Les Deux Agathois are often to be seen moored at the river
bank. The walk down the old fishing port, still very active,
is an interesting one even if somewhat sardine-sprinkled.

The R. Hérault flows broad and deep down toward the
sea, reaching it at the seaside resort of La Grau d'Agde,
4 kms. below the town.

OEUVRE DU LIBRON. Beyond Agde lock the canal passes
through an assemblage of chains, pulleys, girders and sluices.
One can stop and ask the guardien to explain the device,
which is unique in the world. Basically it is a lock with
retractable tunnel-shaped gates through which can run a
vast torrent on a different level. By this ingenious means the
canal can intersect the capricious River Libron even when
it is in violent and heavy flood after sudden rain in the
Cevennes, and navigation is not interrupted. In the same
pound is the marina at CASSAFIERES, where boats may be
hired.

BÉZIERS has plenty of room at the port quay between the
two double locks, a short walk from the centre of the town,
which is perched boldly on a hill overlooking the River Orb
(no longer navigable to the sea). The cathedral of St Nazaire
is a fortified building from the 12th to 15th centuries and
was the scene of the horrible massacre of the Albigensians.
On the feast of St Mary Magdalene in 1209 a vast army of
mercenaries and crusaders, lured by loot and impelled by
xenophobia and promised forgiveness in advance by Pope
Innocent III, broke into the town and murdered the entire
population, right down to children in arms and whether
'heretics' or not. Béziers is also the birthplace of Riquet, and

a statue of him can be seen in the broad avenue which bears his name.

The world's first canal tunnel, the Souterrain de Malpas, is 9 kms. beyond Béziers, and near it one can moor at the bank to take the lane over the top of the tunnel to the Oppidum of Enserune, a recently excavated town from the 6th century B.C. with the remains of houses, grain-silos cut in the rock, and three successive periods of habitation one above the other.

CAPESTANG has good alongside mooring at the quay between the two bridges. In the basin at CARCASSONNE, above the lock, one should moor on the station side where there is more water, and where wine barges are sometimes to be found filling their tanks.

The ancient, triple-walled cité of Carcassonne is probably the most impressive fortified town in France. It was brilliantly restored in the 19th century by Viollet-le-Duc, and no place could give a better idea of the ingenuity of medieval military engineers. It was courageously defended when the crusaders arrived in 1209, fresh from the sack of Béziers, but Simon de Montfort defeated the young commander by the simple device of guaranteeing him a safe passage if he would come out to negotiate, but immediately loading him with chains and putting him in a dungeon. Driven out, the citizens built a new town below it, which was later sacked by the Black Prince on behalf of the English.

Carcassonne originally declined to pay a share of the costs of the canal, so Riquet laid out the line to avoid it. Later the council changed its mind, and the new cutting was dug free – by Prussian soldiers captured at Jena.

CASTELNAUDARY, since the construction of the by-pass, has become a very pleasant and quiet market town perched on a hill beside Riquet's reservoir basin built to equalise the flow for the locks of St Roch. The best mooring for shade is under the plane trees at the entrance to the basin, or there is a good quay at the picturesque old port through the bridge beyond the island.

Ocean lock, NAURQUZE, is close to the point where the

feeder stream enters the canal, the Col de Naurouze being the lowest point on the watershed between Mediterranean and Atlantic. Pass the feeder entry and plaque and moor immediately round the bend, in the right angle, or moor right in the end of the feeder, just below the sill. Nearby is the house of the 'canal guard' where the Duke of Wellington sat at the table to receive the capitulation of Marshal Soult, whose forces he had just put to flight. The guard will lend a mighty key with which one can unlock the gate at the base of the mound which bears the very impressive memorial raised to their great relative by all the Riquets who survived the French Revolution. The obelisk stands on the summit of a cluster of rocks rent and split by the weather. It was by these stones that Riquet is said to have had his sudden inspiration that the secret of the canal lay in bringing to this lowest highpoint between the two seas an unlimited supply of water. The prophet Nostradamus asserted that when the rocks rejoined and formed a single mass again, the end of the world would be imminent. As yet there is no sign of their fusion.

Energetic walkers can explore the feeders or *rigoles* cut by Riquet, but as not every boatman will feel inclined to tramp the entire 65 kms., one can hire a car in Castelnaudary to visit the Black Mountain hamlet of La Galaube and take the trail which starts beside the inn and drops quickly down through the beechwoods to the point where the brook is tapped. A monument put up by General Caraman, himself a Riquet, catalogues the dates of the construction from Riquet's first proposals to the opening of the canal to shipping in 1681. From there the path leads off beside the rippling channel through a forest dense and very still, with only the sound of deer to break the quiet. Wild dianthus glows on the rocks and the brook flashes with trout until, 13 winding kilometres further ahead, it bursts out into the Lampy Lake, the first of Riquet's storage reservoirs.

Further along the feeder and right at the edge of the Black Mountain is the Bassin de St Férreol, the main reservoir of the whole system and large enough to provide a beach with pedalos and sailing craft and trips by motor-boat round the lake. One can penetrate a damp tunnel beneath the dam and admire the giant cocks with which the output is controlled. In the spirit of the golden age of the Sun King, Riquet equipped St Férreol with an ornamental waterfall to cascade through an artificial valley of specimen trees, and a giant gusher.

TOULOUSE. For domestic shopping the Port St Etienne is handy and is used by many barges. Otherwise pass the remaining locks to the Ponts Jumeaux basin. For easy access to the bus-stop (line 22) pull in immediately beyond the branch canal entrance on the left. Otherwise there is a yacht port further down the basin. Toulouse is a rose-pink city full of architectural splendour and supersonic Concorde bangs, but still remarkably Riquet-conscious. A crocque monsieur is in some cafés called a crocque Riquet : a statue of the baron, visible from the canal, stands at the head of the Allées Jean Jaurès and a fine allegorical memorial in Carrara marble adorns the wall of the port he constructed at the Ponts Jumeaux. He is buried at the foot of the massive Orleans pillar in the cathedral of St Etienne at Toulouse, and his own chateau of Bonrepos-Riquet is 25 kms. distant, standing peaceful and decrepit on the edge of a hill. In the dense woodland behind the chateau a solitary elegant column of stone pokes up bravely among the creepers and nettles, but the basins and trial locks and miniature canal built by Riquet as a model on which to work out the details of his fantastic scheme have all vanished beneath the tangle of undergrowth, and patiently await excavation.

St Sernin's church in Toulouse is a famous pagoda-towered building. Begun in the 11th century, it was an important halt for pilgrims on the road to Compostella. On Sundays it is surrounded by a vast market where intriguing bargains of all kinds can be picked up. In the centre of the city the 18th-century Capitole or city hall stretches along one side of a fine arcaded square. Behind it stands the keep of the former Capitole. Old houses survive in many of the streets nearby, and particularly in the Rue St Rome and the

Rue des Changes. The Rue d'Alsace-Lorraine is an excellent shopping street where ladies aboard the ship will probably want to spend half a day.

La Nouvelle branch. This is the short cut to the Emerald Coast and the Costa Brava, from which it is only half a day distant. Leaving the main line of canal 38 kms. along the long pound above Béziers, the side branch drops down 13 locks and through Narbonne to the port of La Nouvelle. The canal is used by grain ships and tanker craft plying to La Nouvelle docks.

Navigation: After the lock (Gailhousty) beyond the two-step lock in Sallèles village, the canal crosses the R. Aude. In flood this needs great care, and in dry weather the course must be correct to avoid stranding. There is a faded diagram on the lock-side – ingeniously sited so that craft coming from the sea only find it after they have made the traverse. Going toward Narbonne follow the cut round the curve and on reaching the river turn hard upstream, keeping 5 to 10 m. from the starboard bank until 15 m. from the overhead cable which once served for a tow-horse ferry. Cut across the river parallel to this, then turn downstream to follow the further shore at 5 to 10 m. *Caution:* In the event of strong current there will of course be more water, so keep well over toward the shore to avoid the draw of the weir.

From the next lock (Raonel) the channel is narrower for 3 kms. and laden barges should be met at dead slow. At Gua lock the canal begins to enter Narbonne.

Caution: Approach the town bridge below Narbonne lock with great care. Being Roman it is old and tired, and a notice to mariners states that captains causing damage will be held responsible. As the bridge carries a double row of houses and shops, to demolish it could prove expensive. The difficulty is that the bridge is immediately below the run-out of the power station and the bridge arch itself consists of two sections, the bores of which do not coincide – quite apart from the pipe fixed to the underside.

From Narbonne the canal narrows again to wind across

20 kms. of bleak salt-marshes and skirt the lagoon of Gruissan before reaching the main port channel of La Nouvelle.

Moorings: NARBONNE has a good quay in the town centre, port side, though by the much-used gents' lavatory. The market is close at hand. Originally on the sea (which has since receded) Narbonne was founded in the 2nd century B.C. and was a busy port. The fortified palace of the Archbishops — one of whom was a fervent supporter of Riquet's canal schemes — was built from the 13th century onward, and restored by Viollet-le-Duc in the 19th. The cathedral itself was begun about the same time, but was constricted by the town walls and never finished. From its tower there is a view across the marshes to the sea, and over to the Pyrenees. In LA NOUVELLE there is no possibility of mooring anywhere beyond the right-angle bend at the end of the canal, but a good stone quay is available just before the corner. *Caution:* Do not attempt to draw in on apparently adequate quaysides in the port channel; in every case there is some very good reason why no ships are there.

La Nouvelle is something of a seaside resort but it lacks all shape or form and might be considered the world's most dismal end, but for the fact that the boulders lining the channel between the moles are covered with extremely large and clean mussels which can be gathered by hand. There is good bathing on a clean sandy beach, to either side of the jetties.

Canal latéral à la Garónne. From Toulouse to the River Garonne upstream of Bordeaux. Length 193 kms. Locks 53. The locks have been lengthened from 30 m. to 38·5 m. Other dimensions are standard French.

The Canal des Deux Mers (The Canal du Midi) originally ended at Toulouse, the ships entering the Garonne for the rest of the journey to Bordeaux. In the 19th century much of the river course was by-passed by a lateral canal, and all navigation now takes this route, the river itself being no longer navigable for more than 51 kms. above Bordeaux.

Navigation: The locks have a pair of tall bars set in recesses, round which a line can be passed. Provided the line is slack enough not to jam, this is an effective if primitive form of rising bollard. *Caution:* the Canal has a copious supply of water from the Garonne at Toulouse, and at each lock a spillway draws off the surplus and returns it below the lock. Unfortunately the design is very bad, both intake and outlet being across the lock entrances. At the upper level a boat moving slowly will have its stern pulled over and a light cruiser steered carelessly can be drawn into the grating and held there. At the lower level the jet shooting across the canal sets up a powerful swirl which is best run over either very slowly or very fast according to taste and experience. A moderate speed is likely to lead to a collision with the bullnose at the entrance.

The locks have no ladders. The lock-winder has to be dropped and picked up on a stone step by the lower gates – an entertainment made even more exciting by the outfall already mentioned.

The canal is unspectacular but most of its route down the Garonne valley is rural and pretty, and besides being part of the cross link from the Mediterranean to the Atlantic this waterway provides an excellent cruising ground. The first 36 kms. below Tolouse are somewhat dull, the course being flanked by the main road and railway, and it is sensible if possible to reach the point where the railway sheers away northward before attempting to moor for a quiet night. At Montech the idyllic Montauban branch (see below) leads off to starboard, and then comes a short run to Castelsarrasin before the canal flies on a magnificent aqueduct over the River Tarn to Moissac, where the boats pass right through the town in a brick-lined trough.

Between Moissac and Agen the canal is at its best, winding along the edge of the limestone cliffs of the Tarn valley then past the immense lake of the headwater of the dam where the two rivers meet, and twisting through the woodland with views down to the turbulent Garonne below. Beyond the port of Agen it leaps the Garonne on another aqueduct 600 m. long, and then drops down sharply to follow the edge of the wide river plain, the locks here being usually several kilometres apart. The course is tree-lined as it passes through the fruit-growing area of the Ageams, and heads toward the land of the white Bordeaux wines.

In spring the entire length from Toulouse to Castets is edged on either side with a broad golden band of water iris, and the copses resound to the call of cuckoo and jay. Even in Moissac and Agen there is likely to be a nightingale within almost embarrassingly loud singing distance, all night long.

Moorings: As the traffic is not heavy, mooring is possible in many places against the bank. Otherwise at GRISOLLES at the quay by the granary, and at MONTECH in the widening before the Montauban arm, close to the first water-slope or *pente d'eau* in the world, opened in 1973. This remarkable mechanism consists of a sloping trough set at a 3/100 incline, up which two locomotives push a plunger, or shield, ahead of which is a puddle containing a barge. Five locks are by-passed, and a barge can make the ascent in 6 or 7 minutes, but for various technical reasons connected with mass and acceleration yachts cannot be taken on the water-slope, but must still use the locks.

Just before Castelsarrasin note the name of Lock 18 (Prades), entirely written in empty wine bottles. CASTEL-SARRASIN has a basin with water up to 1·20 m. at the down-stream end only, and one should lie along that bank at right angles to the canal. Although an easy shopping point the town itself has little of interest, except the quaint public weighbridge and a rather cake-icing town hall.

MOISSAC has a long deep-water quay right in the town, below Lock 25, and this is probably the best lying on all the canal – even if the water tap is on the wrong side of the road.

On crossing the Tarn aqueduct toward the town note the open-work railway bridge nearby, successor to the more solid one which became jammed with debris in March 1930 and formed a dam which diverted the river through the town, washing away houses and causing many deaths. When the water rose right over it the bridge collapsed, and for many months the expresses used the canal towpath. On the bend at Lock 23 (Cacor) one can still see the remains of the temporary railway embankment from that time.

Walking from the quay into the town one passes through the Rue de l'Inondation de 1930 and in the square there is a covered market presented by the city of Paris to the distressed people of Moissac. Further on lies the abbey church of St Peter, the carving on which probably represents the summit of Languedoc art. The portal (1130) is a powerful piece of design, its interlocking winged beasts giving it a decidedly oriental flavour, and the peaceful cloisters surrounding a huge cedar tell many strange tales in the intricate carving on the capitals. Another attraction at Moissac is the riverside *uvarium* where the local Golden Chasselas dessert grape may be tasted, and there is also a stall on the Boulevard Lakanal where in summer bunches of the grape are given away free to all comers.

The two locks leading to the Tarn are most regrettably closed, and the sight of a ruined lock in the river is sad indeed.

The port of VALENCE D'AGEN is a grass-banked basin among the trees and is a particularly peaceful place to lie overnight, with nightingales in attendance. The little town is an unsophisticated and busy place of market squares, and near the port is one of the finest public wash-houses in France, a semicircle of scrubbing bays surrounding a series of elegant stone basins controlled by little sluices.

AGEN is a prosperous town of fruit merchants and prunestuffers, with a long quay at the port, to which one is invited by notices 1 km. on either side. At BUZET, moor either in the entrance of the Descente en Baise locks (long disused, as the Baise is no longer navigable) or against the bank to starboard, just short of the bridge.

Grassy basins with some mud and weed are also available at DAMAZAN, MEILHAN, and at MAS D'AGENAIS, a pleasant little town built behind the ruins of a medieval castle from which there is a fine view of the canal and the Garonne. The

town still keeps its inhabitants up-to-date by means of a
town crier equipped with side-drum and megaphone. At
CASTETS-EN-DORTHE the stopping point is above Lock 52
(*not* 53, where the bank is needed for craft arriving on the
tide). The most notable feature of the village is the terrace
behind the church, from which there is a commanding outlook over the wide plain, the vineyards of Sauternes and
Entre-Deux-Mers, and the tide-locks where the canal comes
to its end.

Montauban branch. Length 9 kms. Locks 9.

This side-trip is compulsive for those with a flair for
adventure. The canal has plenty of water and none of the
awkward outfalls on the main line, and it proceeds splendidly down an avenue of trees and fishermen's rods to a
quiet and grassy basin just short of the River Tarn, the exit
to which is now closed because the Tarn itself is unfortunately no longer navigable. The canal carries some traffic
(about one boat in three weeks, but more during the harvest)
and so the locks are maintained to a standard in which
they can just be opened by brute force and with the
assistance of the old ladies (often crippled pensioners) to
whom they are entrusted. In spite of the hard labour the
keepers are overjoyed to see a boat, and wrestle away with
determination.

MONTAUBAN is very well worth the filling or emptying of
18 locks on the round trip. The basin is only twenty minutes'
walk from the town centre, most of the way being by the
rampart of the high river wall and then along the quay of
the very picturesque medieval river port with a marked
Spanish influence. The sight of a derelict lock on this magnificent reach is enough to make a boatman weep, for when
the Tarn was itself navigable there were altogether 31 locks
and ships could reach Sault-de-Sabo, 109 kms. further upstream.

The 205 m.-long brick and stone bridge was built as long
ago as 1304, and at its western end a flood scale easily
explains its great height. Beyond it the town stands on a
hill, a range of palatial Renaissance residences ending in the

Archbishop's Palace (1664), now the Ingres museum. The Place Nationale is a most picturesque arcaded square of 17th-century brick houses, mercifully not turned into a car park. Near the museum a stall offers local fruit free to all.

River Garonne. Navigable from Castets-en-Dorthe to Bec d'Ambés, where it becomes the Gironde. Length 79 kms. No locks. Tidal throughout.

From the lock at the end of the Canal latéral à la Garonne the river leads broad and determined toward Bordeaux, and it can safely be navigated according to the Thirds Rule. All islands should be left to port except the last one, at the extreme edge of Bordeaux itself.

Caution: The current flows swift and swirling through Langon bridge, and because of shallows the river above this point should only be run at more than half tide.

The Garonne is lined almost all the way to Bordeaux by trees, beneath which stand countless rickety fishing platforms on tall stilts, each equipped with a large drop net for friture, diminutive eels, or whatever may be passing by. Here and there a village with vineyards approaches the water, but most of the course is secluded and shut away until the very edge of Bordeaux.

Moorings: To stop before Bordeaux is not easy, there being no quay of any description. Wine names such as Ste Croix du Mont, Barsac and Loupiac are to be found all along the course but there is no chance of visiting the places except by anchoring and rowing ashore – and this is not very advisable in a strong tideway where the river may also carry a lot of debris such as tree trunks. However, the gravel barges and staging at CADILLAC provide a reasonable mooring close to the Porte de Mer, a gateway in the almost complete range of walls from the 14th century. Centre-piece of the town is the early 17th-century moated palace of the Dukes of Épernon.

BORDEAUX begins suddenly, and from the third bridge it is majestic in its lay-out. This bridge is Napoleonic and has seventeen handsome arches of brick and stone, navigation being through any except those at the extreme edges. Beyond it the long curving waterfront opens out, ships of the West Africa trade and coasters loading Bordeaux wine being ranged along the quay in front of the splendour of the 18th-century Place de la Bourse. (The Customs office for yachts is in the Hôtel des Douanes at its upstream edge.) Mooring space is usually available just beyond the first large hangar on the quay, L.

Bordeaux has in fact all the appearance of a capital — which it was, being the chief city of Aquitaine. By the marriage of King Henry II to Eleanor, divorced wife of Louis VII, Aquitaine and other vast territories of France became English, and the stage was set for the Hundred Years War. It was the English who called the local red wine claret, on account of its clarity.

There is a wreck on the bend of the river opposite the Place de la Bourse, and the corner should not be clipped at any state of tide, but the red buoy scrupulously left to starboard. At the lower edge of the port the Garonne is spanned by the Pont d'Aquitaine, a high suspension bridge opened in 1967. Just before it there is a yacht club, L, but the moorings are exposed to violent tidal current and possible depredations from local vagrants and inebriates, apart from which they are too far out of the city to be convenient. Below this point the river continues featureless to its confluence with the Dordogne.

River Dordogne. Navigable from Lamothe-Montravel to the Gironde at Bec d'Ambès. Length 84 kms. No locks. Depth variable, but at least 2 m. up to Libourne.

Navigation: After the winter snows have thawed in the Auvergne, or after prolonged rain, the Dordogne will rise several feet and become fully navigable to a few kilometres beyond Castillon-la-Bataille. It is a tricky river, but should not deter those with some experience of difficult navigations. The tidal effect persists over the whole course with a *mascaret* or bore at times below Libourne, but in the higher reaches the difficulty is to be sure where the channel is. Until the 1930's, when barges went right up to Bergerac, the navigation channel was about 5 to 15 m. from the towpath. The last published chart (1911) shows the path on the right bank from Libourne upstream, with the channel always close to that shore (port hand going upstream). However, the last dredging was in 1925, and the drag dredgers met on the river at the present time are helping themselves to gravel and are not really concerned with making things better for shipping which does not exist. The deeps they dig will of course alter the flow, and so will silting, reed beds, massive shoals forming round sunken tree trunks, and erosion by spring floods.

Nevertheless, the right-bank channel still survives to some extent. However unreasonable it may appear, all islands and aits should be left to starboard ascending. From Libourne up to the bridge at Branne it is safe to follow the Thirds Rule, but above the bridge keep $\frac{1}{3}$L to about 100 m. below the ait 3 kms. ahead, then cut sharply across to within 10 m. of the wall which supports the road on the tight bend through Vignonet village. Resume the Thirds Rule until round the sharp bend by the bridge of St Jean-de-Blagnac, then imagine the towpath to exist on the port hand and close the shore beside it for the final 9 kms. to Castillon.

The mere name of the Dordogne conjures up a picture of a rippling river cut deep in limestone, its twisting course trickling shallow past cliffs riddled with caves where once our ancestors tried their hand at painting wild life on the walls. Those glamorous upper reaches are only accessible to the kayakist, but further downstream the Dordogne is used by small tankers and other craft up to about 300 tons. A boatman heading from the Biscay rollers toward Bordeaux and the calm of the Canal du Midi will find the Dordogne a side-trip well worth a few days, particularly if he likes to enliven his voyages with some adventure.

Formerly the river was navigable to Bergerac and beyond, with 10 locks in the higher reaches, and the traffic was barges hauled by oxen. A few such craft may be seen as pensioners at Castillon, or wrecked, but the oxen have gone. Although the modern theoretical limit is given as Ste Foy-la-Grande (106 kms.) this would only be practicable in a boat of very shallow draught, and in flood time. At some times of year the limit is Libourne (43 kms.), which can easily be reached on the tide. To that point there is maritime red-or-black buoyage.

At Bourg the river is nearly one mile wide, and it only narrows slowly as it leads up past the land of Entre-Deux-Mers — the two seas between which this wine is produced being not the Atlantic and Mediterranean but merely the estuaries of the Garonne and Dordogne. For the first 35 kms. the scenery is undramatic, and there is not a quay or jetty, nor indeed anything but a few ancient wooden wrecks stuck in the bushes on the bank. Then at Vayres the Dordogne changes its habit and become more mindful of the eye of the beholder, starting with the splendid spread of the Château de Vayres, restored in the 17th century and recently provided with formal garden and topiary in the style of Louis XIII. From Vayres onward the stream twists and turns between magnificent vineyard properties and small hamlets of fishermen.

The Dordogne is the world's best river for lampreys, which ascend the river to spawn in spring. The lamprey is curious in its habits, and so are the lamprey fishermen, of which there seem to be hundreds. Each has a boat which he rows across the river, all the while paying out a long net which floats. The shipping channel seems to be the favourite hunting ground, and wherever there is a little man in a little boat there is sure to be a net stretching from him to a lamp floating on a piece of cork a hundred yards or more away. *Caution:* Lampreys may be delicious enough to have killed King Henry I, but the nets are expensive and should not be run down.

Moorings: Only 3 kms. from the Gironde lies BOURG-SUR-GIRONDE, which oddly enough is *sur* the Dordogne. It is easily identified by the tall and rusted funnel of the wartime wreck of an Italian steamer lying almost in the town.

Bourg is a place of balconied houses of curiously Spanish appearance, the port (with no harbour) lying quiet and sun-faded at the foot of a cliff on which stands the non-marine part of the town, reached by long flights of steps. Mooring alongside the ferry for refinery workers is possible, as the ship only runs across to Ambès at the end of each 8-hour shift.

LIBOURNE was once a flourishing port, and it carries its English connection proudly in the name – for it was called after Roger of Leyburn, English governor during part of the Hundred Years War. Libourne is now a market town with a quay where railway sleepers from the Périgord are loaded into the barges which just occasionally remember to come and collect them, and inviting though this jetty may appear it can be relied upon to provide the most uncomfortable night's mooring in the world, for it is set exactly at the place where two strong tides meet, the fast ebb of the Dordogne already twisted and swirled by the thick buttresses of the handsome Louis XVIII toll-bridge being struck violently in the ribs by the ebb of the River Isle which runs in on its other side. Combined with an evening surfeit of *Lamproie à la Bordelaise* and an overdose of nearby St Emilion the resulting swirls can produce an acute sense of paranoia. Much better is to moor along the quays of the old port in the River Isle and eat the lampreys in peace. Long lines are essential (5½ m. rise of tide). Moor only by a piece of high wall, or the boat may be left on the quayside.

The town is now a busy one, and there may be a cattle market under the plane trees along the Isle. The Grand-Place is arcaded with buildings from the 16th century and later, and one massive gateway survives from the ramparts once manned by the English.

ST EMILION is best visited by bus from Libourne (5 kms.), as it lies just off the river. Clumped on a collection of lime-stone hillocks, it consists of a mass of ecclesiastical ruins built over and under the ground, among which the famous town of rich red wine has grown up. It has a 'monolithic' underground church with three naves – that is, a church cut

out of the solid rock – and there are catacomb-type ceme-
teries. One can visit the cave and spring where St Emilion
is said to have lived after he came here from Brittany in
the 8th century. *Caution:* Married women who sit on his
stone chair are alleged to give birth within twelve months.

The town is surrounded by vineyards, many of them
having famous wine-list names. Château Ausone reminds
one that Ausonius, who praised the Moselle (q.v.), came
from these parts.

CASTILLON-LA-BATTAILLE is neither moated nor fortified,
but merely a country town on a steep rise above the
Dordogne. At its foot lies an old steamer converted to a
crane-stage for the gravel lighters. Once this vessel carried
convicts to the Île de Ré prison but like the handsome ox-
drawn sailing barges still moored in the stream it now has a
quieter life and offers a hospitable mooring to any boat
penetrating thus far up the river. As for the Battaille, about
fifteen minutes' walk along the riverside lane leading upstream is a monument where Talbaud (i.e. John Talbot,
Earl of Shrewsbury) was slain with a battle-axe after being
Governor of Guyenne for 53 years. 'All will be ours, now
bloody Talbot's slain' says Charles the Dauphin, in *King
Henry VI, part I.* Another monument to the battle is about
1 km. distant beside the road N136. Talbot is of special
interest to geneticists because the effigy on his tomb at Whit-
church in Shropshire shows an abnormality of the finger
joints still present in his descendants 500 years later.

River Isle. Navigable from St Denis-de-Pile to its confluence
with the R. Dordogne at Libourne. Length 20 kms. No
locks. Officially it is held to be navigable up to Lock 40
(disused) at Laubardement (31 kms.), but this is very
optimistic. Formerly, the 40 locks fed up to Perigueux, 110
kms. further, and one can only lament the disappearance of
such a fine cruising river.

Navigation: As the Isle is narrow, and trees have collapsed
into it from both banks, the course is up the middle. For the
first 15 twisting kilometres, there are no difficulties. Not

until the bridges at Galgon is one likely to touch down and
have to await an extra foot of flow, and it is only at St Denis-
de-Pile that more extensive shoals may put an end to the
voyage of boats drawing 1 m.

Caution: Fishing derricks may be slung right across the
stream. In the afternoon their owners may be sleepy with
vin rouge. The appearance above Galgon of a soldier waving
hysterically will mean that shooting is in progress round the
bend, the targets on one bank and snipers on the other. An
attitude of non-comprehension should secure a safe passage.

Tidal throughout, the Isle is nevertheless not like the
Dordogne, but is narrow and its banks are generally edged
with copses or meadows. For the first few kilometres the
fishing derricks persist in patches, but thereafter the stream
is deserted except by warblers and an occasional angler.
Immediately above Libourne the river winds round the
foot of the hill of Fronsac, a hamlet known by name from
its red wine, but after that the countryside is not unlike that
of the Upper Thames.

Moorings: LIBOURNE (see under *Dordogne*). Otherwise
none. Anchoring in mid-stream is easy, there being no
commercial traffic.

INLAND ROUTE, CHANNEL TO THE BALTIC

It is possible to reach the Baltic from Calais or le Havre, or even from Marseille, without straying outside canals and river estuaries. Much of the course crosses Holland, which can in fact be traversed by an almost infinite number of routes. The goal should be Groningen, and the course here outlined starts at the R. Scheldt so as to form a continuation of the route described under *Intra-Coastal Waterway* (q.v.). In general, all waterway towns and villages in Holland are so well equipped with proper quaysides that there is no need to give detailed information about moorings. Butcher and baker and grocer are often alongside, or arrive water-borne in their own boats.

Before crossing Northern Holland it is wise when in Amsterdam to call at the Bureau voor Watertoerisme (see p. 14) and acquire detailed waterway maps for the whole intended route. Otherwise you can become lost in a surfeit of canals.

The *Scheldt* estuary (Wester Schelde) can be reached at three points – Vlissingen (Flushing) at the mouth, Terneuzen on its southern shore, and through Antwerp. There is no scheme to shut off this vast tideway in Delta Plan fashion, and because of the number of ocean ships using it one may assume that the Scheldt will always remain open, with a tidal range of 4 to 5 m.

In 1975 the new canal from Antwerp to the Hollandsch Diep near Wilemstad will be open, but this will not affect boats coming from the Channel. They will still have the choice of two waterways leading northward from the

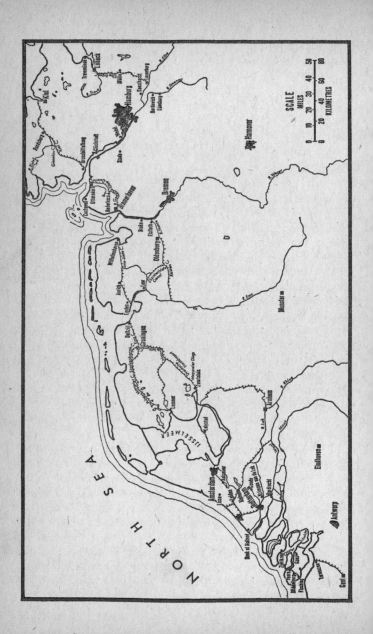

Scheldt. These are the Walcherens Canal and the South Beveland Canal.

The *Walcherens Canal* starts at Flushing and leads straight across the island of Walcheren to Veere, 15 kms., one lock at either side.

Moorings: At FLUSHING in the Dok, a small inlet curving away to the left about 1 km. beyond the entrance lock. This is the only stopping point which is not cut off from the town by the canal itself, which increases the walking distance to the town centre from 300 m. to at least 2 kms. Flushing has a fine promenade with a good sandy beach for those who can contemplate with equanimity a bathe in the North Sea. MIDDELBURG has quays in the main canal and an inlet on the port (town) side which once was part of the complex of town canals and moat. This leads almost into the centre. Destroyed during the Second World War, Middleburg has been well restored. The 16th-century City Hall has a fine belfry, the sound of which dominates the air. A simple way of touring the whole island of Walcheren is to visit the scale model in Middelburg's park. At VEERE pass the lock and turn hard to port into the former sea harbour, now no longer tidal since the Veersche Gat and Zandkreek inlets became the Veersemeer under the Delta Plan. Veere has an air of sadness, as though regretting that its merchants' houses are becoming boutiques, now that the fishing fleet and cloth trade have both vanished. The Schotse Huizen recall the 16th-century connection with Scotland. The vast half-completed church and the delightful spiky town hall of the same period stand out as landmarks across the flat wind-swept countryside.

The *Veersemeer (Veere Lake)* ends in a dam west of Veere, and at a lock in the Zandkreekdam to the east. It is a large dull sheet of water but a good sailing area. 3 kms. beyond the Zandkreekdam lock and on the island of South Beveland is Sas van Goes, with a lock leading to a 5-km. canal which runs to its end at GOES. This is a pleasant side-trip for those who are not in a hurry to reach the Baltic. One can proceed as far as the town quay at Goes itself, where on Tuesdays the market for South Beveland is held on the Grote Markt, which is dominated by the great 16th-century church and the City Hall. Another side-trip is to turn to port out of the Zandkreek, pass through the legs of the immense Ooster Schelde bridge and take the cut up to ZIERIKZEE, 2 kms. with one lock usually open. This town on the island of Schouwen-Duiveland was the scene of fearful struggles against the Spaniards in the 16th century but now is a quiet, half-forgotten spot with gateways and towers and the massive incomplete tower of the vanished St Lieven's cathedral.

The alternative route to the Ooster Schelde is through the *South Beveland Canal,* which leaves the Wester Schelde 32 kms. above Vlissingen, at Hansweert. Length 9 kms. Locks at either end (in each case three in parallel, to cope with the vast mass of Rhine shipping on the Antwerp and Gent runs). The locks are manned night and day at all times. The canal debouches into the Ooster Schelde at Wemeldinge, 6 kms. east of the entrance to the Goes canal. Both termini are small towns of ships' provisioners and nothing else. Moorings are available on piles in the outer harbours, but one is not likely to wish to stop.

Caution: According to the state of the tide you may go up, or down, when locking in either direction. Keep the lines loose until you are sure which. At spring tides arrive well in advance of high water, as the locks have the unusual feature that they cannot be opened when the water is too high, and there may be a wait of 2 or 3 hours.

Zeeland. The channels are well buoyed, and even without *Admiralty Chart No. 192* it would be hard to lose the way amid such an interminable flowing of shipping. The course leads through the Ooster Schelde, Keeten, Mastgat, Krammer and Volkerak channels to the lock at Willemstad on the corner of the Hollandsch Diep. There are no places of note on the way, though harbours of refuge are available at Zijpe and Dintelsas. Beyond the lock the attractive town of WILLEMSTAD lying within its star of moat and ramparts now has permanent deep water alongside, and also has a large yacht harbour. The town basin is a quiet point for an overnight stop. 25 kms. ahead and on the Dordtsche Kil is DORDRECHT (DORDT), situated at the busiest water cross-roads in the world.

Moorings: At all costs out of the stream, which is churned throughout the day and night. There is a yacht harbour reached through the first entry to starboard beyond the Grote Kerk (Great Church), or one may proceed another 700 m. to the next entrance, crossed by a black double-bascule bridge. This gives access to the Wolwevershaven, a quiet dormitory for tugs, police-boats and maybe your own craft. Dordrecht now resounds to the hoots and toots of ships, but once was the scene of the great theological debate (1618–19) which gave birth to the Dutch Reformed and Dutch Remonstrant churches. A statue shows the de Witt brothers, victims of mob fury in 1672.

To port and opposite the Wolwevershaven is the *Noord* (i.e. the Rhine, q.v.) which carries the main bulk of shipping to Rotterdam. After 9 kms. this converges with the *Lek* branch of the Rhine to become the *Nieuwe Maas.*

After 6 kms. the *R. Hollandsche Ijssel* flows in on the starboard hand at Krimpen aan der Lek. Turn into this, giving the point a wide berth, and run up it to the Julianasluis at Gouda, 21 kms. distant. The run can be done at all states of the tide, but is best done on the flood (which begins about 3 hrs. after L.W. Hook of Holland and lasts for 5 hrs.).

Moorings: None in the tideway, but at GOUDA either in the first turn to starboard, $1\frac{1}{2}$ kms. beyond the lock, or by adventurously following the Ijssel round the edge of the city (i.e. to the right before the Julianasluis) and entering the town canal system through the Mallegatsluis, $1\frac{1}{2}$ kms. ahead on the port hand. Gouda is the home of the less soapy of the two main species of Dutch cheese. It also has a church (St Jans, i.e. St John's) from the 16th century, famous for its large number of remarkably fine stained-glass windows – some six dozens in number – mostly of the original period but others showing such modern scenes as the Liberation of the Netherlands in 1945. The City Hall from about 1600 is one of the finest in all Holland, and stands gloriously uncluttered and alone on the market place.

From the Julianasluis the *R. Gouwe* is followed northward through a market gardening and horticultural area for 15 kms. to Gouwsluis, where there is a water cross-roads immediately beyond the two bridges. The railway bridge opens frequently, but only for very short intervals. At the road bridge the Gouwe dues are levied with a tin on a string (by returning south-bound traffic they are paid at the staging just before the railway bridge, and the ticket must be handed in at the Julianasluis). Ahead is the *Aar Canal* which leads to the *Drecht* (1 lock) and the *R. Amstel* (one lock at the entrance to Amsterdam, which is 38 kms. from Gouwsluis).

The route by the Amstel is probably the quickest, but an alternative is to turn left at Gouwsluis into the *Oude Rijn*, which once was in fact the Rhine. This is a down-to-earth waterway of brickyards, wharves, shipbuilding and all manner of busy trades. After a few kilometres and beyond Alphen, turn right under a lifting bridge at 's Molenaarsbuurt into the *Heinmanswetering*, which leads through the wide lake of the *Braassemermeer* to Oudewetering (9 kms.), a long village astride the waterway.

At the T-junction at the end of the village the canal runs into the *Ringvaart*, a ring canal surrounding the Harlemmermeerpolder, which is continually pumped out into it. From this point to the Nieuwe Meer lock at the edge of Amsterdam is 21 kms. if one turns right, 43 if one follows the ring left-handed.

The Ringvaart passes through many of the best of the bulb fields, and on the right-hand course it also connects

with meers which have excellent sailing possibilities. It cuts
past AALSMEER, scene of the daily (not Sundays) pot-plant
auctions which are open to the public and should be visited
early in the morning – about 6 a.m. There are two auction
halls, both accessible from the yacht wharves in the
Westeinder plas (lake) or from the small town cut leading
off the Ringvaart at Aalsmeer itself. A sufficiently persistent
maze-runner can thread the minor canals and cuts and
get within easy walking distance of the auction establishment. Keen gardeners can ask at Aalsmeer's V.V.V.
(Tourist office) for permission to visit horticultural establishments.

Beyond Aalsmeer the canal passes Schiphol Airport, which
actually has a landing stage where yachtsmen can draw
alongside to meet or deposit members of their crews.

Left-handed the Ringvaart passes by the entrance to the
Kager plassen (lakes), a favourite sailing area with an outlet
to Leiden, and then by a side branch of 1 km. leading to
LISSE, centre of the bulb industry and site of the famous
Keukenhof gardens where all the finest varieties are grown
in what once was a kitchen garden. This is a sight not to be
missed if traversing Holland in the early spring. The gardens
are about 1½ kms. distant from the canal end, but a bus
runs frequently from the village.

From the Ringvaart, Amsterdam is reached through the
Nieuwe Meer, north-east of Schiphol Airport, at the further
end of which a lock leads into the vast network of city canals.
Instead of mooring far away from the city in some distant
yacht harbour on the wrong side of the 400 m. broad R. Ij
(or Y), any boatman who follows the directions carefully can
penetrate right to the heart of Amsterdam, and sleep amid
the tinkle of the city carillons. His crew will probably thank
him, for the difference between the two situations is
immense.

Routes through Amsterdam. Leaving the Nieuwemeersluis
(Lock), keep straight ahead along the Schinkel and
Kostverlorenvaart through six bridges in 5 kms. These

bridges are all manned and will open in the daytime (on Sundays also) except during the morning and evening rush hours (7.45 to 9.00 and 17.00 to 18.00). After the sixth bridge fork right at the junction and enter the Kattensloot. At the end (about 300 m.) pass under the bridge and bear left into the Singelgracht, and through three more bridges into the open water of the Houthaven (Timber Harbour). The exit straight ahead is into the North Sea Ship Canal, where you should turn right, pass the main railway station on the starboard hand, and prepare to duck beneath the railway, choosing your route according to whether or not your craft has more than 2·8 m. of freeboard.

Fixed bridge route (2.8 m. clearance). Take the second opening to starboard at the end of the station, pass the road and rail bridges, and enter the relatively peaceful water of the Oosterdok. Cross this diagonally and take the first opening on the further side, under a fixed bridge. This is the *Oude Schans,* a broad waterway of great charm which passes several side canals with possible mooring places. Straight ahead there is one more fixed bridge before the canal reaches a dead end.

Lifting-bridge route. Take the second entry past the railway station, also into the Oosterdok. Harbour tolls are no longer levied for foreign yachts staying under one week. *Caution:* Traffic is heavy through the bridge hole, and the trip-boats are not always intelligently managed.

Cross the Oosterdok diagonally and take the next opening beyond the fixed bridge route. This is the *Nieuwe Heerengracht* which runs under a number of lifting-bridges directly to the Amstel. The bridges open in the daytime except during the two rush-hours.

Moorings: AMSTERDAM. In a city with a spider's web of waterways this is largely a matter of personal choice, but mine is the *Groenburgwal,* a small opening parallel to the Oude Schans. It can no longer be reached from that waterway since the upper end was filled in. But if coming via the lifting-bridge route turn right and then take the second canal on your right. The Groenburgwal is to all intents and purposes a dead end and spanned by the most elegant wooden bridge in the city, hard by the English church. There is easy domestic shopping locally, and the whole of the incomparable network of Renaissance canals can be toured by dinghy. Amsterdam is not the capital but it is the main city of Holland, and one which demands to be explored by water. Its sights, from Rembrandt's House (passed on the fixed bridge route) to the Rijksmuseum, are too many to be described here but are nearly all directly accessible by dinghy or suitably small craft.

From Amsterdam to the North. Return to the Ij, cross to its further side and follow the shore round to the Oranjesluizen (Orange Locks), about 4 kms., manned day and night. The water beyond is the *Ijsselmeer,* or what remains of it now that the polders have been formed. In good weather one can keep to the north and take what open water remains beyond Lelystad, 35 kms., the new town at the centre of the poldering activities. The quickest route is undoubtedly to make for the *Prinses Margriet Canal,* just to the west of Lemmer, and lock through into the main route which crosses the bleak but beautiful Friesland lakes toward the Sneekermeer and the main trunk canal to Groningen (93 kms. 2 locks).

Caution: An up-to-date chart of the Ijsselmeer is essential, as there is no knowing what the engineers may have been up to in the last fortnight.

The Ijsselmeer can be really dangerous in bad weather, and even barges are occasionally sunk by its short sharp seas. It can easily be avoided by taking the alternative sheltered route along the strip of water up to 2 kms. broad which has been left between the new polders and the shore, a long and slowly curving sheet of fresh water which goes by the names of *Gooimer, Eemmeer* and *Veluwemeer,* in succession. Turning eastward to Zwartsluis (127 kms. and 3 locks from the Ij), you can take a variety of routes, but the most direct is by the *Meppeler Diep, Drentsche Hoofdvaart* and *Noord Willemsvaart,* uneventful but rural waterways which lead to Groningen, 83 kms. and 12 locks distant. This course is not very heavily used by barges, and waiting for locks will be unlikely. However, the bridges and locks remain closed on Sundays.

At Groningen, make sure you are leaving the city by the right canal, which should preferably be the *Ems Canal* (*Eems Kanaal*), the main waterway used by coasters; it is no longer possible to enjoy the quiet charm of the adjacent and older *Damster Diep*. Although the Ems Canal is open until midnight it is closed on Sundays, and so is the lock at Delfzijl (26 kms.), which leads out into the harbour on the southern side of the Ems estuary. From this point the alternative routes to the Baltic will be given in greater detail.

River Ems (Estuary). The crossing to Emden (which is *not* the port plainly visible straight across the water but is further upstream, 17 kms.) is easy and can be made at any time in reasonable weather, but a fairly strong tide runs in the Ems, and it is simpler and quicker to leave Delfzijl (Dover + 0.10) at low water to half flood. A sea chart is essential because the Dollart area has plenty of submerged obstructions. Charts can easily be obtained in Groningen or Delfzijl. (*Admiralty Chart No. 3509.*)

Navigation: Keep rigorously to the channel. There are groynes and training walls outside it. Off the entrance to Emden a choice has to be made. One can either take the Ems–Jade Canal to Wilhelmshaven, or proceed up the Ems to the Küsten Canal. Bremerhaven can be reached either way, but the first route involves a coastal passage of some hours round notorious sands ominously studded with towers on stilts, thoughtfully provided for the preservation of shipwrecked mariners.

EMDEN. The harbour entrance lock is accessible at all times. At the inner end of the port an excellent floral mooring in the Ratsdelft is handy for shopping. Emden's interest lies mainly in its history, for it was so close to the Netherlands that it became the port to which refugee merchants easily escaped during the Spanish domination of their country in the 16th century. Once very rich it later declined, but rose again with the cutting of the Dortmund–Ems Canal which made it the port for Ruhr imports of iron ore. Totally destroyed during the Second World War, it has been rebuilt with plenty of open space, but is not worth a special detour.

Ems–Jade Canal. Length 72 kms. Locks 6, minimum length 33 m. There are more than 40 swing-bridges, all of them manned – though distant hooting may be needed to awaken the East-Frisian bridge-swingers.

The canal is a weird and almost deserted waterway built to take coal to the Kaiser's warships, and crossing the strange and lonely East-Frisian countryside, much of which has been reclaimed by flooding the marshes with Ems dredgings. The route crosses tracts of moor and blasted heath, and in parts is a paradise for birds, especially avocets. Half way along lies the county town of AURICH, with a curious custom at Ascensiontide, when children strew a route with flower petals. Possible side-trips along fen waterways exist for the intrepid, through ancient locks with a length of only 23·7 m.

WILHELMSHAVEN is a hideous half-deserted Victorian Prussian naval base with no redeeming features whatsoever. It should be left behind as soon as the weather permits, but not before. There is a ship-lock into the Jade-busen (Bosom of Jade), an inlet much bleaker than it sounds. Sea charts and calm weather are essential for the passage round dangerous sands to the Weser, or direct to the Elbe.

ALTERNATIVE ROUTE

River Ems. Locks to Dörpen two. Although officially termed the Dortmund–Ems Canal even in these lower reaches, the Ems above Emden is at first a typical river tideway, and much time can be wasted by trying to run up on the ebb. The villages are mostly hidden behind the banks and the voyage is pleasant rather than spectacular.

Customs clearance is at the first lock, at Herbrum. There

is water enough for laden craft to lie at piles in the approach channel even at full ebb.

Moorings: A good overnight stop is at LEER, a pleasant town with an inland port on the R. Leda. Turn left into this river shortly after the first bridge, which takes the Europa-road E35 over the Ems. Fork left again into the entrance lock at Leer harbour, and moor beyond it in the town centre, beside the town hall.

A very determined small-boat man can explore through wildest East Frisia by following the Leda upstream, passing the tidal barrage which will be raised on arrival, and losing himself in the maze of drains beyond. The routes are only suitable for boats of less than 1 m. draught, but they are used by local peat barges and the like. One course leads through to the R. Jümme and the Nordgeorgesfehn Canal (8 locks, 50 kms.) which eventually reaches the Ems–Jade Canal at Macardsmoor : another leads to the Elisabethfehn Canal (4 locks) and thence to the Küsten Canal about half way along its course, thus providing a short cut in distance (but more doubtfully in time) on the inland route to the Baltic.

Küsten Canal. From the Ems at Dörpen to the R. Hunte at Oldenburg. Length 69 kms. Locks only at either end. A comparatively straight and uneventful waterway across the moorland and fens, this canal is the main barge route from the Ruhr to Bremen and Bremerhaven, and is much used. High banks shut off the view, which would probably consist of peat moors.

Moorings: Outside Dörpen lock, and in the Hunte tide-way at OLDENBURG, preferably alongside other craft. Oldenburg is a busy centre of agriculture and horse-breeding but has no great architectural features.

River Hunte. Tidal all the way, this river passes through nowhere on its way from Oldenburg to the R. Weser at Elsfleth, 25 kms.

River Weser. Tidal and dotted with commercial ports such as Brake and Nordenham, the lower Weser is a pleasant stream with plenty of traffic – ocean-goers, barges large and small, and fishing vessels and week-end sailors from Bremen. The channel is deep and well marked, but a sea chart is advisable. (*Admiralty Chart No. 3506.*)

Moorings: Apart from commercial quays, at anchor off the long island of the Harrier Sand by Brake, and in the small harbour of Sandstedt on the right bank below Brake.

Caution: Watch for ferries and trawlers emerging from the River Geeste entrance at Bremerhaven.

For an account of the river above Elsfleth, see *River Weser.*

River Geeste. The entrance is obvious, the mouth of the Geeste being between two prominent piers. Round to the right, inside, a twin lock available at any hour gives access to the Fischereihafen, which provides the only serviceable alongside moorings in the city.

Tidal as far as Schiffdorf lock and barrage (5 kms.), the lower Geeste should be run at about half tide on the flood, to ensure water enough in the river but not so much that the lock cannot be entered because of reduced headroom under the structure over the gates. (H.W. = Dover + 1.9).

The lock-keeper will put a rule up the boat to check that it will clear the railway bridge on the Cuxhaven line which, although still a day's journey distant, is the lowest bridge between Calais or le Havre and the Baltic. The maximum headroom at normal water level is 2·95 m. but this can be reduced by floods.

Moorings: At BREMERHAVEN, inside the Fischereihafen, or below the lock. The Fischereihafen contains one of Europe's greatest fish markets, with auctions daily from 6 a.m. Visitors are not expected, but are very welcome. The same basin contains an oceanographical laboratory and fisheries museum. Half the German fishing fleet is based on Bremerhaven, but otherwise it is a typical phoenix town of chain stores ringing up a wealth of cash at their tills. It was originally built by the City State of Bremen to provide a

deep-water port at any state of the tide, the reaches nearer
Bremen having become too shallow.

Elbe–Geste Waterway. Formerly used only by turf boats and
small craft trading to Hamburg, this waterway had its many
bridges raised in the 1960's, only the railway bridge (at that
time not the lowest) remaining unaltered. It is another
forgotten waterway of the North German moors, and
extremely picturesque, winding across heathland and farming country. It consists of three sections : the Upper Geeste,
the Bederkesa–Geeste Canal as far as Bederkesa lock, and the
Hadelner Canal from there to Otterndorf lock. Tolls are
paid at Bederkesa lock, and are not large. Total length 55
kms. Locks 3 – a tide-lock at each end, and the lock at
Bederkesa.

Caution: The low speed limit is strictly enforced, and
boats are timed on their passage. Those covering the ground
too fast are immediately fined. In fact the speed permitted
– about 2 to 3 knots according to the section – is slower than
many boats can accomplish at dead slow, so it is advisable
to save face and money by halting for lunch, indulging in
bird watching, or shopping at Bederkesa. The second section
of the waterway also happens to be narrow as well as
shallow, which produces an interesting phenomenon of
hydrodynamics. In this part of the route an oncoming barge
should be met only at dead slow and with fenders over the
side, as the water will draw off and probably throw the boats
together.

Moorings: Above Schiffdorf and below Otterndorf locks,
and at the quay in BEDERKESA, or at anchor in the romantic
pine-fringed Bederkesa See, which has an entry from the
canal.

OTTERNDORF is a market town on the River Medem, which
is navigable for small barges and can be reached by anyone
adventurous enough to dart out of the Hadelner Canal
when the gates to the tunnel under the vast sea-dike open
at high water (Dover + 0.50), and double back through the
adjacent rabbit-hole into the River Medem. The dike itself

with its flood marks and underground lock is weird and impressive. There are fine views across the watts toward Schleswig-Holstein.

Alternative route. Boats too high above the water to pass the Cuxhaven railway bridge are obliged to make the long and not always comfortable sea voyage of 80 kms. from Bremerhaven to the Elbe at Cuxhaven. An intricate and shorter passage leads over the sands at just the right moment of tide, but as the course continually changes it is inadvisable to risk this trip without local (fishermen) assistance. There is the added disadvantage that the Knechtsand is used as a bombing range.

There is *no* other inland route to the Elbe apart from the Mittelland Canal, which leads through the German Psychopathic Republic and so should be avoided. (See note 2 on p. 283.)

River Elbe. The estuary channel is buoyed. From the Otterndorf tide-gates at the end of the Hadelner Canal a row of birch perches marks the twisting course of the narrow bed of the Medem out into deep water. From the beacon at the end of the row, follow the buoys upstream. (*Admiralty Chart No. 3261.*)

Caution: After high water, the level falls away very rapidly. Do not delay, but run out at once, keeping the perches to port (that is to seaward) and not more than 3 m. distant.

The entrance to the Kiel Canal is 26 kms. upstream. The roadstead will be dotted with big ships of all nationalities waiting to enter. Following a coaster at a cautious distance is easier than trying to decipher the message of the flapping signal arms.

Caution: In the lock you may rise or fall, according to the state of the tide. Make fast only to the floating pontoons along the lock-side. Customs and canal dues are dealt with while locking through.

Kiel Canal (Nord–Ostsee Kanal). Length 98 kms. Locks at

either end only. Opened in 1895, this is a masterpiece of engineering, one single *gate* of its locks being larger than an entire lock on the Thames. In places there is a wide vista over toward the low, rolling hills of Schleswig-Holstein and the endless flow of traffic fills the canal with throbbing life. (*Admiralty Chart No. 2469.*)

Navigation is simple – keep to the right and the devil take the hindmost. *Caution:* Do not attempt to exercise your libido by overtaking a giant ship – and getting sucked into the propellers. Do not stop in the canal or you will be pounded to pieces. Watch out for ferries. Keep well clear of the ship entering the lock ahead of you until its propellers have finally stopped.

Moorings: At BRUNSBÜTTELKOOG, immediately beyond the entrance locks, on the port side. This is an excellent place from which to watch the ships passing through, and to wander over the lock installations without let or hindrance. Otherwise make for the *Gieselau Canal* – km. 41 on the port hand. This short canal (4 kms.) leads through one lock to the River Eider, an unusual side-trip. The Eider is navigable up to Rendsburg (23 kms.) but in that town it is dammed by a railway embankment, and there is *no* through passage. Downstream from the Gieselau junction it is navigable to where the tideway begins at Nordfeld. Locks 2.

At RENDSBURG, beyond the town and transporter bridge double back on the port side of the Kiel Canal at km. 67 into the Upper Eider, navigable easily for 3 kms. Rendsburg was Danish until the 19th century and the 13th-century church of St Mary has many of the painted heraldic memorials one associates with Denmark. Formerly it was the terminus of the Eider Canal, fore-runner of the Kiel Canal and built by the Danes in order to avoid the dangerous passage round Skagen (the Skaw), but most unfortunately the Germans placed a railway dam across the river and so cut the link to the sea. The town has walks along the cutting of the Kiel Canal so that visitors may watch the ships, and there is good bathing on sandy beaches in the Eider. Engineering enthusiasts can spend a happy hour examining the ingenious loop

railway with its underslung transporter bridge, built to solve
the problem of how trains could clear the masts of the shipping and yet arrive at a ground-level platform. The town
also has several mellowed buildings miraculously surviving
from the 16th century, and one can see that it was once an
island but later surrounded by vast fortifications designed on
the French style. HOLTENAU is too swept by wash to provide
good mooring, but from the harbours in the Kiel fjord one
can visit the remaining portions of the Eider Canal, which
are close to Holtenau lock. A walk across the Holtenau high
bridge gives a most impressive bird's-eye view of the ships
passing below.

KIEL. Plenty of moorings exist in this yachtsman's Mecca,
with its Kiel Week. In the Church of St Nicholas, rebuilt
after the tremendous air-raids, a side-altar has a plaque
with the one word 'Coventry'. But already we are in the
Baltic and outside the scope of this book.

Side-trip: 13 kms. short of Holtenau, a lock on the starboard hand leads to the Ring Canal, navigable for 3 kms.
along the edge of the Flemhuder See, once an ancient
portage route. There is no through connection to the Baltic.

ALTERNATIVE ROUTE FROM OTTERNDORF

River Elbe. Continue up the estuary to Hamburg (75 kms.)
and carry on upstream to Lauenburg (131 kms. from
Brunsbüttel). One lock, at Geesthacht (head of tideway). The
frontier line between the German Federal and German
Democratic Republics crosses the Elbe a few hundred metres
upstream of Lauenburg.

The Elbe tideway (*Admiralty Chart No. 3292*) is relatively
unexciting in its lower reaches, which can be a bad place to
be caught by a strong north-westerly wind. Short of Hamburg the shore rises on the port hand to the cliffs of fashionable Blankenese. At Wedel a loudspeaker entertains visitors
by playing the national anthem of each passing vessel –
including yours if no larger ship is near enough. It is polite
to appear flattered.

Navigation: Above Hamburg the river should be run only on a rising tide. Customs must be cleared in the city (see below) and again at a jetty on the port hand beyond all the docks. The nooses hanging from gibbets on the staging need not cause alarm. They are not for visiting yachtsmen, but to help the officers climb aboard unladen craft.

The passage of the Elbe can be tricky, the river often being deep on the bends and very erratic on the cross-overs. Here and there poles can be seen on the dikes, bearing diamond-shaped boards which are red-and-white on the port hand going upstream, black-and-white on the starboard hand. If the division between the colours is *horizontal* the message is 'aim for here'; if vertical, 'beat it to the other side of the stream'. These marks are helpfully stated to be 'usually correct'. In fact, the Thirds Rule ($\frac{1}{3}$L or $\frac{1}{3}$R on the bends, the $\frac{1}{3}$ being nearer the outside of the curve) is adequate on a rising tide. The river is navigable right up to Lauenburg for craft drawing 3 m., and as barges run up to Czechoslovakia one may encounter Czech and East German craft.

Caution: The shores are groyned all the way, except on the outside of the bends.

Moorings: At various small harbours in the estuary below Hamburg (Glückstadt, Stade, Wedel and several tidal creeks).

HAMBURG has a maze of waterways to explore in a small boat. The main port is strongly tidal, and to reduce the flow through the various links between the Norder Elbe (on which Hamburg itself is situated) and the Süder Elbe (flowing past Harburg) a number of watertight doors are installed which will open if you approach them, like automatic doors in a big store.

On arrival in Hamburg, customs must be cleared. Pass the St Pauli passenger landing-stage with prominent clock-tower (port hand) and watch for the first main opening on the same side, just before the two main harbour basins opening obliquely to port. The customs jetty is at the entrance to this opening, which leads into the Binnenhafen.

After clearance, leave the docks to starboard, duck under two bridges, bear left and pass under a bridge carrying trams to reach the entrance of a lock below the roadway. A convenient mooring is through the lock, near the third bridge, in the Alsterfleet. Craft small enough to clear all the fixed bridges can pass right through into the Alster lakes, or explore the various town canals and moor wherever they wish – though to land is not always so easy.

Hamburg is the largest German city except Berlin, and was once a separate city state and a main prop of the rich Hanseatic league. It is best seen from the northern side, where the Alster lakes provide the chance of a voyage in your own craft (if small enough) or in a trip-boat to see the famous view of the row of elegant spires over 100 m. in height. The port used to have many links with England, and Hamburg fashion modelled itself on London, even to such things as afternoon tea. Nowadays the city has all the robust noise and fun of a cosmopolitan port, and though sociologists and pornographers may wish to visit the famous Reeperbahn, a rather sleazy area with tarts in glass showcases, more pleasant excursions are to be had beside the Alster, or across the two branches of the river to the Lüneburger Heide. Young members of the crew should insist on being taken to Hagenbeck's Zoo, one of the best in the world and renowned for its skill in educating animals for the circus. After almost total destruction the city is mainly modern in style. The most picturesque part still remaining is along the Nikolaifleet, next entry upstream of the Alsterfleet.

Above the city there are no convenient moorings until beyond the tidal influence, after which GEESTHACHT has a harbour (entry in the upper lock-cut, port hand). Geesthacht is a miserable town, but the hills are pleasant and the up-and-down electric works with storage reservoir is considered a great attraction. At LAUENBURG it is possible to moor on other craft in the canal entrance, or rather better immediately above the lock.

Caution: Under no circumstances should one attempt to proceed beyond the canal and cross the frontier in a yacht, even if barges may do so. East German guards shoot first and ask questions afterwards.

Lauenburg was formerly important because of its position at the entrance to the Stecknitz Canal, Europe's oldest watershed canal and part of the route by which salt was taken to Lübeck. It has a shipping museum with models of canal craft from the 14th century onwards, and an ancient lock of the former canal is preserved on the edge of the town. Lauenburg is also one of the checkpoints for crossing into the Eastern Zone or German Democratic Republic. An interesting if depressing experience is to walk down to the checkpoint and talk to travellers, but on no account should one stray into the grim No-Man's Land minefield. The checkpoint has an exhibition of Communist murders of would-be escapers to freedom.

Elbe–Trave Canal. From the Elbe at Lauenburg to the Baltic inlet of the Trave estuary at Lübeck. Length 60 kms. Lowest fixed bridge, 4·20 m. Locks 6 (2 up, 4 down).

For several kilometres the canal runs close to the course of the Stecknitz Canal of the 14th century, now the frontier line of the two Germanys, and watchtowers and barbed wire dominate the scene on the eastern side. Half way along, the waterway skirts Mölln and then drops slowly to reach the River Trave. Lübeck is 5 kms. down the river, which passes round the edge of the city in an elegant cutting which was once the moat. A further 22 kms. beyond Lübeck the broadening waters are suddenly constricted at Travemünde. Through this strait with its quays and yacht harbour lies the open Baltic.

Moorings: At the locks. From the second lock (Witzeeze) a lane leads to the Dückerschleuse inn, a picturesque Holstinian farmhouse with a good view of No-Man's Land at the end of the garden, where there is also the ruined pen of a 14th-century Stecknitz Canal lock. At GÜSTER (20 kms.) extensive gravel pits in a woodland setting have been made into a yachting centre, complete with landing-stages and every facility. MÖLLN is a real challenge to the adventurous,

for the canal skirts a lake which has been bisected by a high
railway embankment. The lake is deep and without obstructions, and a search along the further shore will reveal a gap
in the willows. Pushing through, one finds a waterway leading under a rustic wooden bridge to a right-angle bend so
abrupt that one may have to pole the boat round. A high
culvert tunnels under the railway to emerge from the bushes
in the other half of the lake, with the water-girt old town
of Mölln cramped tightly on an island hill. Anchor in the
lake or moor at the landing-stage when the trip-boat is not
in residence. Mölln's brick church of St Nicholas from the
13th century has on its outside the tombstone of the medieval
joker Till Eulenspiegel (see also Damme). Nearby is a pump
with bronzes of Eulenspiegel and George Bernard Shaw.
There are shady woodland walks to other lakes, and an
excursion to the even more remarkable island town of
Ratzeburg (10 kms.).

At LÜBECK there are abundant quays with a peaceful outlook upon the old merchant houses and the city of tall brick
spires. After joining the Trave and passing under the second
of two railway bridges, keep always to the right at each
junction of waterways until the lifting-bridge at the edge
of the docks. Beyond the bridge turn sharp left and help
yourself to a good berth.

Lübeck was the founder of the Hanseatic League, and
somehow it has managed to preserve the atmosphere of a
bustling medieval city. The approach by canal gives one of
the finest views, and looking along the willow-hung moat to
port one has a sight of some of the tall pointed spires of
pink brick on the great Gothic churches which are such a
feature of the city. In St Mary's the bells, melted and broken
in the heat of the 1942 air-raid are left on the floor as a
memorial; St Nicholas has a battered lifeboat of the ill-fated
training ship *Pamir*. The massive gateway of the Holstentor
(1477) stands beside the gabled salt warehouses, and the
City Hall is a remarkable mixture of styles from the 13th
century onward. The city has associations with Thomas
Mann (d. 1955) and particularly 'The Buddenbrooks'; the

house of this fictional family in which Mann was himself born, being now the Volksbank. The Schiffergesellschaft or livery hall of the Guild of Seamen is open to the public as a restaurant and vividly recalls the customs and life of Hanseatic days. Lübeck's modern specialities are shipbuilding and marzipan fish.

TRAVEMÜNDE is a seaside resort, yachting centre and fishing port, with plenty of berths. It is pleasantly situated on the narrows, just short of the open sea.

Caution: If proceeding further to seaward, keep west of the line of buoys marking the aquatic frontier, or else prepare to be arrested.

River Ilmenau. From Lüneburg to the R. Elbe at Hoopte. Length 29 kms. Locks 3. Draught restricted to 1·10 m. – but this only applies within the upper 400 m. of the waterway, which otherwise is considerably deeper.

Navigation: The entrance is immediately above the ferry stage L, on the R. Elbe at Hoopte, some 9 kms. downstream of Geesthacht lock. At low water it almost dries out, and one should allow the tide to flood for at least two hours before leaving Hoopte, otherwise one will overtake the tide and have to slow down before reaching the head of the Ilmenau tideway at Fahrenholz lock (9 kms.). Beyond that point there are no problems until above the timber yards at Lüneburg. At the fork (where the water is becoming shallow and fleet) take the right-hand arm and proceed gently over the clean sandy bottom until prudence and grating sounds suggest you have gone far enough. On the starboard side there is a quay all along this part, and you can pick your own mooring. It is certainly possible with a draught of 1·10 m. to reach the derelict iron crane outside the former salt warehouses. Boats of shallow draught can penetrate further, but already one is almost in the town centre.

The Ilmenau was for centuries the route by which salt from the Lüneburg brine pits was conveyed to the Stecknitz canal and so to Lübeck. Though this trade has long since ceased the river has slight traffic above the locks and rather more on its tidal stretch, where there is a loading station for potash below Fahrenholz weir. The Ilmenau is a rural waterway of great charm, winding hesitantly across open meadows and past small farming hamlets. Above the tideway the banks are low, and cattle and storks look with surprise and perhaps suspicion at a passing boat. After the bustle of Hamburg and the R. Elbe, the river provides a restful side-trip for any boatman heading for the Baltic by way of the Elbe–Trave Canal (p. 260), and his crew will appreciate the chance of a dinner in one of the many pleasant inns in the centre of one of the finest and most unspoiled among all the smaller cities of Germany.

Moorings: Above the tideway almost anywhere. Traffic is slight – about one barge per day to the timber yards. At BARDOWICK there is a run-down cathedral (12th century), relic of greater days. LÜNEBURG, at the very edge of its famous heath, has an air of resting contentedly upon the enormous wealth which derived from the salt trade. Its City Hall is beyond all doubt the finest in Germany, its rooms rich in carved and painted decoration, some of it commissioned work by Hans Memling (d. 1494). The market is a good place to buy strange edible fungi from the heath, but the Am Sande square is the one with the finest buildings in delicate pink brick fashioned into surprising shapes. The old port area, with an abbatial mill still in use, is as picturesque as any, and if the port is no longer used the old warehouses are a vivid reminder of the days of the Hanseatic League. Outside the Kaufhaus (Merchants' Hall), recently rebuilt after a disastrous fire, there is a magnificently restored wooden crane from the 18th century.

GÖTA CANAL AND CONNECTIONS

This name is usually applied to a string of waterways which begins at Gothenburg and crosses Sweden to Stockholm, a distance of about 630 kms., although only 190 kms. of this are the Göta Canal itself.

The idea of a trans-Sweden waterway is said to have originated with Bishop Håns Brask, who produced a plan in 1516 and was actually responsible for a section of the present waterway near the eastern end of the present canal. Under Charles IX another portion was cut below Vennersborg, and the section by Lilla Edet lock was added in the reign of Gustav II. Other sections were planned at intervals, but it remained for Baron Baltzar von Platen to complete the route in the 19th century.

The constituent waterways of the Göta route will here be described from west to east.

River Göta, or Trollhätte Canal. From Gothenburg to Lake Väner at Vennersborg. Length 82 kms. Locks 6.

Navigation: The Göta river has a modest current, but not enough to cause any difficulty to the boatman. Throughout its length it is navigated by ocean-going ships which ply to the lake ports, and the whole course is lit for night navigation. By day it presents no problems, but for a night run it is essential to have *Swedish Chart No. 86 'Göta Älv'*. This is also useful in the daytime, to give some idea of where you are.

There is one lock (Lilla Edet) before the Trollhättan flight and another at Brinkebergskullen, 4 kms. short of

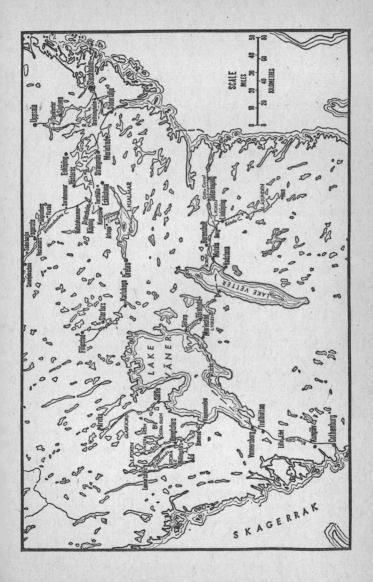

Vennersborg; and at Kungälv (16 kms. up from Gothenburg) there is an alternative outlet to the sea through the
Nordre Älv (North River), but the depth is limited and this
access is not suitable for craft drawing more than 1·8 m.

There is nothing else in Europe quite like the Göta river,
which leads up a broad valley often flanked by typical
Swedish forests of birch or matchwood until, just short of
Trollhättan, the hills close in and the course becomes a
gorge at the head of which are the mighty Trollhättan falls,
by-passed by four deep ship-locks. The sight of smart modern
cargo vessels steaming across the meadows or dropping down
the giant locks is one never to be forgotten.

Moorings: At KUNGÄLV pass the long thin ait, leaving it
to starboard, and continue past the junction with the first
channel on the port side to round the broad flat island of
Sävtuvan edged with reed beds, giving the northern point
a wide berth. Passing down behind the island take the
narrow creek on the starboard side, leaving Bohus castle to
port. There is at least 2 m. of water in this channel, which
runs to a dead end at moorings beside one of the most
delightful hotels in Sweden. Along the road past the hotel
is the modern Kungälv new town – an awful warning to
architects. From near the hotel a path leads up to the hilltop ruin of Bohus castle, once the strongest fortress in
Sweden, and the scene of several battles.

Apart from occasional chances of mooring at lumbering
jetties (of which there are not many) there is no proper
facility until TROLLHÄTTAN, where there is a long quay about
3 kms. above the locks. This is a compulsive stop for any
boatman, the collection of navigation works scattered about
the hillside near the falls having no equal in the world. One
can examine the remains of no less than four previous
attempts – two of them successful – to by-pass the falls with
locks, and marvel at the tenacity of the engineers who
tackled such a formidable problem. The present locks were
built in 1916.

The falls, more than 1½ kms. in length, are likely to be
almost dry, the water being usually diverted to pass through

the power station, which is open to the public. A rock bears the inscribed names of all the monarchs who have come to see the place.

At VENNERSBORG there are also good quays, not on the main shipping canal, but in the town itself. Follow the main route through the swing-bridges, and after 500 m. turn to starboard round the buoy and enter the town channel. This mooring is convenient for shopping and away from the wash of large vessels, but the town itself is of little interest.

Lake Väner (Vänern). This vast sheet of water is the third largest in Europe, and most of it is comparatively shallow. Half way up its length Vänern is constricted by skerries, and as it is well sprinkled around the shores by rocks and shoals it should not be crossed without the *Swedish Charts Nos. 295 and 293,* which cover the Göta route and also the entrance to the Dalslands Canal (q.v.).

Vänern should always be treated with reasonable care. It is as broad as the English Channel and can mount a nasty sea in strong winds. It is well equipped with lighthouses and has a number of commercial harbours, but it can also be fog-laden on summer nights.

Moorings: On the route to the Göta Canal at Sjötorp, there are only two possible stops. One is in the Ekens Skärgård (skerries) at LÄCKO, where there is a landing-stage at the foot of the splendid castle built for the bishops of Skara and taken by the crown in 1528. The second largest castle in Sweden, Läcko was redecorated in the 17th century and the Hall of Knights is painted with scenes from the campaigns of Gustavus Adolphus in the Thirty Years War. MARIESTAD has a proper harbour, but as a town is pleasant rather than memorable. The Maria in the name was the Queen of Charles IX.

Other waterways approached from Lake Väner are :

The *Säffle Canal*, a cut with one lock (42 m. × 7·8 m.) leading through the paperworks town of Säffle into the River By, which with the Glafsfjord lake provides a navigation route of 75 kms. right up to the timber town of Arvika. Navigation is quite possible but one may encounter great masses of floating timber.

The *Karlskoga–Filipstad Waterway*. This remarkable channel does not actually connect with Lake Väner, but is useful for trailer craft. It passes up the River Tims, and threads a maze of lakes to Storfors. There are 5 locks (21 m. × 3·6 m. with a depth of 1·2 m.) in the course of 70 kms., but because the railway bridge at Nässund is no more than 1·9 m. above the water the channel is only available beyond this half-way point to really small craft. Further information can be obtained from the Karlskoga–Bofors Motorbåtklubb or the Storfors Båtklubb, which together have produced an excellent and detailed guide to the navigation. *Chart: Swedish Map No. T. 2381.*

Göta Canal. From Sjötorp on Lake Väner to Mem on the Gulf of Bothnia. Length 190 kms. Locks 58 (32 m. × 7·1 m. with a depth of 3 m.).

Because of the lake crossings (25 kms. in the case of L. Vetter) *Swedish Chart No. 81 'Vettern och Göta Kanal'* is essential.

This is the Göta Canal proper, the route having been open since 1832. After various earlier attempts a survey was made by Thomas Telford for Count Baltzar von Platen, who pursued the work with tireless energy until his death in 1830. 86 kms. of the total are artificial canal, the remainder being lakes, of which Lake Vetter is the largest.

After suffering a decline the canal, which is largely subsidised by the timber concession granted along its length, was acquired by one of the Swedish banking houses, and the future of this excellent cruise-way seems assured.

It is the custom on this waterway for the crew to work one half of a lock, leaping to activity whenever the keeper blows his whistle. The machinery is in good order, and the canal has sufficient traffic – mostly yachts and steamers – to keep the works in trim.

The Göta Canal starts splendidly with a short flight of locks at Sjötorp, where dues must be paid. It then climbs steadily through a gentle countryside to Töreboda before passing through the Bergskanal, a narrow rock-cutting with meeting places, and passing the summit lock into L. Viken, a wild and twisting sheet of water which connects through a short canal cut at Rödesund with L. Vetter. This lake is deep, unobstructed, and capable of generating a really dangerous sea in bad weather. It is devoid of shelter and should only be crossed under good conditions.

From Motala on the eastern shore the canal takes up the course again and drops down the famous lock staircases of Borenshult into L. Boren and Berg (where there are 11 locks) into L. Roxen, at the southern end of which is the entrance to the Kinda Canal (q.v.). Beyond Roxen the canal passes through the small L. Asplången, but nearly the whole of the remaining route by Söderköping to Mem is pure canal.

Moorings: At SJÖTORP in the basin above the first flight of locks. There is a quay close to the station at TÖREBODA, but apart from mooring against the bank there is no facility at TÅTORP lock, which leads into the summit level of Lake Viken. At Landhöjden nearby there is a canal memorial. RÖDESUND at the entrance to Lake Vetter (Vettern) has a quay where waiting is possible. Overlooking the lake is the massive arsenal of the Carlsborg (named after Charles XIV). There are four other guest harbours on this half of the canal.

VADSTENA, some 5 kms. south of the direct crossing to Motala, is perhaps the most attractive mooring on all the route. Renowned for lace-making, Vadstena is a pleasant town which surrounds the convent established by St Birgitta (Bridget) in the 14th century, the 'blue' church of which can be visited, as can the cloisters. The berth is at a good quay, almost at the door of the magnificent castle erected by Gustavus Wasa in 1545, from the window of which his son Magnus cast himself into the arms of an imagined water sprite. *Caution:* Diaphanous female forms rising from the lake should be disregarded.

MOTALA has quays at the entrance to the next canal sec-

tion. The workshops which originated as shops for making
canal gear now produce heavy machinery and locomotives.
A statue of von Platen is in the market-place, and a short
distance along the bankside path is his tomb, at a spot
chosen by himself. From BERG locks it is only a short walk to
Vreta, where the abbey – rebuilt after a fire in 1298 – was
saved from pillage at the Reformation because the mother-
in-law of Gustavus Wasa had retired to it.

SÖDERKÖPING has a good town quay and was founded at
the site of a spring said to have gushed out at the foot of the
block on which St Ragnhild was beheaded. The 13th-century
St Lars church in pink brick has a detached belfry, and
across the canal there is a Bronze Age fort. At MEM there is
mooring just below the final lock, which has an inscription
from Psalm 127.

At Mem the salt water begins, and *Swedish Charts Nos.
251, 239 and 238* are necessary for the long but sheltered run
through the thousands of skerries along the inlets of the
east coast of Sweden toward Södertälje.

Södertälje Canal. Length 3 kms. 1 lock of sea-ship dimensions. This ship canal cuts through the narrow neck of land
which separates an inlet of the sea from another of Lake
Mälar (q.v.).

From the lock, Stockholm is only 37 kms. distant along
the lake. *Swedish Chart No. 240* is essential, '*Mälaren,
Ostradelen (Eastern part)*'.

In summer, the steamers of the Göta Canal Company ply
over the entire route, and the three-day voyage is certainly
the finest inland waterways trip in the world. Because of
demand, early enquiry and booking is essential. For those not
wishing to make the round trip there are facilities for return
from either end by train.

Dalslands Canal. From Köpmannehamn on Lake Väner to
Lake Stora Le, with a connection to the Västra and Östra
Silen lakes. Total length about 254 kms. Locks 29. Dimen-
sions : length 22·7 m., breadth 4·2 m., depth 1·8 m. The

first lock at Köpmannebro is double width.

Navigation: The entrance of the Dalslands Canal is extremely hard to find, but in about the expected position on the western shore of L. Väner a solitary blocky and rather faded warehouse may be sighted. This is in fact on the tip of the tongue of land behind which the channel runs in.

The locks, many of which are in staircases, have the unusual feature that in some cases they are blasted in the rock and only tailored round the upper edge. It is easy to scrape or snag a boat on the protruding crags and combs of rock, and great care should be taken with fenders. The locks should also be filled slowly to avoid damage.

Developed in the 1860's for bringing rafts of timber to the paper mills, this waterway is beyond any doubt the most remote in Europe. Although at one time abandonment seemed likely, its future as a cruising ground is assured since the decision in December 1971 to spend 1·3 million Swedish crowns (about £125,000) on improvements, about 70 per cent of the money coming from the state. Although very few craft used the canal in 1958, by 1971 the number passing through in the summer was over 12,000. However, this should not deter a visitor, for there are many hundreds of kilometres of lakes and sounds in which to lose oneself.

One can often travel for an hour or two without any sign of habitation, and the forests along the shores of the lakes which make up all but 8 kms. of the total are dense and often without tracks. Most of the lakes are deep (up to 100 m. in the Stora Le) and marks are not necessary, but in shallow areas and narrow sounds the course is clearly staked or buoyed. It is essential to have the *Swedish Chart No. 296, 'Dalslands Kanal'*, or within the first hour one will already be lost in the maze of inlets and side arms which run off on every hand.

Lake Stora Le is partly in Norway, the frontier line passing down the centre and leaving one long arm in Norwegian territory, but customs officers are rarer than the eagles in this area. The whole complex of Dalsland lakes is extremely beautiful and can provide a week or two of exploration, but

as repair and salvage facilities are virtually non-existent the
boatman will need to be self-reliant and have a craft which
will not give trouble. So remote is the countryside that the
mail used to be carried by boat.

Villages with shopping facilities are extremely few and
one should bear in mind that for a day or two no provisions
may be obtainable. However, there are fish, crayfish, strawberries and bilberries to fall back on, and the water in Lake
Stora Le is so pure that it can safely be pumped into the
tanks. *Caution:* Do not be startled if you think you see an elk.
That is just what it is.

Two side branches are navigable. Below Upperud a
channel, leads to the *Snäcke Canal*, 17·4 kms., 2 locks of
similar dimensions, which leads to the Ånimmen and Ärrsjö
lakes; and beyond the final flight of locks at Lennartsfors
one can head north along Lake Foxen to reach the *Stora
Le–Östen Canal*, 21 kms. and 2 locks, 22·6 m. by 4·2 m. Both
canals have a minimum depth of 1·8 m.

Moorings: Anchoring may be feasible where the water is
not too deep or the bottom too smooth, but it is often possible
to find a bank or jetty close to a lock. At KÖPMANNEBRO there
is staging by the lock, close to a village store. HÅVERUD has
a good quay in the widening above the locks and beyond
the memorial to Nils Ericson, engineer of the Canal.
Håverud aqueduct, an iron trough which carries the waterway over the river, is one of the great canal sights of Europe,
and here one may see river, canal, rail and road (and maybe
aircraft) all crossing each other on different levels. A canal
museum is close by, at the foot of the locks. Altogether there
are more than a score of guest moorings on the waterway.

In Råvarpen Lake one can anchor off HÖGSBYN, where
there are Bronze Age rock-carvings by the shore. At DALS
LÅNGED, there is mooring in the cut, and also above the lock
at LÅNGBRON. At BILLINGSFORS, with a period theatre belonging to the factory, the paper works has a yacht harbour.
BENGTSFORS has good bankside mooring in the cut at the
foot of the locks. On the Maiberg hill there is an excellent

open-air museum to which typical wooden houses of the
Dalsland province have been transported intact. STRAND has
a sheltered inlet with a jetty and a shop. ED is a mountain
and forest resort on a narrow tongue of land between two
lakes, but the ski-jumping is better than the mooring. In
Norway there are no moorings at all but one may be able
to come alongside at OTTEID saw-mill, or anchor nearby, and
walk up the bank to see the side arm of the Norwegian Tiste
Canal within a stone's throw. A really small boat can be
man-handled over the divide.

A steamer plies in summer, usually between Bengtsfors
and Köpmannebro.

Kinda Canal. From Lake Roxen to Horn on Lake Åsunden.
Length 80 kms. Locks 15. Dimensions length 24·5 m., beam
4·5 m., maximum permitted draught 1·3 m. Height at lowest
fixed bridge 3·09 m.

Navigation: The restoration society (Kinda Kanals
Vänner) has produced a detailed chart in two sheets, *Kinda
Kanal och Dess Sjösystem,* with up-to-date soundings.
Because of the shoals and rocks in some of the lakes, this
should be obtained before proceeding beyond Linköping,
where the harbour office is at the town quay.

The railway swing-bridge at Risnäs (above Vist) opens to
permit the passage of the trip-boat, and can be passed daily
between 11.00 and 13.25. At other times it is necessary to
make an arrangement by telephone – preferably with the
help of some person who can speak Swedish.

Originally built to transport lumber from the area of the
Kinda Lakes, the Kinda Canal was not opened until 1872,
since which time it has remained unaltered. After a time of
prosperity it went bankrupt, was revived during the Second
World War, and then suffered a relapse. A solitary trip-boat
ran during the summer months but otherwise the waterway
was deserted until a local restoration society was founded to
work for its preservation. In 1971 it was re-opened to navigation, and provides an excellent cruising ground through a
gentle, undulating landscape of meadows and birch woods

18

with here and there a splendid mansion or baroque chateau to be glimpsed through a gap in the woodland.

The Kinda Canal has the usual low proportion of artificial cuts for a Swedish waterway (7 kms. out of 80 compared with 14 out of 100 for the Strömsholms Canal and 8 out of 254 for the Dalslands). These cuts are nearly all concentrated between Linköping and the first of the large lakes, Stora Rängen, but further ahead there are many twisting and narrow sounds of great beauty. Another feature of the canal is the surprising number of movable bridges, lifting, swinging or sliding as the case may be. Good exercise can be had working all these devices.

Moorings: All the moorings and jetties are marked on the charts, so they will not be given in detail here. However, it should be remembered that the jetties are used by the trip-boat and should not be cluttered when it is due. The only place of much consequence on the canal is LINKÖPING. Upon entering the waterway from Lake Roxen there is a sailing-boat harbour about 1½ kms. up the canal and a motor-boat harbour 1 km. further. ahead, both on the starboard hand. The town quay is about ½ km. beyond Nyqvarn lock.

The city is a centre of aircraft and motor manufacture, but it is also an ancient episcopal see. The cathedral dates from the 12th century, but suffered terribly at the hands of 19th-century restorers. In the market there is a notable fountain by the sculptor Carl Milles (d. 1955) and the park of the Trädgårdsföreningen (Gardeners' Association) has an old farmstead restored. Linköping is a good hunting ground for regional handicrafts.

A trip-boat runs between Linköping and Horn during the summer months.

Lake Mälar (Mälaren). Mälaren is the third largest lake in Sweden, with a length of about 117 kms. and a greatest breadth from north to south of 45 kms. It is included here for two reasons. Firstly, it is the connecting link between the sea, the Göta Canal (q.v.) the Hjälmare Canal (q.v.) and the Strömsholms Canal (q.v.), and in its own right it must be one of the finest cruising grounds in the world, for both sail and motor craft.

Whereas Vänern and Vettern are large sheets of water comparatively unbroken, Mälaren is sprinkled with about a thousand islands, some of them very large and many extremely beautiful. In spring they are white with lily of the valley and some glow with the violet bells of the pasque flower. Ospreys can often be seen overhead, or perched on dead trees on isolated rocks.

There is always good shelter available and the lack of long fetches means that no sea of dangerous proportions can be raised. The maze of isles is a favourite boating ground for the Swedes themselves. Large ocean-going vessels pass up the lake on their way to the modern port of Västerås, to which an ice-free channel is kept open throughout the winter. Cargo-ships of considerable size also penetrate to Köping.

Historically, Mälaren is at the heart of Swedish life. The present capital is sited upon it, and no less than three former capitals are scattered around the lake. There are castles, cathedral towns, and an endless supply of interest. In summer, steamers ply from Stockholm to various destinations on the lake, and the ships of the Göta Canal Company pass through Mälaren for about 30 kms. of their total route.

From the sea there are two entries, at Stockholm and Södertälje. At Stockholm, yachts normally use the smaller lock at Slussen (The Lock) which is situated under an immense road junction, but craft with tall masts may have to use the Hammarby ship-lock. At Södertälje there is no small-boat lock, but all craft are passed without delay (see *Göta Canal*).

The Stockholm approach is covered by *Swedish Chart No. 88*. The lake itself requires *Nos. 240 (Mälaren East)*, *241 (North)* and *242 (West)*. Without these one could become lost in the maze of channels and creeks.

Moorings: In the case of Mälaren it can be assumed that every port or town, large or small, is provided with good alongside mooring facilities capable of handling steamers or modest cargo vessels, and that there will be no difficulty in finding a good berth. Here and there, yacht harbours or anchorages are also available.

No attempt has been made here to describe in detail the delights of STOCKHOLM; but that part of the city which flanks the lake as opposed to the sea and is accessible from the inland side includes the Norr Mälarstrand with alongside berthing close to the famous City Hall of 1923, which started a new trend in architecture. Its fine tower topped by three golden crowns can be seen in the distance as one approaches the city by the Göta route, but even this imposing sight is only a foretaste of the wealth of craftsmanship in metal and stone, brick and paint which is contained within the building. Every episode in Swedish history or legend seems to have its place.

On the adjacent island of Riddarholmen is the Riddarholms Kyrka (church) with the tombs of Swedish monarchs from the 13th century onward, including Gustavus Adolphus. A small bridge leads to the island of Staden (the City) with the Royal Palace (early 18th century) and enough State Apartments and statues and portraits of eminent Swedes to make one wonder whether it is not time to watch the changing of the guard and then go back aboard ship.

DROTTNINGHOLM on the island of Lovön some kilometres west of the capital is a Swedish Versailles, lavishly ornamented with all such treasures looted by Gustavus Adolphus from Prague and Bavaria as were not lost at sea on the way to Sweden. The baroque Court Theatre is a real delight, and stage performances are given in the summer. The mechanical works, including a thunder machine and an artificial sea of rollers, are intriguing.

The island of BJÖRKÖ is the site of the ancient Viking stronghold of Birka. The burial grounds with two thousand mounds as well as the ring ramparts can still be seen. A chapel and a memorial commemorate the founding by Ansgar of the first church in Sweden, c. 830 (see Corvey, under *R. Weser*).

The route to the north leads through the Stäket Sound swing-bridge to SIGTUNA, said to be the oldest town in Sweden. It has three 11th-century churches and was once the capital, but in 1187 it was sacked by the Estonians and has not yet really recovered. It has a tiny 18th-century town hall, but in modern times Sigtuna is more renowned for its two excellent public schools (in the English sense). Next comes SKOKLOSTER, the magnificent 17th-century castle of General Wrangel of the Thirty Years War (d. 1676). More relics of the sacking of Prague are here on view, and a collection of arms and armour from Wrangel's days and earlier. The end of the run is at the weir in the River Fyris, at the foot of the castle hill in UPPSALA. The cathedral was fearfully restored in the 19th century and one can only guess how splendid it must once have been. The University Library has on view the Codex Argenteus (about 500), a translation of the Bible inot Gothic – looted, of course, from Prague. The castle of pink brick was restored in the 18th century, and from a nearby bell the curfew is daily rung, though not heeded. The garden of Linnaeus, arranged according to his own principles of botanical orders, is still just as he kept it. Outside the town are the 6th-century tumuli and the Disagården open-air museum at Gamla (old) Uppsala, and the workshop and residence of Linnaeus at Hammarby, with many of his sketches and other material. For those with scientific interests this is a most interesting excursion, and here again one can see a garden of a rather different kind planted on strictly botanical principles. At Hammarby the spot is also preserved upon which the Kings of Sweden were formerly elected.

The routes along the southern shore of Mälaren leads past the island of Kungshatt (Kings Hat) where a giant iron hat on a pole marks the spot where a former monarch is said to have escaped from his would-be murderers by spurring his steed to leap into the lake. His hat was all that was left to his pursuers. Beyond this the first inlet is a dead end, the second leads to Södertälje and the Göta Canal, the third to MARIEFRED, originally the site of a Carthusian monastery (the name means Peace of Mary). The market square was devised by the stage-struck Gustav III as a set for dramatics. The village faces Gripsholm Castle, restored in very good taste in the 1890's and once a royal residence. The building with its turrets and moat and courtyard is very appealing and a good sample of what a Scandinavian royal residence would once have been like. There is another excellent baroque theatre, the work of Gustav III. Other monarchs were imprisoned at Gripsholm and one was born in the dungeon.

Caution: There are more than two thousand portraits of royalty, royal children, royal horses and royal dogs, few if any of them being artistically notable.

Further west is STRÄNGNÄS with a cathedral in pink brick at the top of the hill above the wharf. Dating from 1291 it was well restored in the present century and contains some rune-stones set in the exterior walls. Adjacent is the splendid Archbishop's Palace, built in the 15th century.

At SUNDBYHOLM there is a narrow-wooded promontory with moorings. Nearby on the Ramsundsberg is the Sigurds-ristning, the largest and most notable rune-stone memorial in the world, on which the whole saga of Sigurd the Vol-sung is set out so clearly that it can all be easily identified and understood. A little further west, craft can run up the Törshällaån to TORSHÄLLA, a small town which once was a considerable port, but it is to be regretted that the Torshälla Canal which led to ESKILSTUNA (7 kms. 3 locks) was abandoned in the 1960's. However, the journey can be made by bus. The town is named after the English monk Eskil but is more famous for steel manufacture. It contains a number of 17th-century smithies built for Charles X by a Netherlands ironmaster named Rademacher. Five have been assembled as a museum of period iron-working and the exhibits range from arrest-tongs to armour for bear-hunting dogs. The primitive domestic arrangements for these one-man or two-man factories are also of great interest.

At the mouth of the R. Arboga is KUNGSÖR, and further up ARBOGA, a charming little town with grassy streets and little wooden houses set beside the river (see also *Hjälmare Canal*).

In the north-west corner of the lake lies KÖPING, a considerable port trading with Russia and Germany. The apothecary's shop of Carl Scheele (d. 1786), the chemist who discovered oxygen, chlorine and prussic acid, can still be visited.

Further east are two other ports. ENKÖPING is accessible up 4 kms. of river and is a market town of about 10,000 inhabitants, with a museum which has good collections illustrating the ordinary life in the area. VÄSTERÅS on the other hand is a large and modern city which has engulfed the original older town cramped on the banks of the Svartån (Black River). Its prosperity derives from A.S.E.A., which is based there. The cathedral was brilliantly restored in the late 1960's, and the neighbourhood converted into a semi-museum of little alleys and old houses which are actually lived in. Västerås is a good shopping centre and it has facilities for the many hundreds of small craft based there.

Strömsholms Canal. From Lake Mälar at Kvicksund to Smedjebacken on Lake Norra Barken. Length 100 kms. Locks 26. Dimensions length 20·1 m., beam 5·0 m., depth 1·35 m. minimum. Lowest headroom, 2·5 m. (at the bridge leading to Strömsholm castle).

The canal was completed in 1860 to carry coal, iron ore and the products of the steelworks which drew power from the waterfalls between the lakes which make up 89 of the 100 kms. of waterway. Abandoned after commercial traffic ceased in 1945, the whole waterway was completely restored between 1962 and 1970, vast sums being spent on the new lockgates alone. Mooring facilities were added, and the canal brought into excellent conditions throughout.

The Strömsholms waterway is probably the least remote of any in Sweden, for it passes by a number of small towns. To say that these are foundry communities gives an impression of smoke and dirt, but in fact the places are clean, and because they were founded long ago in a very un-populated area of lakeland and forest, the steelworks were developed on the 'bruk' lines, where the management administered forests, agriculture, houses and all the needs of the people. Steelworks are spread at intervals along most of the valley, and yet the canal passes through some of the most idyllic scenery in central Sweden. Sombre forests, delicate churches and the elegant wooden mansions of the ironmasters are mirrored in the clear, clean water of the Bergslagen lakes, and there is provision for bathing and camping and swimming. Some hundreds of small craft are based on the marinas along the waterway.

Moorings: Throughout, as there is no commercial traffic. Guest harbours with jetties and every facility are available at Borgasund, Hallstahammar (below the locks), above Surahammar, at Virsbo, Vestanfors, Semla, Söderbärke and Smedjebacken. There are also mooring facilities below or above most locks. At STRÖMSHOLM one may visit the royal castle rebuilt in the 17th century. Above the HALLSTA-HAMMAR locks on the port hand is the original house of the canal overseer, now one of the most detailed and interesting canal museums to be found. At SURAHAMMAR the original works has been converted to a steelworks museum where all the iron-working machinery of the early days can be seen *in situ.* Surahammar manufactures wheels for railway rolling stock, and the original wheel forge is also on view, together with an early locomotive and a Vabis car of 1904 (the motor company was owned by Surahammars Bruk). At ÄNGELSBERG there is an early blast furnace in a works dating from 1590.

The booklet *Strömsholms Kanal Informerar* is issued free and gives full details of everything from guest harbours and restaurants to banks and hire cars. It can be obtained from the Strömsholms Kanal AB, 73400 Hallstahammar, Sweden, who can also supply a detailed chart (also obtainable in bookshops in Sweden).

Hjälmare Canal. From the R. Arboga at Gravudden to Lake Hjälmar at Notholmen. Length 13 kms. Locks 9. Dimensions length 32·1 m., beam 7·1 m., draught 2·1 m. Speed limit 5 knots. The locks are open in Summer from 8–10, 12–14 and 16–19.

The existing canal dates from the 19th century, replacing an older one opened in 1639, of which some traces can be found nearby. After being closed for a few years it was acquired in 1965 by the Swedish Forestry Commission and re-opened as a cruising waterway. The condition is good and navigation easy.

The waterway consists of an artificial cut which passes across a few kilometres of meadow and farmland before reaching the birch-woods. From there its course is partly through long and narrow natural lakes until a further canalised section and a descending lock completes the line. A deserted canal passing through no villages at all, it is one on which no supplies can be obtained. However, it is a romantic cruising waterway for real explorers, and it also provides a route to Lake Hjälmar (see below).

The canal is reached from Lake Mälar (q.v.) at the western end of which the R. Arboga flows in through the town of Kungsör. The river channel is well marked with the usual Swedish brooms and sticks, and is used by coasters and similar craft right up to the quayside in Arboga itself, a few kilometres beyond the canal entrance, which is some 19 kms. upstream of Kungsör railway bridge, on the port hand.

Moorings: Throughout the canal, there being no commercial traffic. Otherwise below the locks at either end, or at HÄLLBY DOCKA, where there is a basin. In the woods below the canal bank a former canal building has been set out as a museum of the canal.

Lake Hjälmar is a wild, deserted sheet of water in central Sweden, renowned for its pike. It is navigable over a total length of 75 kms. from Skogstorp sawmill in the east to Örebro in the west, but the lake should not be attempted in bad weather or poor visibility, nor at night – when certain vital lights may well not be showing. It is open to a build-up of considerable seas in a south-westerly wind and is flanked along all its shores by immense numbers of isolated rocks and miniature skerries. There are some moorings, but it is possible to anchor for shelter in the lee of islands, par-ticularly Valö, though the holding is not good in a wind.

The course is well marked, all narrows being picked out with sticks and brooms, but a reliable compass is essential and one should not venture into the lake without *Swedish Chart No. 87, 'Hjälmaren'.*

At the western end the marked channel leads to the mouth of the *Örebro Canal*, a cut of 2 kms. with one lock of Hjälmare Canal dimensions, leading to ÖREBRO, where moor-ing is possible below the lock, or above it if the gates can be opened. The city is a manufacturing centre which owes its prosperity to the cutting of the Hjälmare Canal, and it is also the capital of a province. In the park there is a memorial to the Petri brothers, who initiated the Swedish Reforma-tion in the 16th century. The massive 16th-century castle standing on an island contains a regional museum. For a good view of the lake one can ascend the tall modern water-tower ('Švampan' – the Mushroom), which has a restaurant. Örebro was the birthplace of the national rising led by Engelbrekt Engelbrektsson in 1434 against Danish domina-tion. The hero was murdered on the small island which bears his name and is situated about 1 km. SE. of Björksund leading lights.

NOTES

1. The Canal de la Marne au Rhin between Toul and
   Nancy is to be closed, and the Liverdun aqueduct
   demolished. The first six pounds of the Canal de l'Est,
   branche Sud will also be abandoned. Instead the R.
   Meurthe has been opened up from a large new port at
   Nancy to its confluence with the Moselle, which is being
   canalised to Europaship dimensions right up to Neuves
   Maisons, 24 kms. above Toul. The total navigable length
   of the Moselle will then be 363 kms.

2. The Nord–Sud Canal, due to be completed during the
   1970's at a cost of more than £90 million, will connect
   the R. Elbe above Hamburg with the Mittelland Canal
   near Wolfsburg, east of Brunswick, and so provide an
   inland route to the Elbe entirely within West German
   territory.

INDEX

Moselle, R., 91, 172, 283
Motala, 269
Mouzon, 145
Mulhouse, 191
Münster, 116

Nahe, R., 83
Namur, 142, 147
Nancy, 173, 283
Narbonne, 229
Nassau, 100
Naurouze, 225
navigation hours, 25
Neckar, R., 109
Neckargemünd, 111
Neckarshausen, 110
Neckarsteinach, 111
Neckarsulm, 112
Nennig, 95
Nete, R., 131
Neuburgweier, 86
Neuf Brisach, 88
Neumagen, 96
Niederlahnstein, 99
Niederwalluf, 84
Nieuport, 67
Nieuwe Maas, 245
Nieuwe Meer, 247
Nijmegen, 80
Noord, 245
Nouvelle, La, 229
Nuremberg, 107

Oberlahnstein, 99
Obernhof, 100
Oberwesel, 83
Oberwinter, 82
Ochsenfurt, 106
Offenbach, 102
Oise, R., 151
Oldenburg, 252
Olfen, 116
Oppenheim, 84
Örebro, 282
Ostend, 68
Otteid, 273
Otterndorf, 254
Oudenaarde, 136
Oude Rijn, 246
Ourthe, R., 141
overtaking, 40

paddles, 48
Palavas, 218
Papenburg, 117
papers, 22
Paris, 169

permis de circulation, 23
Pierres de Ternay, 203
Plasschendale, 67
Plombières, 184
Poincy, 155
Pont d'Arles, 218
Pont d'Avignon, 212
Pont-à-Mousson, 94
Pontoise, 152
Pont de l'Ouche, 184
Pont de Pany, 184
Pont Royal, 184
Pont-sur-Yonne, 179
Port Maria, 168
Port St. Louis du Rhône, 214
Porta Westfalica, 123
poste restante, 59
Pouilly-en-Auxois, 184
Pouzin, le, 209
Pronfondeville, 142

Quillebeuf, 166

Ravières, 183
Regnitz, R., 107
Reims, 153
Remich, 95
Rendsburg, 256
Revin, 144
Rheinfelden, 89
Rhinau, 194
Rhine, R., 73
Rhone, R., 203
Rinteln, 123
rising bollards, 50
Roche-de-Glun, La, 208
Roche Guyon, La, 168
Roches-de-Condrieu, les, 208
Rotterdam, 79
Rouen, 167
Rüdesheim, 84
Ruhrort, 81
rule of the road, 34
Rupel, R., 127
Rupelmonde, 135

Saale, R., 104
Saar, R., 93
St Andries, 139
St Denis-de-Pile, 239
St Emilion, 238
St Florentin, 182
St Germain, 169
St Gilles, 218
St Goar, 83

St Jean-de-Losne, 184, 197
St Mihiel, 145
St Nicolas-du-Port, 174
St Omer, 157
St Pierre, 210
St Romain des Îles, 199
St Thibault, 184
St Valéry, 161
St Vallier, 208
Sambre, R., 146
Saône, R., 195
Saverne, 175
Scheidt, 98
Scheldt, R., 135, 241
Schierstein, 84
Schwedsbengen, 95
Schweich, 96
Schweinfurt, 106
Schwetzingen, 111
Sedan, 144
Seille, R., 201
Seine, R., 162
Seligenstadt, 102
Seneffe, 130
Senheim, 97
Sens, 179
Sète, 222
Seurre, 198
Sierck-les-Bains, 95
signals, 35
Sigtuna, 277
Sjötorp, 269
Skokloster, 277
Sliedrecht, 79
Söderköping, 270
Soissons, 150
Somme, R., 160
Sondernheim, 85
sound signals, 35
speed limits, 34
Stenay, 145
Stockholm, 276
stoppages, 26
Strand, 273
Strängnäs, 278
Strasbourg, 86
Strömsholm, 280
Stuttgart, 112
Sundbyholm, 278
supplies, 57
Surahammar, 280
Suresnes, 169

Tancarville, 166
Tanlay, 183
Tarascon, 212
Tåtorp, 269
Tauber, R., 104